Chicken Soup for the Soul.

Christmas Is in the Air

D0051414

Chicken Soup for the Soul: Christmas Is in the Air
101 Stories about the Most Wonderful Time of the Year
Amy Newmark

Published by Chicken Soup for the Soul, LLC www.chickensoup.com
Copyright ©2020 by Chicken Soup for the Soul, LLC. All Rights Reserved.

The publisher gratefully acknowledges the many publishers and individuals who granted
Chicken Soup for the Soul permission to reprint the cited material.

Front cover illustration of buildings courtesy of shutterstock.com/Shafran (©Shafran),
illustration of Santa courtesy of shutterstock.com/AVA Bitter (©AVA Bitter), illustration of
snowy hill courtesy of shutterstock.com/Nopi Pantelidou (©Nopi Pantelidou), illustrations
of children courtesy of iStockphoto.com/Vect0r0vich (©Vect0r0vich)
Back cover illustration of snowy hill courtesy of shutterstock.com/Nopi Pantelidou
(©Nopi Pantelidou), illustrations of children on sled courtesy of iStockphoto.com/
Vect0r0vich(©Vect0r0vich)
Back cover and interior illustration of Christmas tree courtesy of iStockphoto.com/Maria
Voronovich (©Maria Voronovich), interior photo of Santa hat courtesy of iStockphoto.com/
ZaharovEvgeniy (©ZaharovEvgeniy)
Photo of Amy Newmark courtesy of Susan Morrow at SwickPix

Cover and Interior by Daniel Zaccari

Distributed to the booktrade by Simon & Schuster. SAN: 200-2442

Publisher's Cataloging-In-Publication Data
(Prepared by The Donohue Group, Inc.)

Names: Newmark, Amy, compiler.
Title: Chicken soup for the soul : Christmas is in the air : 101 stories about the most wonderful time
     of the year / [compiled by] Amy Newmark.
Other Titles: Christmas is in the air : 101 stories about the most wonderful time of the year
Description: [Cos Cob, Connecticut] : Chicken Soup for the Soul, LLC, [2020]
Identifiers: ISBN 9781611590708 | ISBN 9781611593044 (ebook)
Subjects: LCSH: Christmas--Literary collections. | Christmas--Anecdotes. | Miracles--Literary
     collections. | Miracles--Anecdotes. | Gifts--Literary collections. | Gifts--Anecdotes. | LCGFT:
     Anecdotes.
Classification: LCC GT4985 .C456 2020 (print) | LCC GT4985 (ebook) | DDC 394.2663/02--dc23

Library of Congress Control Number: 2020942115

PRINTED IN THE UNITED STATES OF AMERICA
on acid∞free paper

25 24 23 22 21 20   01 02 03 04 05 06 07 08 09 10 11

Christmas Is in the Air

101 Stories about the Most Wonderful Time of the Year

Amy Newmark

Chicken Soup for the Soul, LLC
Cos Cob, CT

Changing your world one story at a time®
www.chickensoup.com

Table of Contents

❶

~Feeling that Christmas Spirit~

❷

~Tales of the Tree~

3

~The Joy of Giving~

4

~Through the Eyes of a Child~

5

~Gratitude & Grace~

❻

~Homemade Holidays~

❼

~Holiday Hijinks~

8

~The Perfect Gift~

9

~It Takes a Village~

10

~Treasured Traditions~

Chapter 1

Feeling that Christmas Spirit

Christmas in New York

Blessed is the season which engages the whole world in
a conspiracy of love.
~Hamilton Wright Mabie

When my daughter Jessica and daughter-in-law Kathy proposed an early December trip to New York as my Christmas gift, I jumped at the chance. A life-long Midwesterner, I'd never been to the Big Apple but had always dreamed of visiting.

As we planned our itinerary, I discovered that New York was a prime Christmas destination, which meant bookings filled up fast. This knowledge doubled my excitement but added a touch of apprehension. I've never been fond of wall-to-wall crowds, even back then before the pandemic. If thousands of strangers crushed into one small area, would it make our visit a less pleasant experience? I didn't mention my worry to the girls, and we penciled in activities for every moment of our brief stay.

On departure day, we waited at the gate to board a full flight. A group of women around my age chattered non-stop. They wore matching green T-shirts printed with the New York skyline and "Girls Trip 2019." I struck up a conversation with one of them. She said, "We do a Christmas trip every year. This one has been on our bucket list for a while." We began to compare notes on what we planned to do.

By the time our plane landed in New York City, I felt like the ladies had morphed into friends.

After checking in at our hotel, Jessica, Kathy, and I headed for Times Square. The place was crammed with people, but that didn't interfere with me admiring the huge video billboards that surrounded us. We snapped selfies on Broadway, and I ogled the ball that drops every New Year's Eve. Then we moved along with a sea of people to Rockefeller Center, where an enormous decorated evergreen tree astonished me. A stranger from Japan took photos of us in front of the tree, and we did the same for her.

We met a British couple and a family from Mexico. I'd never heard so many different languages in one place. French, Italian, German, Japanese, British English, and Spanish were all represented, plus languages I couldn't begin to identify. Despite the crowded conditions, people smiled and waved as though they were recently connected family members. The girls and I joined the throng as we bustled through famous department stores that I never dreamed I'd see in person. We oohed and ahhed in front of countless windows decked out in holiday themes as we walked down Fifth Avenue, and then we strolled down legendary 34th Street toward Macy's.

One evening, the girls and I bundled up against the crisp night air to make our way to Radio City Music Hall. The Rockettes put on a captivating show to a full house. Everyone in the audience was given a Santa cap to wear. We all had something in common… a funny hat and a huge smile.

The next day, we embarked on a whirlwind trip through the city on the upper level of a double-decker bus. We tourists scooched over to make room for each other and then all of us craned our collective necks to see the sights. Once again, we helped each other. Language wasn't a barrier at all. Someone would point to a camera and grin. Everyone got the message. At the end of the frosty ride, most of us ended up in the same place—a crowded restaurant serving cups of steaming hot chocolate topped with fresh whipped cream.

On our final afternoon in the city, the girls and I waited for a cab to take us to the airport. I got emotional and a bit teary. The past few days had been more than an amazing experience. I'd been given the unique opportunity to meet fascinating people who represented more countries than I could count. Here we were, all of us together celebrating the most wonderful time of the year in one of the most iconic cities on the planet. No barriers. No politics. No arguments. Only a sense of peace and joy.

In the soft glow of the season, my small-town Midwestern heart learned that even an ocean of people could become companions instead of strangers. We were fellow travelers who shared the same path, creating countless memories in the magical yuletide spirit of one unforgettable Christmas season in New York City.

—Pat Wahler—

Priceless

Truly wonderful the mind of a child is.
~Yoda

I had set up our artificial Christmas tree from the previous year, and the children — ages eleven, seven and five — had decorated it. Many of the ornaments had been made by them at school over the years and they earnestly placed them as high as their little arms could reach. The old, artificial tree, with its bunched-up branches and half the lights not working, wasn't looking too good, though. And we had no gifts to place under its branches either.

Friends' and neighbors' homes were beautiful, with fresh Douglas firs or good-looking artificial trees, nicely wrapped gifts, and pretty home décor, but I couldn't seem to get in the spirit to decorate. Our financial burdens were weighing heavily on me as Christmas approached.

One evening, my seven-year-old daughter came home from playing at her best friend's house down the street. After seeing her friend's tree, she was very concerned that we didn't have any gifts under ours. She scurried to her room and gathered little toys, books and trinkets that she knew her brothers would like. Then she used a roll of left-over wrapping paper and carefully wrapped her treasured items. Finally, she proudly placed them under the tree.

The next day, her little brother Julian woke up and found the gifts. His face lit up. Inspired, he ran to his room, gathered some of his special possessions and wrapped them to give as gifts — not knowing that his sister was responsible for the ones under the tree. The tree still lacked beauty, but now several little gifts were beneath it, awkwardly but lovingly wrapped by my children.

One weekend, after finally doing some Christmas shopping, I looked at this imperfect tree, with its little gifts of trinkets, used toys and books, and felt compelled to wrap a working string of lights around the tree. Then I moved some of the ornaments to the higher branches that the kids hadn't been able to reach.

As I rearranged the handmade ornaments, I began to appreciate each little handprint made into a Rudolph, each snowflake with pictures from kindergarten and preschool, and all the other ornaments made by little hands and then signed in crooked print by Juan, Jazmyn and Julian.

As I moved the children's gifts to make room for the ones I had bought, I got a close look at what each package contained: a bouncy ball that Jazzy really liked but Julian liked to play with; a little car that Julian owned but Jazzy liked to use with her Barbies; a Pokémon card that Jazmyn owned which Juan had been trying to get from her; and a broken pen without any ink that Julian saved because it had a purple feather his sister really liked. I noticed a picture for Juan that Jazmyn had drawn. It was a portrait of our family. I shed happy tears and felt an indescribable tenderness knowing that my children understood the meaning of giving.

It's not the price, the quantity or the beauty of the gift that matters. It's knowing that it will make someone smile. It's the time you've dedicated to let them know their existence is meaningful to you and they are appreciated. My children had learned that sacrificing something special to ensure a smile on another's face was the most important thing. Love brewed within their little, innocent hearts.

The new store-bought gifts I was about to wrap seemed so worthless compared to the treasures I'd discovered. The classy ornaments on neighbors' trees were nothing like the years of handmade memories from my precious three.

I sat there proudly, knowing we owned the most valuable tree. It was decorated in abundant love. Beneath its branches were the gifts of caring, compassion, and innocence — all priceless.

— Lucy Rodriguez —

Old Becomes New

The excellence of a gift lies in its appropriateness
rather than in its value.
~Charles Dudley Warner

"What do you kids want or need for Christmas?" I asked my two daughters when we were out for lunch on one of those rare days when the three of us getting together was possible. Both are married and working, with kids in their teens.

"We don't need anything," they replied, nearly in unison.

"What do you *want* then?" I asked.

"Mom," one said, "just come to Christmas dinner and bring a pie. Your presence is present enough. No need to buy us anything — or the kids, either. They're teenagers. They'll tell you they want a Mercedes or a trip to Paris or something just as goofy. They've outgrown what we called the 'magic' of Christmas."

Outgrown Christmas? Say it isn't so. I'm a grandmother to teenagers, and I haven't outgrown the magic, tradition or meaning of Christmas.

I went home totally discouraged after our lunch. Images of Christmases past filled my mind — my little daughters on the top step, fidgety on Christmas morning, peeking and wondering what Santa might bring.

I felt sad, and I still had no clue what to get everyone. Humbug or not, I would somehow gather a collection of gifts, each one wrapped, beribboned and ready for the family's grand opening event. Luckily,

Christmas was still a couple of months away, so I had time.

Meanwhile, I had my own tasks and "must-dos" — getting rid of a lifetime of "stuff," for instance. I had a closet filled with those old things one keeps forever. The kids had already turned down the good china and some grand old pieces of furniture. No one wants antique silver or lovely furniture from long ago. If it isn't microwave- or dishwasher-safe, no one can use it. I had a beautiful coat with a fox collar I had to give away because my daughters wouldn't wear fur. I couldn't blame them. I gave up wearing that coat myself for the same reason.

I spent my spare time that fall going through closets and the garage, selling, giving away, and tossing out things I once thought I could not live without. The used-clothing-and-houseware places got carloads of my donations. A garage sale reduced my "keepsakes" as well.

I spent an entire week going through old photo albums — not just mine but also those my parents had left for me. Oh, the memories I looked back on as I turned the old, yellowed, curling pages.

I stopped at one. It was a very old, somewhat cracked photo of our farmhouse.

We moved there as a young couple, my husband and I. The original house was built in 1900. It was the place where we raised our children. This photo showed the original house and the family that built it. It had been given to me by our neighbor, an old woman who was born in that house. She told me the story of the farm's beginning. It was a grand tale, filled with adventures and tough times.

As I looked at that old photo, I wanted to frame it and keep the memory alive of that lovely, old house and its history. My children had been raised in that house. A bit of our family history is woven there, too.

Now one of my children lives there, and the old farmhouse is now a modern one, with new everything, but it retains the old feeling and a thousand memories. Our story continues. Suddenly, I knew what to get the kids for Christmas. There was actually something old that they *would* want! I had the photo duplicated and framed — one for each grown child and one for me.

The framed photos turned out quite lovely, and they were a hit. The kids had tears in their eyes as they opened them, and we shared some of our stories about the house. Not only did it remind them of the years we lived in and loved that place, but it made all those years memorable again. I look at my picture often. They were good years. And that photo and those memories made Christmas magical again.

—NancyLee Davis—

Chicken Soup
for the Soul

The Most Festive Neighborhood in Town

Then the Grinch thought of something he hadn't before!
What if Christmas, he thought, doesn't come from a store.
What if Christmas... perhaps... means a little bit more!
~Dr. Seuss, How the Grinch Stole Christmas

Ever since my mom began working as a teacher at the neighborhood school, she dreamed of moving to Haggin Oaks so she could be a part of the Christmastime festivities. A few years back, her dream came true, and our family moved to a large, red-brick house in the prestigious neighborhood.

Each Christmas season, nearly every house in the neighborhood is decked out in sparkling strands of lights and a wide array of decorations ranging from sentimental mangers to jolly Santa Clauses with bulging sacks of toys. Neighbors admire each other's fabulous displays, which are generally put up the day after Thanksgiving. Some neighbors engage in a bit of friendly competition and try to outdo each other, but it is all in good fun. Some of the most extravagantly decorated houses are featured on the local evening news and in the newspapers, so it is no wonder people try so hard to make their yards look spectacular each year.

One man in our neighborhood dresses up as the Grinch (green

face paint and all), and his wife dresses up as Mrs. Claus with a red dress and white wig. The cheerful old gentleman rides around in a lime-green Grinch-mobile that blows bubbles, giving rides to excited crowds of people. The man also has a Santa house in his yard where people can go to have their picture taken for free with Old Saint Nick himself.

The house next door to the happy Grinch holds a fundraiser called Dustin's Diner every year. They sell hot chocolate and baked goods for one dollar apiece to raise funds for the homeless shelter. My mom taught the original Dustin (he no longer runs the diner) in her fourth-grade class many years ago. Since Dustin and his brother Daniel first started Dustin's Diner in 1993, the small stand has raised more than $250,000 for the shelter.

Our front yard is pretty full of Christmas cheer as well, with striped candy canes lining either side of the walkway, colorful lights rimming the roof, and glittering reindeer in the yard. We decorate our windows with glowing Charlie Brown displays that are always much-admired by the long procession of passing cars that tour the neighborhood. Each night, we enjoy peeking out the window as people eagerly pose for photos in front of the manger and Christmas dog inflatables that grace our front lawn.

Horse-drawn carriages clomp merrily down the streets, carolers sing joyful Christmas tunes, and residents play holiday songs for all to hear. On some nights, old-fashioned cars and trucks decorated with lights and ornaments parade throughout the brightly lit neighborhood. There is even an annual holiday bike ride where everyone adorns their bikes with lights and dresses up in Christmas sweaters to ride the streets of Haggin Oaks together.

People who do not have the means to do expensive things at Christmastime enjoy being able to ride and walk through the streets at night with their families. I have warm memories of riding through this same neighborhood when I was little, drinking hot chocolate as I gazed out the backseat window at the displays. Not everyone can afford to have their picture taken with Santa at the mall, so countless people pose in front of the Christmas displays in people's front yards.

Our neighborhood helps bring holiday cheer and happiness to the entire town, which truly captures what the heart of the season is all about. I am so thrilled to be a part of an extraordinary community that really gets into the spirit of Christmas!

—Baylie Jett Mills—

Gift of Life

We can only be said to be alive in those moments
when our hearts are conscious of our treasures.
~Thornton Wilder

The vice president at my new job made it known that he expected our entire department to participate in the company's annual blood drive, so I signed up. I'm not a fan of needles, but the process was relatively painless — a prick less annoying than a bee sting. Fifteen minutes later, we were treated to bakery cookies and a plethora of beverages. I exited with a sticker proclaiming that I was a "hero." Heady stuff.

I wore that sticker proudly all day and became a regular donor for the next forty years. Sometimes, I just donated whole blood. Most often, I donated platelets. The process took longer, but I could donate more often. There wasn't a lot I could do for others while holding a full-time job, raising five children and maintaining a large home. But this I could do. The cookies were delicious, and I could sit in an adjustable contour chair for a couple of hours while gracious phlebotomy techs fawned over me.

A few years later, I signed up for the bone-marrow program. I was never a close enough match for marrow donation, but my blood was compatible with a young boy battling leukemia. I was called in often, especially during chicken pox outbreaks; something in my blood protected him from the disease.

One of my call-ins occurred on Christmas Eve day. I sat in the lounger, watching tubes transfer my blood out of one arm and return red cells in the other, as donors and staff came and went. It was nearly noon when I finished. The last remaining phlebotomist chatted with me as he removed the tubes and cleaned up. He fed me chocolate, baked goods and juices. Then he leaned in and whispered, "You gave him Christmas."

My heart skipped and then raced. Wow! To think that a couple of hours of my time could extend a life was euphoric. That made my Christmas.

Designated donation calls stopped after that. When I went in for my next regular donation, I asked why. Specific information about recipients is confidential, I was told, but generally if someone no longer needs blood, it's either because of recovery or... death.

I never met that brave little boy or his family, but I had been connected to them for years. I felt a personal loss. I thought of them every time I went to the blood center. I thought of how his last Christmas made mine fuller.

That's when I decided that I would schedule my last donation every year on December 23rd or 24th. To honor his struggle. To keep me grateful for the gift of health. To keep me mindful that not all families gather around a lighted tree, open presents and sing carols. Some families gather around a hospital bed to say goodbye.

My Christmas traditions now include prayers for all those who are celebrating their last Christmas on earth and the loved ones who will miss them. I pray for blood donors and phlebotomists, and that more people will be moved to donate. And I thank God for giving me the opportunity to touch that child's life, and have mine so touched in return.

— Diane C. Perrone —

Santa Has Left the Building

A little magic can take you a long way.
~Roald Dahl

When I was five years old, I met the "real" Santa. Well, *almost* met.

It was Christmas Eve, and my ears had just picked up the sound of unidentified, soft footsteps moving through the house. I say "unidentified" because I'd taken the precaution earlier of closing my bedroom door. (The rumor at school was that if you see Santa delivering your presents, he takes them back.) So, as tempted as I was to throw caution to the wind and go out into the living room, I was also smart enough to know it could be my mom up with my baby sister, Nancy. Compromising, I cracked the door open and peeked out.

The house was dark, which meant it wasn't my mom and Nancy. I could hear my dad snoring, and my sister Karen was sleeping in the bunk above mine. That left just one other possibility!

Opening the door a little wider, I heard the rustling of wrapping paper as packages were moved from one location to another. I pictured Santa in his red suit and hat, gently tucking gifts under the tinseled branches of our Christmas tree. As the noises began to fade, I heard the soft click of the front door closing. Santa had left the building.

The next morning, while my dad set up his movie camera, and

Karen and I waited for my grandparents to arrive, I began to think about how and when to share my big news. Should I do it right away or wait until we finished opening presents?

In the end, my mother made the decision for me. Popping her head in the door, she said, "When I count to three, you can come out. But no pushing and no running. One..." Karen pushed me out of the way and ran down the hall. Not far behind her, I entered the living room just in time to hear the first rip of wrapping paper. Thoughts of Santa's visit flew out the window as I focused on a Barbie doll with black, bubble-cut hair.

Later that morning, I perched on the edge of the sofa as the adults settled in for coffee and homemade cinnamon rolls. I evaluated every pause in the conversation, waiting for the right time to share my news. When it finally came, I said with aplomb, "I heard Santa in the living room last night! I have proof he was here." Letting that bombshell drop, I sat back and prepared to be the center of attention.

The clock ticked loudly. Nancy burped. Karen continued playing with empty boxes and wrapping paper. Sounding suspicious, my mom said, "What do you mean you have proof? Did you get out of bed and see him?"

Not wanting erroneous reports getting back to Santa, I answered quickly, "No, I definitely did not get out of bed and see him. But I heard him."

My parents and grandparents looked at me with varying degrees of skepticism, so I went to Plan B (which I didn't even know I had) and placed into exhibit Santa's empty cookie plate and milk glass. Then I pointed out that the carrot we put out for Rudolph was gone, which meant that it was Santa I heard in the house because nobody else would take the carrot. Finally, with a dramatic pause, I delivered the definitive evidence: a thank-you note from Santa in his own handwriting.

Christmas, much like life, is as magical as we allow it to be. At sixty-one, I still see its magic. But now I see it through older, wiser eyes. Christmas isn't just about tucking gifts under the tree. It's about tucking them in our hearts. And Santa's biggest magic? Why, that's the illusion that he disappears at the end of the night. Because, you know, he never really leaves.

— Crystal Hodge —

Dream Job

Nothing else in all life is such a maker of joy and cheer
as the privilege of doing good.
~James Russell

I t was the beginning of the Christmas season. Our small town on the Mississippi was decorated with lights crisscrossing the streets and huge wreaths on the lampposts. They thumped in the frigid winds that roared off the river.

But I was not focused on that. I was hearing the voice of the lady from Sears who had called the day before: They had a job for me, working on the sales floor every night until 9 p.m. and a full day on Saturdays.

It was my first job, and I was happy about that, but it was not the job I dreamed of having. That job was the one my best friend had had at Vogue, the most fashionable dress shop in town. She had worked wrapping gifts, tying up boxes covered with silver and gold foil. She topped them with generous amounts of red and green ribbon, which became bows and curlicues with a twist of her hand. She looked so grown-up and accomplished in that setting, and I wanted to be just like her.

That fall, as my friend went off to college and I turned sixteen, I had applied for the job at Vogue. But I didn't get it.

As I passed Vogue, I could see my friend's replacement busily working with ribbon and paper. I was jealous.

I reported to the Sears personnel office and was escorted to my department: Toys. I cringed. I knew nothing about toys and had no interest. How much nicer Vogue would have been: wrapping beautiful pieces of clothing, chatting with the customers, but I did not let my frustration show. I did, after all, have a job.

My supervisor was a cheerful man about my father's age in a white shirt and a tie. "Have you ever sold anything before?" he asked.

"No," I admitted. "My first job."

"It's a tough one, toys. Lots of merchandise." He waved his arm over a wilderness of trucks, dolls, playhouses, and football gear. "Hope you have a good memory." He smiled as he talked, his voice warm with encouragement.

"Take a look around. Learn as much as you can. If you cannot find something, come to me. We do not want a customer to leave empty-handed." He showed me how to operate the cash register and figure out sales tax. "It's our best department; you will need roller skates."

He was right. The amount of merchandise was daunting, and people were already shopping, picking up merchandise, looking at it carefully, and putting it back. Before I walked up the first aisle, I had a customer — a young man who wanted a tractor-trailer truck for his cousin. "My parents gave me one years ago. I want one just like it." We arrived at the truck section, and he found what he wanted in a few minutes. I rang up my first sale.

I had just turned from the cash register when I had another customer who was looking for a baby doll that wet. Another sale. The next customer wanted a paint-by-number set. We looked through the game section and found one she liked. I had to smile. It was very much like one Santa had put under the tree when I was in third grade. It had brought me hours of creative happiness.

As I helped my customers leave the store with trucks, kitchen sets, and dolls, I remembered the Christmas Eves of my youth. After church, we would drive home, my brother and I straining at the windows for a glimpse of a reindeer or a man in red, and then open the front door to a surprise of lights and presents.

Now, years later, I was at Sears at Christmas, in a whirlwind of people all trying to create that same magic. But this time, I was very much a part of it, searching, looking, finding — the happiness of my customers motivating me to put all my effort into it.

About mid-evening, a couple came up to me. They were older, wore business clothes, and spoke to each other in a foreign language. They had a picture cut from a magazine. "This," they said. "Like this." It was a train. The hours on my feet paid off. I knew exactly where to find it.

"Yes, that one," the couple said as we looked at the trains. They smiled at each other and put away the picture. The gentleman turned to me. "Not now," he said. "Come back." He pointed to his wallet. "Later. Come back," he repeated. I nodded that I understood.

They left, and I went back to my job. It got busy as the evening wore on. Several times, I checked on the train sets. About an hour before closing, I checked again. Only one was left. I pulled back the door to the small storage space under the shelves where the surplus merchandise was kept. Nothing. This was the last train. I had to do something. I took the train off the shelf and shoved it far back in the storage space. It could be seen only by crawling around on hands and knees. I knew it was safe.

Toward the end of the evening, I saw the couple enter the store. They recognized me, and together we went straight to the train aisle. Before they could panic, I brought out the train set. The woman took the box in her arms, hugged it as if it were a lost child and smiled at me. The couple pointed at the hiding place and then at me. They laughed and smiled. They understood. As we walked to the cash register, I imagined a child tearing off the wrapping paper, giving a shout of surprise. What fun! I rang up the sale and started back to the other customers. The couple followed me, speaking to each other rapidly, and then running to catch up with me. In the hand of the woman were some dollar bills. "You, for you. Take," she said.

I was bewildered. Was this a tip? I was not at all tempted to take it. A stillness, quiet as light, had come over me. I knew something clear and eternal as the dawn: Joy had nothing to do with money.

I motioned for the woman to put the bills back in her purse. "Thank you, but no," I told her. I smiled again, shook their hands, and together we went to the door. I watched as they walked down the street under the Christmas lights, past Vogue and all the things I had wished for, now so unimportant. Good things were happening right where I was — at my new dream job.

— Nancy Roenfeldt —

A Two-Dollar Miracle

Kindness, like a boomerang, always returns.
~Author Unknown

I was nine years old, but I still remember it like it was yesterday. I was in Grand Central Station with my mom, dad, and brothers around Christmastime. We were heading back to Connecticut after fulfilling our annual tradition of seeing the Christmas tree at Rockefeller Center.

My dad had taken my older brother to get a snack while my younger brother and I stayed with my mom. We sat on a bench, mesmerized by the constellations on the station ceiling. After a little while, I overheard a man arguing with his friend. "I don't have enough money for my train ticket home. I only need two more dollars!" he said.

His friend responded, "I don't know what to tell you, but I have to go." He rushed to catch his train, leaving his friend behind.

My mother must have overheard them too because she held our hands and walked over to the man. I saw her pull out her purse and hand him two dollars. He looked flustered, thanked her quickly, and ran off to buy his ticket and catch the train. In that moment, my mother sat us back down and explained to us the importance of kindness and helping others. I was listening intently, while my younger brother got distracted by the escalators.

"Can we go up and down the escalators?" he asked while half-listening to the lesson my mom was trying to teach us. My mom agreed, and we headed to the escalators. As we stepped on, a middle-aged man in a suit stepped on behind us. He watched as my brother and I giggled on the escalator and then reached into his pocket. The man pulled out his wallet and put a dollar in each of our hoods. When we reached the top of the escalator, the man smiled and went on his way. My mom reached in our hoods, realizing that the man had put a dollar in them — two dollars in total, the exact amount she had just given to someone in need. My mother froze, stunned by what had transpired. She always talked to us about karma but had never experienced it so instantly.

Ten years later, I'm still astounded by what happened that night. My mom has told that story time and time again, and each time she says that she felt real Christmas magic that day. Sometimes, it really is the little things that make the biggest impact. My mother helped out the man who was two dollars short with a small gesture, and the man in the suit made a big impact on our lives with his small gesture. We learned that it is important to put good into this world because you get out what you put into it. This instant magic is rare and may not happen to everybody, but there is little magic all around us every day. We just need to know to look for it.

— Anissa Deshpande —

The Nativity

For the spirit of Christmas fulfils
the greatest hunger of mankind.
~Loring A. Schuler

I was doing my rounds, checking for anything that might be amiss in the senior citizens' apartment building where I work as a night security guard. All was calm and peaceful as I moved silently through the building, stopping occasionally to admire the holiday decorations on the display shelves outside each apartment in the hallways. There were glittering Christmas scenes with miniature figures gliding on tiny mirrors, colorful menorahs, majestic angels made of porcelain and lace, miniscule Christmas trees with tiny presents beneath them, and numerous bowls of colored candies and confections for friends and visitors to take as they passed by.

Some residents really decked the halls, so to speak, while others decorated more simply, obviously being of the belief that less is more. Either way, it was a treat to behold them all as I performed my nightly inspection.

Although it was late, I happened upon an elderly gentleman and his middle-aged son cleaning his shelf to get it ready for the seasonal display. The son brought out a beautiful nativity set, piece by piece. The resident, dressed in his bathrobe and slippers, held each piece lovingly and proudly explained to me that his now deceased wife had painted them years ago.

"They are beautiful," I exclaimed, and stood back quietly to watch the scene unfold. The elderly gentleman was on a mission and very specific about where each piece was to be placed. "The animals need to be closest to Baby Jesus," he explained, "so they can watch over him. They were there first!" His very patient son smiled and winked at me as he placed each piece carefully where his father told him it belonged. He made the mistake of putting the three wise men too close to the baby, and his father quickly moved them. "That's not where they go," he told his son. "They arrived last! They can't be in front of the animals."

Again, the son and I shared a private smile, and he obediently placed the rest of the figures where his father indicated. I bid the two gentlemen goodnight and quietly continued on my rounds, feeling as if I had just witnessed something very special, but not quite knowing what.

As I walked around, it occurred to me that I had perhaps witnessed the true meaning of Christmas in that little setting up of the nativity set. The father was being ever so careful to preserve the work of his beloved wife, all the while making sure that the scene accurately portrayed the simple beauty and significance of a baby born in a manger and heralded as a king. The son displayed love in its purest form, patiently helping and guiding his frail father, and understanding the importance of this nativity set to him.

Before I left for the night, I went back to take a look at how it had all unfolded. Some of the figurines were in a slightly different place, and I presumed the father had deferred to some of his son's suggestions about how they would look best.

Looking at the nativity scene, I felt overwhelmingly engulfed by a trinity of love: a husband's love and pride in his wife, a son's love and patience for his father, and a father's love for his son, displayed in his willingness to compromise in the placement.

What a quiet night of wonder it was in a place where magic and wonder became even more evident during the holiday season. I walked outside, and the sounds of Christmas music filled the crisp air as I did my final walkaround, making sure all were safe and accounted for on this magical winter night.

— Joanne Padley —

Finding Peace

May the spirit of Christmas bring you peace,
the gladness of Christmas give you hope,
and the warmth of Christmas grant you love.
~Author Unknown

It was March 2020, and I was quarantined in my assisted-living facility in Southern California, doing my part to stay isolated and avoid the coronavirus that is sweeping the world. Also, I didn't want to inadvertently pass the virus on to anyone else, as the residents here are in a high-risk age group. I longed for the moment when I might hear "All is well with the world."

This morning, as I sat alone in my bedroom, I noticed a Christmas gift bag sitting in the corner, still bulging with its bounty of holiday cards. I set about to reread the cards, praying for each person who thought enough to wish me goodwill and peace on earth.

As I stared out my window, feeling lonely and isolated, memories of my worst Christmas crept into my thoughts. I tried not to think of them, but my eyes soon filled with tears.

I remembered sitting on my couch in the family room on Christmas Day two years earlier. I watched the twinkling lights on the Christmas tree blink on and off in Morse code fashion, wishing a M-e-r-r-y C-h-r-i-s-t-m-a-s to all. The tree and holiday decorations didn't have the sparkle they had in years past, and I had little Christmas spirit, if any. My son and I were alone. My husband had died, and my daughter was on her Christmas break from her teaching job, visiting our Italian family in Milan, Italy.

"I'm sorry, Christopher," I said. "I didn't prepare anything for lunch." I felt terrible. It was Christmas, and I had let him down.

This was the first Christmas that the table wasn't laden with plates boasting a homemade dinner and cut-out sugar cookies for dessert. I simply didn't have my heart in it.

"That's okay, Mom. I'll go out and get us something to eat."

We called restaurant after restaurant to see if they were open on Christmas Day. No luck.

"Something's got to be open, Mom. I'll go out and look."

I watched my son get on his bike and disappear up the street. He appeared an hour later holding a bag that contained two fish filets and two orders of fries.

"Nothing was open, Mom. Only the place with the golden arches."

I thanked him for his bike ride and blessed the cooks who made us a Christmas dinner. But the day dragged on as we had a heart-to-heart conversation about life's letdowns and our unfulfilled dreams.

For months, I felt sad and guilty. But one day, I decided I didn't want to carry this guilt around any longer. I decided to look at that Christmas with a positive attitude instead of a sorrowful one. I began seeing it as a sacred time I shared with my son. It had been a day when we had all the time in the world to talk, cry, and reminisce about things past, present, and future. It became our Christmas gift to each other, mother and son.

Later that day in March my son called to see how I was handling the quarantine and isolation.

"Fine. I'm doing okay."

"I'm so grateful, Mom, that you are where you are. I feel good that you are in a controlled environment and being taken care of."

At that moment, I promised myself that Christmas 2020 would be extra special. After all, the fish sandwiches and French fries that my son and I shared two years earlier on what I thought was the worst Christmas ever had taken on a special meaning, leaving me with a heart full of gratitude. My son's call gave me peace and hope for the future, one in which the world will recover from this invasive virus and social isolation, and we will have Peace on Earth and Goodwill to All once again.

—Lola Di Giulio De Maci—

Chapter 2

Tales of the Tree

Ashley's Tree

*Small acts of kindness can make a difference in other
people's lives more than we can imagine.*
~Catherine Pulsifer

I was driving home after attending an EMT meeting down in the village of Monument when my headlights picked up the glimmer of tinsel and coloured baubles. Was that a Christmas tree around the corner? This was at the edge of a county road with no residence in sight.

It turned out to be a scrubby little juniper, more like a bush than a tree. Who on earth had decorated it? I couldn't help but grin every time I came up that hill during the month of December and saw that little Christmas tree. As mysteriously as it was decorated, it once again became a scrubby, little juniper tree at the end of the Christmas holidays. If you knew what to look for, you'd see that a little straggle of tinsel remained.

The following year, I waited to see if the little tree would once again be adorned in Christmas glory. Lo and behold, it was! I heard that the tree was being decorated by a middle school girl named Ashley Mund who lived with her family a few miles farther up the road from "The Tree" and just a mile or so from our own farm. From then on, I waited impatiently for Thanksgiving to roll around and looked for my headlights to pick out Ashley's Tree when driving home in the dark. It never failed to make me smile.

The years went by, and that little juniper flourished. Each holiday season, it sported its Christmas decorations.

Then the day came when Ashley graduated from high school and was off to start a new life in college. Imagine my surprise and gratitude when I was driving home in the dark from an EMT call only to have my headlights pick out the tinsel and baubles on Ashley's Tree! How delightful that this wonderful tradition was continuing.

A few more years went by, and Ashley got married and started a new chapter in her life. Surely now would be the end of Ashley's Tree. Yet, each year around Thanksgiving, when I came around that corner on my way home that tree would sparkle at me, bigger than the year before.

This year, the county road department went on a tree-trimming and roadside-tree-hazard eradication project. Coming down our hill the day they started this project, I was fretting and fuming to my husband Darrell as I drove, fearing that Ashley's Tree would be cut down. The cutting stopped before they got to it, so I thought Ashley's Tree had been spared. But then they resumed cutting a few months later, and that was it. Ashley's Tree was unceremoniously cut down and dumped in the ditch at the side of the road, a stray wisp of tinsel still amongst its boughs.

That Thanksgiving, Darrell and I were returning home from Bend after he spent the night in the hospital following an angiogram and stent procedure. Imagine our surprise and delight when our headlights caught a glimmer of tinsel off to the side of the road.

It was another Ashley's Tree! It made tears come to my eyes. Ashley, now grown-up and married with a life of her own, had decided to continue her tradition of so many years. Despite the loss of the glorious old tree, she had found another to fill its role, a bit scraggly but splendid nonetheless. It sits right on a fence line so the county road department surely cannot take it down. Ashley's new tree, decorated in its tinsel and baubles, is a fine tree to behold, proudly carrying on her tradition of many years. God bless her!

— Rose Howe —

12

A Tree Named Apollo

The perfect Christmas tree?
All Christmas trees are perfect.
~Charles N. Barnard

I was living in San Francisco's Sunset District in 1980 when I purchased a six-foot-tall, eleven-year-old avocado tree in a large clay pot at a garage sale. I paid twenty dollars for it — contingent on the two sellers' ability to maneuver the tree in its pot up the narrow, winding stairway to my second-floor flat. It was a precarious process, involving sweat, grunts, and groans, but the tree arrived in my living room without losing a leaf.

Brad and Doug, my teenaged sons, were delighted by the presence of a live tree in our living room. I was too, having imagined that owning a houseplant taller than the man I was dating was a luxury reserved for rich people, not single moms like me.

We set the tree before the front window where it would bask in the afternoon sun. We gazed at it worshipfully, sitting cross-legged on the floor beneath its large, flat, tear-shaped leaves. Light green veins ran through each darker green leaf, with smaller veins branching from the main one to their edge — like country roads branching from a highway. The tree trunk was brownish gray and rough to the touch. Smaller, smoother branches were a vivid, tree-frog green. I inhaled deeply with satisfaction and exhaled strongly, blowing carbon dioxide upward into the tree, causing a slight stirring of its lower leaves. I could almost feel the gift of oxygen pouring from those leaves in exchange.

I named the tree Apollo after the Sun God. "Cool," my sons said.

The conflict began in December when I suggested that, rather than buying a Christmas tree this year, we should decorate Apollo.

"This tree is part of our home," I said, "so why cut down another tree to use for two short weeks and then throw it away?"

My suggestion horrified my sons. It was bad enough when I divorced, when we moved across the country, when I started dating, when I legally chose my own last name — but this, they insisted, was over the top!

Brad shook his head, like he couldn't believe what he'd heard. "We've always had a Christmas tree," he said reasonably, as his brother nodded in agreement. "It's family tradition. Ask Grandma."

When I was a kid in the 1950s, each December my mom hung a handmade evergreen wreath, decorated with pinecones and tiny red bells, on our front door. A week before Christmas, my parents drove to a tree lot in town and bought a fresh-cut pine tree, chosen by me. I inspected every tree on that lot before pointing dramatically at my choice, which my dad then paid for and dragged to the car.

My dad secured the tree in a stand in front of the living-room window. He draped strings of multi-colored bubble lights around the branches and set a silvery star at the top. My mom and I hung delicate, round, pear-shaped glass balls and red-and-white-striped candy canes.

We draped red paper garlands and added tinsel. We hung four glittery bird decorations. Their wings caught the light as they swung gently in flight. Finally, we placed holiday cards we'd received onto selected branches of the tree. The result was breathtaking, even before the lights were turned on.

As a young, married adult with small children, I didn't question Christmas tradition. Even after divorcing my husband and moving with my sons to San Francisco — where I considered myself an untraditional person — I bought, dragged home, and decorated a tree each year. This was the first time I'd considered doing otherwise. But feeling pressured by my sons and preferring not to discuss this with my mother, I went out and purchased a tree.

Far be it for a divorcée to mess with childhood traditions.

The Christmas tree was a five-foot-tall, bushy evergreen chosen by Doug. Brad secured it in a stand in the front part of the living room near the fireplace — as far as possible from Apollo. Then we draped garlands, and hung ornaments, tinsel and candy canes. Brad set the star on top and turned on the lights. The tree looked great, but we all kept looking across the room at Apollo — the tree we lived with year-round — left out and undecorated.

A week after Christmas, we took down the tree, and dragged it downstairs and out the front gate. We dumped it in the gutter where it would stay until Sunset Scavengers carted it away.

"Maybe next year we'll decorate Apollo," I said, regarding the discarded tree. There were no objections.

I never bought a Christmas tree again out of loyalty to Apollo.

We decorated Apollo the next holiday season with silvery garlands and round, pear-shaped glass balls. We added candy canes and tinsel. Carefully, Brad set the shining star on Apollo's top branch. Doug hung the two shimmering, flying birds my mom gave me from her set of four. We placed our festively wrapped, beribboned gifts in and around its pot. On impulse, I placed holiday cards onto selected branches.

"Just like Grandma," Doug said with satisfaction while Brad nodded in agreement.

I may not be so nontraditional after all.

— Lynn Sunday —

13

Chicken Soup for the Soul

Thrice Blessed

You will do foolish things,
but do them with enthusiasm.
~Colette

I suppose that my brother and I should have realized that it was our turn. As young adults, we needed to show some responsibility for our Christmas celebrations. But it was never actually mentioned, so on December 24th, the Christmas tree, which had always magically appeared in past years, was still not in its place. I now imagine that our parents were making a point, but I am quite sure that by the morning of Christmas Eve, they were wondering if they had miscalculated and the lesson hadn't penetrated our brains.

My brother had disappeared, so I stood there alone looking at the corner where the tree should now be standing. It seemed that the moment was mine, as clearly nobody else was prepared to produce a Christmas tree.

"Well," said my friend Marlys on the phone, "I guess you better go on a hunt." She offered to accompany me.

Together, we headed to the local tree lot, only to find that it was sold out. We began to walk and walk and walk. The sun began to slip westward, and I began to panic. It seemed there were no Christmas trees to be found — anywhere.

"Sonny might be home," Marlys suggested. Sonny was her brother and the owner of a ramshackle Volkswagen. He might be willing to drive us to check some other tree lots that were farther away.

Several lots later, with Christmas Eve now upon us, we still had not been able to purchase a tree. "There's no other choice," said my friend's brother. With an axe and a cross-cut saw, we approached a wooded area on the outskirts of town.

"We'll just cut this one down and then lop off the top," he said. But, no, I refused to take the easy route. So, between us, with Sonny climbing through snow-laden branches and cutting, and Marlys and I clearing and dragging, we loaded the top of a tree, which I had refused to allow Sonny to cut from the bottom, into his Volkswagen. With Marlys in the front and me in the back, we stuck our arms through the windows and held the tree to the side of the car as Sonny drove home carefully.

While we had been hunting, it seemed that my parents had relented. As my friends and I carried our trophy through the door, my mother said, "Oh!" Where there had been a bare corner only a few hours before now stood a quite elegant, artificial tree awaiting decoration. "Never mind," it was decided. "We'll use both." There was plenty of tinsel and several strings of lights.

As we decorated, our tradition of hot chocolate was revived and we wondered where my still absent brother might be. "He's been gone ages," we worried. "Hopefully, he's okay."

And then with a thump on the porch and a bump on the door, we heard, "I've had to go all over, but I finally found one. It's not much but at least it's a…" He pushed inside a bedraggled and bent Christmas tree, definitely one of the leftovers.

That three-tree Christmas has become a favorite family story. It was definitely a lesson well learned for us kids, and the beginning of our new roles as contributing adults.

— Robyn Gerland —

The Brightest Little Tree

*Some Christmas tree ornaments do more than glitter
and glow, they represent a gift of love
given a long time ago.*
~Tom Baker

It was nearly dusk on Christmas Eve when I started to cry. Our tiny rented house on the beach in Massachusetts was cold, ugly, and devoid of any decorations or presents. I had been adamant that I would be happy celebrating Christmas by simply having a nice meal and relaxing together.

We had just moved in the fall and barely had enough money from our temp jobs to make rent. I was trying to be tough. But as the wind whipped the waves into a gray froth beyond our kitchen window, I felt all the loneliness of being away from my family in Tennessee.

My husband Jason took my hands in his and said, "Why don't you go take a walk with the dogs? You'll feel better." I decided he was right. I bundled up, clipped leashes to collars, and headed out to the desolate shore.

An hour later, though, I still wasn't looking forward to a holiday in the dark little house. I opened the front door and was moved to tears again. Waiting for me on the kitchen table was a tiny, two-foot Christmas tree, complete with cheap plastic gold decorations. Jason stood sheepishly nearby. "I made it to the grocery store just before they closed," he said. "It was the last one they had. Don't worry about the money—they gave it to me for half off."

The next day, his brother, who was training to be a chef, came for a visit. The two of them took over the kitchen, telling stories, roasting a small turkey, and making cream puffs for dessert. I put on my coat and took the squirmy dogs out again just as the sun was setting. The evening was calm, and the long stretch of beach was empty for most of my walk. The sound of each wave seemed to wash away another layer of my unhappiness. At the end of the path, where the Merrimack River poured into the Atlantic, I saw a family of three picking mussels off the rocks and putting them into buckets. They smiled at me and said "Merry Christmas." I smiled back, said "Happy New Year," and headed for home.

This time, I opened the front door to steamy windows, the sweet smell of warm pastry, and the loud laughter of brothers. With my hand still on the doorknob, I counted my blessings: a safe place to live, a nice meal, a beautiful view, and the love of a man who wanted to make me happy. For the first time in my life, I felt the true peace we're supposed to know at Christmas. The little tree on the table seemed taller and brighter than it had the night before.

That was twenty years ago. Ever since then, Jason and I have only bought each other one present each Christmas: an ornament for our tree. Sometimes, we find one that reflects the past year, such as the one with a painted picture of Boston's Public Garden from our first year in the city. Other times, they're just pretty—glass globes, intricate woodcuts, and hand-embroidered stars. As we dig them out from boxes and unwrap them, we tell our two children the stories of where they came from and why we gave them to each other. Our tree is enveloped in happiness, warmth, and light. And every time I uncover those cheap plastic gold ornaments from our little tree, my eyes well up with tears, and I remember the peace, love, and gratitude I felt that very first year.

—Regina Velázquez—

15

Chicken Soup for the Soul

Christmas Spirit in a Stand

What one loves in childhood stays in the heart forever.
~Mary Jo Putney

"What?" I gasped. "You have to have a Christmas tree!" I looked at Papa, shocked and dismayed that he hadn't planned on getting a tree. I was six, and it was the first year that I would be having two Christmases since my parents had separated nearly a year earlier. I was fine with spending the weekends with Papa, but not having a Christmas tree? It was unacceptable!

Papa had very little money in those days, and a tree was obviously low on his priority list. But he saw that it was greatly important to me, so we went to Kmart and bought a scruffy, three-foot tree, a string of lights, some garland and a small box of ornaments. I assured him that I would make some ornaments for him, too. We spent the evening transforming the tree and his small living room into a Christmas wonderland.

I jumped into his arms, and we sat back together and marveled at the little beauty we had created. Later, he said that it was one of the best ideas he'd ever had — getting the tree — because in those darker days, he would sit in his recliner, look at the lights, and be thankful for me and Christmas.

Now, thirty-five years later, we are celebrating our first Christmas without Papa. The little tree has been stored up in our attic for many years.

Before Thanksgiving, I brought it down. My daughter, Sarah, was away at her first year of college, and she asked if she could have the little tree in her dorm room. She remembered it from her very early years of visiting Papa at his house before he moved in with us. I doctored it up, but the stand was broken. I commissioned my handy son, Daniel, to build a new stand for it.

I figured he would go out to the garage and find some scrap wood. Instead, he drew up a plan and asked his shop teacher if he could use the wood and tools in the woodshop at school. He went far above and beyond what I thought he was going to do. Sarah thought he was doing it for Papa, so Papa's tree could reign once again. I thought he was doing it for Sarah because he misses her, and this was something nice he could do for her. Either way, it was a nice dose of Christmas spirit.

After Thanksgiving, we returned Sarah to college. The little tree rode along in the back of our van with her clean laundry. She asked if I would like to help her decorate the tree. We stood it in Daniel's finely crafted stand. With each ornament that we hung, I felt as if I were six again, happily adorning Papa's little tree for the first time. We stepped back to look at it together. I pulled Sarah in tight. She said it was the best idea she ever had — rediscovering the scruffy, little tree.

— Jesse Neve —

16

The Perfect Christmas Tree

The best Christmas trees come very close
to exceeding nature.
~Andy Rooney

When our children were young, we started our own Christmas tree tradition. Bundling up in hats, boots, scarves and gloves, we went tromping through the snow at the local Christmas tree farm to cut down our very own real Christmas tree. Afterward, at home, we would have cookies and hot chocolate topped with marshmallows to warm us up while we admired our defrosting treasure.

Although we always considered ours perfect, we knew we had to leave the most perfect tree behind in the forest on the tree farm. The farm was owned by Bob and Lois, who also owned a roadside grocery store just four blocks from where we lived. Every year, at the beginning of the holiday season, Lois would scout through her forest of trees and find the perfect tree for her family. She would tie a strip of red plastic to signify her family tree. All other trees available for cutting would have an orange tie strip. Every year, we teased Lois that we almost cut down her tree, and each year she threatened dire consequences if we did.

As Christmas approached one year, getting a tree was the furthest thing from our minds. It had not been a good year. In the summer,

I had a miscarriage. Then in November, I had to have all four of my wisdom teeth removed. About a week before the surgery, I developed a large swelling on the right side of my jaw. I thought my teeth were infected and had become abscessed, but I had the mumps!

On the eve of Thanksgiving, I began to feel very tired and had a strange headache. I felt achy, was running a fever, and my neck was very stiff. My husband had come home from a second job and went to bed. But by morning, he realized something was very wrong. He had to check in at work, but then he returned to call the doctor. I was hospitalized with mumps encephalitis meningitis.

After a week's stay in the hospital, I was allowed to go home and told to rest and take things easy. Then, I discovered I was pregnant with our fourth child. Although the pregnancy turned out fine, I lived in terror of what the mumps might have done to the fetus.

In the middle of all this illness and terror, the holiday season was fast approaching. We had managed to purchase a few gifts for the children, but we had not been able to go to the tree farm for our annual Christmas tree hunt. The children were very disappointed.

I still tired easily from being ill, and my husband had been doing the grocery shopping at Bob's store. Bob and Lois were very concerned about all that had befallen our family during that year. They were sorry I didn't feel up to coming out for our annual Christmas tree hunt. One evening when he returned from the grocery store, the children were watching for him at the window. They came running to tell me, "Daddy has a Christmas tree! Daddy has a Christmas tree!"

Sure enough, he had a Christmas tree, but it would take a while to dry out as it was soaking wet from all the rain we had been having. "Get a lot of newspapers and pad the floor in a large circle," he ordered. "This tree is big and wet. And get the tree stand to stand it up in!"

We did as he instructed, and he went out into the rain and brought in the tree. We got pretty wet making sure it was secured in the tree stand. Only five feet tall but very round and full, the tree had lovely, long green needles. It was beautiful! The children danced with excitement as we stood back to admire it.

"Where did you get such a wonderful tree?" I asked. "This close to Christmas, I thought the best ones would be taken."

Holding the tree secure in the tree stand, he told this story:

"Yesterday, when I went to the grocery store, Lois told me to stop after work tonight — she had a little something for the children for Christmas. I told her that wasn't necessary, but she insisted I stop by. When I got there tonight, she told me, although it was a little wet, our Christmas tree was leaning beside the store and to please take it home. She wouldn't let me pay for it. She just smiled and said, 'No, it's for the children.'"

A big smile lit his face as he continued his story. "As I was putting the tree into the back of the station wagon to bring it home, I found something."

He removed his hand from the top of the tree. After a gasp of disbelief, I began to weep tears of gratitude. Nestled in the top of the tree's branches was the tree farm's small tie strip of plastic, but its color was not orange. The strip of plastic was a bright Christmas red! Lois had given us their personal family tree, and it was the most perfect Christmas tree of all!

— Helen L. Burgess —

17

Miracle on Cherry Street

*The smell of pine needles, spruce and the smell
of a Christmas tree, those to me,
are the scents of the holidays.*
~Blake Lively

A friend of mine recently posted an exasperated note on social media. It read, "Stop with the Christmas decorations... and music... and commercials before Thanksgiving!" Many people commented with remarks like: "There should be a law!" and "I agree. It's SO annoying!"

I must confess, I don't agree.

I love everything about Christmas, so I really don't mind that the season has been lengthened. I love the baking, decorating, specials on TV, concerts at schools and churches, office parties, gingerbread lattes and, yes, even shopping. But of all the holiday activities, my favorite has always been decorating the tree. I believe the Christmas fir perfectly embodies the excitement and magic of the season.

When I was first married, my husband and I shared a very small studio apartment in New York City. It was cramped, but I still wanted a tree. Christmas just wouldn't be right without one. My husband agreed. The only ornaments we owned were the few we received as wedding gifts, so we purchased a few more. My husband didn't care about decorating the tree, so I rushed home from work one day to set up the tree before he got home. When he walked through the door that night, I gestured and exclaimed, "Ta-da!" He responded with all the appropriate "oohs" and "aahs."

Four years later, the first Christmas after he left me, I was still determined to make the holiday special. It was a tough task because I was terribly sad and living alone in a drafty, upstairs apartment on Cherry Street in Syracuse, New York. I was working two jobs, and money was tight. But I really wanted a tree, even if it was tiny. After all, Christmas just wouldn't be right without one. Somehow, I was going to manage it.

I arrived at the tree lot late one night after work. It was already cold and dark outside, but the illuminated string of light bulbs signaled it was still open. There was a trailer nearby, and an older bearded man wearing a red flannel shirt, overalls, and tweed cap came bounding out, waving to me.

"Can I help you?" he asked with a kind smile.

"Just looking for a small tree," I chirped back, heading for the "3-foot" sign.

I was running my hand over the bristles of a small pine when the man appeared again, carrying a much larger Fraser fir. It was beautiful. Straight as an arrow with full, symmetrical branches. I knew I couldn't afford it, so I smiled and said, "Pretty!" Then I turned back to the three-footer, which now looked extra puny.

"You don't like it?" he asked.

"Oh, yes, I like it very much. It's just a little... extravagant for me right now." I tried to sound nonchalant.

He looked at me for a long beat and then sighed, "Ten bucks."

"Really?" I asked.

"Sure," he shrugged, his smile growing larger. "Go inside the trailer and pay my wife. I'll tie this to the roof of your car."

I decided to go before he changed his mind. I thanked him profusely and practically skipped to the trailer.

The woman who greeted me inside had white curly hair framing her kind face. She pointed to a seat and poured a cup of hot chocolate while I wrote out a check. Then we wrapped our hands around our warm mugs and chatted until her husband came bounding back into the trailer, saying, "She's all set!" I smiled for the first time in weeks. How could I ever repay them?

By the time I arrived home to Cherry Street, it was very late, but I couldn't wait to get started. I wrestled the tree up the narrow staircase to my small main room and placed it in the stand. I strung all the lights and then paused before I opened the small box of ornaments. These were ornaments that my ex and I had picked out together, ornaments I assumed we'd be unwrapping with old, wrinkled hands someday, years in the future. Now it was just me. I took a deep breath and threw open the lid. Only a few tears fell as I placed each one on its designated branch. That finished, I added red ribbon from my craft bin for garland. Then I stepped back.

Suddenly, there, in the middle of my sad, empty apartment, was Christmas. I pulled the rolled-up futon mattress from the closet, set it there on the living-room floor, and fell asleep looking at my beautiful tree. I slept soundly for the first time in months. In fact, I slept there every night for the entire season. I'd leave all the lights on, and when I woke in the morning, there it would stand, shiny and bright, saying, "Merry Christmas!" Yes, divorce was crippling—but it was no match for the magic of my Christmas tree.

A few years later, I married the man who has become the great love of my life. We have a marvelous time celebrating life together, especially Christmas. He and I will be decorating our enormous tree this season, as always. We'll hang our cherished ornaments, bought during all our travels over the years. But I'll still pull out one or two others that were purchased for that first tree more than thirty years ago. I'll hang them to remember that December long ago on Cherry Street, when a gorgeous, ten-dollar tree reminded me of the miracle of Christmas, delivering the assurance that everything was going to be okay.

—Joan Donnelly-Emery—

Healing

To live in the hearts we leave behind is not to die.
~Thomas Campbell

I t was going to be a very difficult Christmas. After only two years of marriage, I had lost my husband Gerry in a car accident a few months earlier, and I didn't feel like celebrating Christmas or anything else.

It had been a second marriage for both of us, and he had made me feel loved and whole again. He was truly my best friend and helpmate. He did nearly all the cooking, getting up early every morning to fix me breakfast before he went to work. He helped with the housework, laundry and yard work. He loved telling jokes (long, drawn-out, corny jokes) and was known as a practical joker. He definitely embraced life.

I missed all those things so very much. But most of all, I missed hearing him tell me, "I love you infinite times infinite and just a little bit more." In the two short years we were married, I had come to depend on him so completely that I couldn't imagine living my life without him. And I didn't know if I even wanted to.

It had been our tradition (if you can call two years a tradition) to go out the day after Thanksgiving to a Christmas tree farm to pick out the perfect Christmas tree. At first, after Gerry died, I sort of ignored it, wishing the whole "Christmas thing" would just go away. Why couldn't I skip Christmas this year? But my teenage son kept asking me, "Are we going to have a tree this year?" He expected this Christmas to be like every other Christmas. So, I decided I should buy a tree and do my best to give him a "normal" Christmas.

One night on my way home from work, I stopped at a stand that had Christmas trees for sale. When the gentleman came up to me and asked if he could help, I said, "Where's the shortest, cheapest tree you have?" I didn't want to spend any more than I had to, and I felt that a small tree (maybe three feet) would be less work and would reflect how I was feeling about Christmas that year. He said, "I just put a short one behind the building; I'll go get it."

He came back with a tree that was just under five feet tall and was quite smashed. I thought, *Perfect… an ugly tree for an ugly Christmas.* I bought it, and he helped me shove it into the trunk of my car. At home, I had trouble getting it out of the trunk. *Just what I need,* I thought, *more trouble with this stupid tree that I didn't really want in the first place!* I left it lying in the garage until the next evening, when I dragged it up to the house. (It was heavier than I expected… more work!)

That night, I set it up in the tree stand. *Boy, what an ugly tree!* It was still very smashed, and I noticed that it had a huge, gaping hole in the back. *Well, that is perfect.* It somehow seemed so appropriate that my Christmas tree had a big hole in it to match the big hole in my heart. But I didn't have time to decorate it, so it would just have to sit there "naked" at least until tomorrow.

When I got up the next morning, I saw that a surprising thing had happened. Because of the warmth of the house, the branches of the tree had lowered, and it no longer had the smashed look. It was fat and full, and the hole in the back was not nearly as noticeable anymore. In fact, it was now a very nice-looking tree!

But I ignored the tree for another week. After all, I was busy and didn't have time for this "Christmas stuff." When my son finally asked me, "Are we ever going to decorate the tree?" I decided I might as well get it done since I'd already spent the money for it.

So, one night when I was home alone, I got out the Christmas decorations. I decided that I wasn't going to go all-out decorating as I usually did. I would just put lights and a few balls on the tree. I started sorting through the box to find what I wanted. That box held so many memories! My husband always liked to go shopping with me, so there were lights and ornaments that we had bought last year at the after-Christmas sales. There was the Christmas decoration that he had sent to me at work the year before. And there were the special, loving Christmas cards that he had given me.

With tears streaming down my face, I looked through the box of decorations and remembered Christmases past. I missed him so much! God had indeed blessed me with that special man in my life. And I realized that he would always be a part of my Christmas as I trimmed the tree with the decorations that we had picked out together. And by the time I had finished decorating, I decided it was a beautiful tree. The branches had fallen and made it one of the fattest trees I had ever seen! And that hole in the back no longer showed.

As Christmas approached, another special thing happened. Christmas cards began to arrive from family, friends and my husband's relatives, many of them containing words of encouragement, as people understood that this would be a difficult Christmas. They all meant so much to me. And although I still miss Gerry very much, I realized that in time, with the help of God and the support of family and friends, the hole in my heart, like the hole in the back of that Christmas tree, was beginning to heal.

— Cindy Bear —

19

A Towering Tree

*Our hearts grow tender with childhood memories
and love of kindred, and we are better
throughout the year for having, in spirit,
become a child again at Christmas-time.*
~Laura Ingalls Wilder

I stood at the base of the tower, using my hand to shield my eyes from the sun as I tried to see what all of the fuss was about. What was at the top of Dad's humongous tower? Why did people drive by at night and stop and stare up into the sky above our house?

At night, all I could see were some Christmas lights, so I was trying to get a good view of what was up there in the daylight. The tower was so tall that I couldn't make it out. When I asked what was up there, Dad just smiled and winked at me, leaving it to my imagination.

My mind pondered. Santa and his sleigh? A Christmas angel? I wasn't really sure at that point, but I would soon find out.

Dad's adventurous soul had no fear of heights — a trait that was helpful when climbing that tower.

One day, I learned that my mystery was a Christmas tree adorned with lights atop a 128-foot ham-radio tower. This was before the days of elaborate holiday lighting displays. The most anyone did in our town was trim their house with lights or put up a Christmas tree in the front yard.

Our home was a place where people gathered. Dad was a gracious, generous host, and Mom was an excellent, adventurous cook. Together, they created a space where their adult friends, as well as our childhood pals, felt comfortable. Everyone wanted to hang out at our house.

Apparently, the tree-tower idea sprang from a drunken dare with Dad's card-party gang who met regularly at our house. After a night of drinking and wagering, they wandered outside to have a look at the tower. As they gazed up and realized what would be involved with this adventure, his buddies fell away one by one, and he alone won the honor of "Tower Climber/Tree Planter." He was a strong-willed man from stubborn German stock and was not about to admit that he was not up to the task, so he set out to figure a way to do it.

He picked the ugliest, cheapest tree he could find and put the old bulb-type Christmas lights on it. Then he attached a rope and strapped himself onto the tower with the sort of safety harness that linemen use to climb poles. With the tree rope in one hand, he climbed until he neared the top. Attaching a pulley system, he hauled the tree up with the rope, fastening it to the top section of the tower. Several really long extension cords were employed to enable it to be plugged in at the base. From that height, it didn't matter if the tree was ugly because the lights were beautiful, and that was all people would see.

Mom was quite the worrier. While my brother and some of Dad's friends helped with the tree-perching activities, she and I stayed in the house, playing music loud and hoping not to hear a thud if Dad missed a step and fell off that very high tower. Thankfully, that never happened.

The only close call I know of was related by my brother years later. One year, as Dad neared the top, he noticed the final section of the tower was moving, and not just from the wind. The bolts securing that section had somehow worked loose. It was a disaster waiting to happen! From then on, he made sure to check that the next section of his climb was secure before climbing it.

As Dad aged and grew weaker, he decided to give up his tower-climbing Christmas tradition. At thirteen, my brother Rob decided to be the new tower-climbing champion.

My brother now says that he was never afraid to make that climb.

He said the view was amazing from up there. Per Dad's advice, he was mindful to notice that the bolts attached the sections as he climbed the intimidating tower. Truthfully, Rob would have done anything to make our father proud. To me, they both seemed very brave.

Some years later, Dad's kidneys failed. After some weeks on dialysis, he decided to keep living his adventurous life. He made plans to take his yearly fishing trip to Canada and take a portable dialysis machine with him. After all, he was a doctor and could figure out how to deal with this new challenge.

Regrettably, his body did not hold out for that adventure. He died peacefully in his sleep a few days after making that plan. He truly enjoyed his life and made the most of the short amount of time he had with us. It broke my heart and changed my world when he died. He was my best friend and strongest supporter. He always showed us how much he loved us, even if he didn't say it a lot. Our biological father had abandoned us when we were very young. After Dad married Mom, he adopted us and gave us his name. He was a real father to us and couldn't have loved us more if we had been his own blood.

Our mother has passed on now as well. I stayed in the Midwest with my husband, and Rob and his wife moved to the Northeast. We went to visit them one year at Thanksgiving. They lived about an hour from the airport in the heart of Pennsylvania's Amish country. As we were riding in the car from the airport to his house, I admired the scenery. It's a beautiful part of the world, with winding roads and rolling hills. My brother kept grinning as if he were keeping a big secret. I wondered at his behavior but didn't say anything.

"We're almost there!" he said with more animation in his voice than usual. I gazed out the window as we pulled onto his street. It was becoming dusk. Up in the sky, I could see something glowing. "What is that?" I wondered aloud. My brother just smiled and winked at me, reminding me of Dad.

As we got closer, I realized what it was. Although not as tall as the one I remembered, my brother had constructed his own ham-radio tower and put an ugly, cheap tree with beautiful lights at its top. I am sure his wife had something to do with the fact that it wasn't 128 feet tall. It was still a sweet, glowing tribute to our childhood!

My brother and I had had some rocky times in our relationship over the years. That Thanksgiving we spent together changed and bonded us in ways we never imagined. I came to realize that Rob is a true reflection of all the good things about Dad, including his passion for adventure and family.

That holiday season, we agreed to appreciate the love and adventure of having a crazy family and to remember only the good stuff. The rest isn't worth holding onto.

— Stephanie Pifer-Stone —

20

A Living Memory

A Christmas tree teaches us that we can create magic
with happiness and unity of the loved ones.
~Author Unknown

"The Christmas tree is dying," said my father. How he could see it from the hospital bed we had set up for him in the front room still mystifies me. But he was right. It was dying.

The Christmas tree had been part of my family's Christmas tradition for twelve years, ever since Dad had purchased a Christmas tree permit from the Arizona Bureau of Land Management for fifteen dollars. He and I had driven to our assigned area, near Pinetop, Arizona, to hunt for a Christmas tree, cut it down and return with our trophy. I was eighteen years old, had just graduated from high school and was slightly indignant about being asked to go.

"Why don't we just buy one at the corner?" I asked smugly.

"Well, we could do that," he explained slowly, as if to a child, "but then I wouldn't get to spend this time with you and create some memories."

Chastised, I slouched down in the seat and resolved to be miserable for the next three to four hours.

We stopped in Pinetop for lunch at the Lumberjack Café (Best Burgers on the Rim!) before proceeding to our designated area, approximately 100 square miles of rocky outcrops covered in junipers, sycamores, wild vines and thousands of pine trees, any of which, I was quite certain, would be willing to sacrifice itself for the benefit of our Christmas celebration.

"There's a good one," I remarked, as Dad negotiated our 1984 Chrysler minivan along a Forest Service road. "Or that one, that's a good one. Or how about that one right there, Dad?"

My dad smiled. "Here's the thing, son," he finally spoke, his words as measured and slow as the frustratingly slow pace at which we were driving. "They all look good because they're where they belong. They fit here. But take one out of the forest, like that one there, for example," Dad pointed to a tree we were passing, "and you'd have to buy a new house in order to get it through the door."

Having no suitable retort, I determined to keep any future observations to myself.

We drove on for what I considered to be an interminable amount of time but was, in reality, probably only about ten minutes, when my father slowed the car and stopped.

"There," he confidently pronounced, "there's our tree."

It was about 100 yards away, standing alone on a hill, a delicate dusting of snow causing its branches to sparkle in the receding sunlight.

"C'mon," he announced. "We haven't much time. It'll be dark soon."

My father opened the rear hatch and produced two shovels and some burlap. We were halfway to the tree when the obvious suddenly occurred to me.

"Dad, don't we need a saw to cut it down?"

"We're not cutting it down, son."

"Why?"

"Because if we cut it down, it'll die."

For over an hour, we chiseled and pried at the cold earth. And then, in one desperate levered effort of our two shovels, the ground yielded and the tree emerged, its root system largely intact.

Whoops of joy and high-fives followed, our cheers absorbed by the dense, darkening forest. A light snow began.

Our fingers numb, we wrapped the roots of the tree in burlap and carried, dragged, and coerced it to the van. While the tree was barely four feet high, it resisted our clumsy efforts to corral it through the rear hatch. Finally, the tree succumbed to our efforts, and we were on our way home.

Now, twelve years later, the tree was dying. I asked my father what he wanted me to do.

My dad sighed deeply, the congestion in his chest making it difficult for him to talk. "I want you to take it back."

"Take it back where, Dad?"

"To the forest, son. Where else?"

Sidling up to the hospital bed, I leaned over and studied my dad. He was as alert as ever, his eyes sparkling.

"The pot's too small," he continued. "Has been for a while."

"In that case, Dad," I countered, "I could just transplant it into a bigger pot."

"Nope," my dad insisted. "You've got to take it back to where we got it. It's time."

Not wishing to agitate my father any further, I remained silent.

"Do you remember when we brought it home?" he asked suddenly.

I laughed. "When I saw Mom's reaction, I understood why you didn't cut it down."

"It was her last Christmas with us," my dad recalled sadly. "I think she knew it might be." My dad paused, his voice struggling. "Is the necklace still hanging in the tree — the pearl necklace I gave her?"

"Of course, Dad. It's been hanging there every Christmas since you gave it to her."

"She so loved Christmas," my father observed quietly.

For several days, my dad held on. We reminisced about Little League games, throwing a Frisbee on the beach, catching sunnies on a mist-shrouded lake in Minnesota — all things that, at the time, seemed so ordinary and mundane. Now, the memories of our times together shimmered like myriad stars against the backdrop of the fading light still apportioned to my father.

And then quietly, simply, with a gentle sigh, he was gone.

Weeks passed. I was busy settling my father's financial affairs and thanking friends and relatives for their support when my six-year-old son approached me and asked, "What about the Christmas tree, Dad?"

"What?"

"Grandpa said you might forget. He asked me to remind you about the Christmas tree. That's all he said."

I hugged my son. Somehow, it felt as if I was hugging my dad at the same time.

"You're right," I admitted. "I had forgotten. We'll take care of it this weekend. Thanks, son."

On Saturday, we rose early and loaded the Christmas tree in its too-small pot into the car. We passed through Pinetop, which looked exactly like it had twelve years earlier. I knew I'd never locate the exact spot where Dad and I had found the tree, so I turned down the first Forest Service road we came to, and the search began.

"I think it should be near the other trees," my son observed quietly. "It'll be happier that way."

The dense forest surrounded us on all sides until we rounded a bend and came upon a clearing with a small creek meandering through its center. Pine trees, just like ours and about the same size, bordered the creek.

"What do you think?" I asked my son.

"Perfect," he answered, smiling.

We unloaded the Christmas tree and wheeled it like a barrel across the clearing until we reached a spot next to the creek. The soil was rich, and there was plenty of water nearby. Here, our Christmas tree would thrive.

My son and I took turns digging, making sure the hole was big enough for the roots to expand. After an hour, we were covered in dirt, exhausted and sweaty.

I hadn't felt this good in a long time.

Surprisingly, it wasn't difficult to get the Christmas tree out of the ceramic pot. I had brought a hammer in case we needed to shatter the pot to free the tree, but it wasn't necessary. We lay it on its side, gave a quick jerk at the base, and it popped out. Slowly, almost ceremoniously, we lowered the tree into the hole we had dug and scooped in the dirt.

Our Christmas tree had come home.

Then I pulled Mom's necklace — the one Dad had given her that first Christmas — out of my shirt pocket.

"Are you going to leave it with the Christmas tree?" my son asked.

"Yes, with one addition." I opened the clasp of the necklace, slipped my dad's wedding ring on and closed the clasp. "Here, son. Hang it on the tree."

Slowly, my son approached and took the necklace, cradling it as if it were a rare, fragile gift. After studying the tree closely, he hung the necklace on one of the lower branches.

We stood silently for several minutes, admiring our handiwork. During this moment of reflection, I suddenly realized why my father had been so adamant about returning the Christmas tree to the forest. It wasn't just about the tree. It was about giving my son and me the opportunity to create some precious memories of our own, just like he and I had done so many years ago.

"Thanks, Dad," I said quietly to myself.

"I think we should come back every year and visit the tree," my son observed.

"Good idea," I agreed, tidying up the area around the tree. "As for now, I seem to recall my dad and I stopping in Pinetop several years ago at a restaurant that claimed to have the best burgers on the Rim. Interested?"

"Yes! I'm starving!"

As we made our way back on the forest road, I made a mental note of the mileage and landmarks. I knew that my son and I would return to visit the Christmas tree and relive the memories it had helped to create for years to come.

— Dave Bachmann —

Chapter 3

The Joy of Giving

The Tree Angels

An effort made for the happiness of others
lifts us above ourselves.
~Lydia M. Child

My daughter was five the year I climbed out of a financial hole. I'd been a single mother since she was just nine months old, and we were always skating close to the poverty line. The previous Christmas, everything she got came from a thrift store. From toddlerhood on, she had a much better understanding of budgeting and the value of a dollar than her peers. She didn't ask for much because she knew we couldn't afford much.

But, finally, this year there was something left over at the end of the month. Not much, mind you, but I slowly grew less worried about whether our electricity would be turned off, and I didn't cry every time her feet grew into the next shoe size.

In November, we were checking out at the grocery store when I spotted a small tree by the registers. All over the tree were Salvation Army tags with the names and ages of local children in need. Each tag named one present the child wanted. I knew what it was immediately because I remembered picking a tag off the same type of tree in a mall with my mother when I was a child. We had bought a sack full of gifts at the time, and my mother explained that sometimes Santa needed our assistance to provide for kids who were in the most need.

In adulthood, I developed pride in America for just this kind of deed: We were a generous nation who cared for others, both at home and around the world.

"Let's pick someone to help," I told my daughter. Her eyes lit up, and she helped me scan the names and ages. I read off several to her, and she asked me what each child wanted.

A few were luxury-type items (a game system or electronic device), but many were much simpler than that: My Little Ponies, board games, Thomas the Tank Engine figurines. One just asked for pajamas, which broke my heart. In the end, we settled on a little girl my daughter's age and set out to find the best presents we could on about a twenty-five-dollar budget.

We began at the dollar store, where we found an enormous stocking — perfect to fill with presents! We also found a Care Bears puzzle there. Then we moved on to a crafts store and used coupons to stretch the next ten dollars almost unbelievably far; by now I was a pro at making the most of what I had. Finally, we headed to the toy section of a department store and got the main item on her list: a baby doll. We went home, and I wrote the little girl's name in glitter glue on the stocking. We added some candy canes and little trinkets. I had to admit, I thought we did a pretty great job.

My daughter was so excited to get back to the store a few days later to hand in our present. When I asked a cashier where to take it, though, he looked confused. I pointed to the tree, which was still right near the register, and explained again.

"We took a tag off the tree and bought presents for someone. I'm just asking where to drop them off."

"Oh. No one's asked me that yet. Let me ask a manager."

After a couple of minutes, the manager came over and thanked us, leading us to a storage room where she put the stocking on a nearly bare shelf.

"Have you gotten many donations?" I asked.

"You're the third."

"Oh. How long has the tree been there?"

"Two weeks."

"Maybe people are just waiting until the last minute."

"Maybe."

As soon as we walked out, my daughter looked at me seriously and said, "Can we look at the tree again?"

I agreed, understanding that we probably had the same thought. Sure enough, every tag that we had read last time was still on that tree. In the four or five days since we'd been there last, not one person had taken a tag. My heart sank.

"Mom, Alicia is still there," she said.

Alicia had been our runner-up choice the first time around. She was ten, with a modest request for a latch-hook kit.

"I don't think we should leave her there, Mom. Can we help her, too?"

Again, we filled an oversized stocking. And again we found the tree nearly unchanged when we brought it back to the store.

"Mom, look… Jose is still on the tree. What if no one buys him any presents?"

She handed me the tag and looked at me with puppy-dog eyes. I sighed and decided this was my limit. My daughter had no idea how close she had come to being one of those kids on the tree; we were not in a position to spend recklessly. One more big stocking. One more trip back to the manager. We were happy to see a few more tags gone, but more than half were still on the tree.

I asked her what would happen if any of the tags were left after the deadline, which was just a week away by this point. Would they get moved to another store?

"No. I told the Salvation Army not to send us so many, but they said there's no one else. They already extended the deadline by five days because so little came in so far."

I tried avoiding eye contact with my daughter. I knew I was sunk the minute we walked out of that little room.

"We have to help them, Mom. There's no one else."

"Honey, we can't…"

"Just two more. Please? Kaitlyn and Christopher. You can give them all my toys."

So it was that we wound up with five angels that year. I took on extra work to do it, not only because I cared about those kids on the tags, but because my own kid needed to know what our little family was all about. I'd been talking to her about kindness and generosity since she first learned to speak; now it was time to prove that I meant it.

One day before the extended deadline, we made our final delivery and found six tags still on the tree. I couldn't take another and still pay rent, so I turned to my Facebook friends. I explained the situation: Six kids were left behind, and there was just one day left. I didn't know how I was going to sleep that night until I got a message from a friend who had driven far out of his way to make it to the store. "I took the last tag," he wrote.

Every year, we hang those tags on our tree at home and say a prayer that those children are safe and warm and having the best Christmas ever. Picturing them opening their stockings made our own holidays so much brighter.

— Jenna Glatzer —

22

Chicken Soup for the Soul

The Shopping Spree

You can't live a perfect day without doing something
for someone who will never be able to repay you.
~John Wooden

I was searching for wrapping paper in the local big-box store three days before Christmas when I saw a young mother with two toddlers in tow. She was pushing a shopping cart up and down the aisles of the toy department while trying to calm the fussy youngsters, a boy and a girl. Their clothes were inadequate to keep them warm against the cold December weather.

I had been praying for God to tell me how to spend windfall money that had come my way, and I felt this might be an opportunity. I went over to the little family, stood behind the mother, and tapped on her shoulder.

"Ma'am, my name is John. I am sorry if I alarmed you, but I want to ask you a question if I may." I saw she was even gaunter and paler than I first thought. The kids looked pretty thin, too.

"Oh, that's okay. You did not frighten me, but why do you want to ask me something?"

"Well, I couldn't help but see that you have been pushing your cart up and down the aisles, and there are no toys in it. You are Christmas shopping for the little ones, are you not?" She lowered her head and was quiet for a minute before responding.

"Yes, I want to get something for the children's Christmas, but... I don't know what to do."

Anguish and sadness filled her voice. She and the children appeared so unhappy. "Excuse me for being personal, but you don't have enough money, is that it?"

"I have just seventeen dollars, and I still need to buy food for the kids," she exclaimed. Tears filled her eyes, and she rocked from one foot to the other. Her body was filled with anguish.

"Where is the children's father?"

"I don't have a husband, and I don't know where their father is."

"Please don't be upset, ma'am. I understand your dilemma, and I have a remedy. Let's go shopping!"

I grabbed our carts and motioned for her to follow me, but she just stood there with a look of confusion on her face. With tears flowing over her cheeks, she agreed to go with me.

"But, mister, I don't expect you to solve my problems," she said as we walked.

"No argument, please. This will be a fun shopping experience. Now, let's shop!"

I wanted her to become enthusiastic and enjoy the experience, yet I did not want to be too pushy.

"But, mister, I'm not sure. I don't know where to begin."

"You bet. When the kids look interested in a toy, put it in the cart. Come on, we're wasting time."

In an hour, we filled her cart and mine with every imaginable toy. The looks on the children's faces were priceless, total disbelief. Mom still had doubt but was getting into the spirit of the moment. Other shoppers were noticing us; I think they knew what was going on, but we paid no attention.

"Let's check out and take these toys to your car. Then there's something else I want us to do."

"I don't have a car, mister. I will call my sister to pick us up."

"Don't fret now. We'll put everything in my truck, and I'll drive you and the children home when we've finished here."

At the checkout counter, the store manager met us. He had picked up on what we were doing. "Sir, I know what's going on here, and I'm giving you a ten-percent discount on your purchases." It surprised us, and we felt blessed as we thanked him.

"Well, it looks as if we are finished shopping," she said.

"Not yet. Remember, I told you there was something else I want us to do. Now, let's go back inside where it's warm, and I'll explain what we will do next."

I led the family to the children's clothing department.

"Okay, now, your job here is to select warm clothes for these kids. When you have completed that task, we'll go over to the women's section where I want you to load up the shopping cart with clothes for yourself."

"B-but…"

"No buts, please. It's getting late, the children are tired, and we're not done yet."

She completed loading the cart with clothes for herself.

"Now, if you will follow me to the grocery department, we can finish up this wonderful evening,"

She had soon learned that resisting me was pointless.

"Sir, I thank you for what you are doing, but you're doing far too much."

"Nonsense. I can afford it, I want to do it, and you need it, so there's nothing more to be discussed."

We finished our shopping, and I drove them home with the children asleep in the back seat.

"This is the place, second trailer on the right."

Before me sat a dilapidated mobile home that was no longer mobile. My heart was heavy. I suspected the place had no heat or electricity.

We unloaded everything on a porch attached to the trailer. I understood she did not want me to see the inside of her home. No one spoke as we concluded this final activity. She gave me a quick hug and then hurried inside with the children, leaving her gifts on the porch. I think she was just too embarrassed to prolong my departure.

I drove home feeling better than I had in months, but I couldn't get that little family out of my mind for a long time.

Three months later, I was grocery shopping, and someone behind me tapped me on the shoulder. I turned around, and there stood the mom. She hugged me and whispered in my ear.

"You cannot imagine how your generosity made our lives so happy. I can never repay or thank you enough for your kindness."

"Young lady, I did nothing but allow God to use me for something he wanted to be done. Thank Him — He blessed us both."

—J. Ross Archer—

23

A Lesson in Joy

To give and then not feel that one has given
is the very best of all ways of giving.
~Max Beerbohm

I knew to stay close and look left and then right before crossing the parking lot toward the St. Louis Union Station. Mom had brought me and my three siblings to this bright, bustling mall to Christmas shop. Armed with a budget and a vague idea of a wish list, I entered the main doors.

Even at thirteen years old, I had an awareness that moms shoulder a lot of responsibility without a lot of reward. My mom was no exception. She brought us to Union Station to help us buy Christmas presents for each other — and for her. Because of Mom, my siblings and I would get to experience the joy of giving. I wanted to find her something special.

The rich aroma of chocolate wafted toward me from the Fudge Factory straight ahead, and I wanted to linger. Normally, when we came here, the singing candy makers were my favorite spectacle, but today I had a mission. So, we walked on.

As we passed a rubber stamp specialty store, Mom casually mentioned, "We'll come back here after we look around for a while." She had told me before the trip about wanting a stamp to personalize her book collection.

We browsed a few mall carts offering jewelry, purses and toys, and then turned down the next corridor. Store after store offered trinkets, clothing and treats, but nothing caught my eye. I wanted something unique for Mom. I didn't know what, but I knew I would recognize it when I saw it. Meanwhile, I wondered, *Really, even though she promised to not look while we shop, how will whatever I pick be a surprise?* I knew moms, and especially my own, have extra senses for what kids are up to.

All of a sudden, there it was, the perfect gift for her! On one of the kiosks in the middle of the corridor sat a figurine of a lion and lamb lying down together. It would complement a drawing of a similar scene Mom had hung on the wall. I had heard her talk about how long she had owned the picture and who had drawn it for her. I knew it was very special.

I turned the figurine over to check the price and couldn't believe my eyes. I could afford it! Mom didn't know it, but I had tucked some extra money in my pocket from babysitting the neighbor kids, so I had more money than what she had given me. But she was standing nearby. No way could I make the purchase without her knowing. I put it down quickly, hoping she didn't see me holding it.

A moment later, she noticed the very same figurine. I watched her eyes light up. I overheard her tell my brother that it reminded her of that picture she had at home. She picked it up and turned it over, just like I had done. But then she set it down disappointedly after seeing that it would cost more than any of us had to spend. Seeing her interest, I knew it was the perfect gift. But how could I possibly make the purchase while she was so close?

As I walked away, I noted where the mall cart was, hoping I could sneak away. To my dismay, we kept getting farther and farther from the cart, turning down the next hallway and toward the exit. I began to think about finding a replacement gift, even though I knew nothing would be as wonderful as that little statue.

We were almost back at the entrance; it was time to finish our purchases and head home. The last stop was the rubber stamp store, as Mom had planned. She showed us a few things she was interested in before leaving us alone to make our final choices. She didn't seem particularly in love with anything but seemed to be calibrating her wish list to the budget she knew we had to work with. Nothing at that store even came close to the lion and lamb figurine.

Then I saw Mom was distracted helping my youngest sister. Suddenly, I knew it was my chance to sneak away. My stomach fluttered with excitement. It was a long way back to the kiosk with the prized gift, but I had to buy it. I raced out of the store, down the hall and around the corner, all the way back to the mall cart with the lion and lamb statue.

There it waited, exactly where I had set it down. I took less than a second to pick it up and carry it to the attendant. She carefully wrapped it in tissue paper, and I paid for my purchase. My heart was pounding as I thought about what a surprise this would be on Christmas morning. I tucked the package inside my coat so Mom wouldn't see it.

Then I rushed back the way I had come, all the way back to the rubber stamp store. I peeked around the corner of the entrance to see where she might be.

Had I been fast enough so she wouldn't notice I was missing?

Her back was turned. *Good!* I thought. I snuck to the back of the store to pretend I had been there the whole time, praying my heavy breathing wouldn't betray my recent exertion.

Not a moment later, she turned and saw me, asking if I was finished in the store. It wasn't a lie when I said, "Yes."

Did she suspect anything?

I left Union Station with my family, exhilarated that I had acquired an unexpected gift for Mom. As we walked through the parking lot to the van, I could feel the hard edges of the little animals against my side. I squeezed my arm tighter, holding the package safely in its hiding place.

Once home, I wrapped my prize, placed it under the tree and settled in to wait for Christmas morning.

The day finally came. Of course, my siblings and I tore into the treats and treasures our parents had lovingly tucked inside stockings and brightly wrapped packages.

My parents waited for the flurry to be over before opening their own gifts. Gleefully, we began presenting gifts to one parent or the other. I was sure Mom thought she knew what was in the box I handed her because she genuinely seemed surprised at its weight. It was much heavier than a rubber stamp.

She opened the box and gasped. Tears came to her eyes. "How did you…?"

I relished retelling how I had managed to make such a significant purchase so secretly.

Then Mom stood up and carried the little lion and lamb over to the sentimental drawing that had been in the room watching this all unfold. She placed the statue on a shelf just below the framed picture.

The warmth I felt proved something I thought I understood before, but this experience made the concept much more real: Many times, giving is more rewarding than receiving. I don't have a clue what I received that year. Instead, my happiest memory is having surprised my deserving mom with a special gift.

— Stacey Sisk —

24

Memories to Go

*Gifts of time and love are surely the basic ingredients
of a truly merry Christmas.*
~Peg Bracken

My great-aunt Joyce has always loved Christmas. The home she shared with her husband, Gilbert, was always impeccably decorated. She had a different Christmas tree in every room, each with its own theme. There were s'mores decorating the tree in the guest bathroom, woodland creatures in the hallway, reindeer in the kitchen, and ornate Old World ornaments in the living room. As kids, we would always look forward to Christmas Eve dinner at her home, where we would rush to see who would find the ceramic pickle ornament that she'd hidden in her tree. The winner always received a prize, not just some little trinket; her prizes were the best!

Each of the ornaments came with a memory that Joyce shared with anyone who would listen. They came from friends who traveled to exotic locations, gifts from loved ones at Christmas, places she adored, and animals that she treasured. She told me that Santa Claus himself brought her one every year.

Even the kitchen table had its own Christmas tree. We gathered around it, year after year, sharing Christmas Eve dinner and stories of the past. I grew up surrounded by a love for Christmas and the knowledge that family was what made it so special. The house was filled with laughter, usually caused by a joke at someone's expense and food so good we couldn't help but go back for seconds. My uncle sometimes made it back for thirds.

But this year would be different. A few months earlier, my great-uncle had passed away, and due to her declining health and trouble with her memory, Joyce was moved into a senior living community. The home that she always decorated so beautifully for Christmas was sold, and her belongings were put into storage. Her new home only had room for the essentials.

My mom and I decided that a woman who loves Christmas as much as Joyce would need a Christmas tree. We gathered up all her favorite ornaments and a new, smaller artificial tree and snuck into the facility while she was busy at recreation. We closed the door of her new home and hastily assembled the tree, worried that she might return before we could finish. Mom and I unwrapped each of her delicate ornaments and carefully placed them on the tree. Mom snuck in some room decorations as well and busied herself with placing them on the bed and dresser, while I put the finishing touches on the tree. Everything we brought that day was from Joyce's collection, each one a memory of days before.

My great-aunt has good days and bad days. Sometimes, she remembers things clearly. Other days, she struggles to recall why she cannot go home. She has always had a strong wit, and her sense of humor helped her cover the decline in her memory for many years. Yet, even on bad days, she still has a joke to crack. She claims the title of "great-aunt" describes her accurately since she is great, and she always whispers to each of us that we are her favorite. She has a lot of favorites, and she doesn't whisper very quietly, so we all know it.

As she walked into the room that day, she took in the tree and the decorations, and the tears in her eyes twinkled from the lights on the tree. Today was a good day, and she called us both "stinkers" for sneaking into her room, and then proclaimed that everyone else was going to be jealous of such a beautiful tree.

As she surveyed her room, she stood a little taller and smiled. She checked on all her little creatures: the stuffed pig now placed under the tree, her Santa Claus ornament, her little angels watching from the dresser, delighting in each. She remembered. She remembered the stories she once told about the hot-air balloon ornament and how Santa snuck it on her tree. She told us about her little Christmas village and the people she remembered sharing it with. She laughed, remembering us rushing to find the hidden pickle as children and then later as adults. Maturity doesn't run in our family, but silliness absolutely does. What can I say? We competed for those pickles prizes long after we should have grown up.

She invited the other residents in to see her tree and she smiled broadly when they complimented her tree. She is tiny, not even five feet tall, but that day she seemed bigger than anything else in that place, and she was sparkling just like her tree. We sat with her that day, and together we remembered Christmases past. While Great-Aunt Joyce's memories may fade, that day is a blessing that I will never forget.

—Shannon Scott Poteet—

25

Paying It Forward

Christmas is the spirit of giving
without a thought of getting.
~Thomas S. Monson

For years, I struggled to buy wonderful presents for my four daughters. One year, though, I had nothing. How do you buy gifts when you can barely provide food?

A call from a local church restored hope. They wanted to adopt my little family, and they did it well. On Christmas Eve, I pulled a few black bags out of the attic and placed the donated presents under the tree. My gratitude mixed with sadness at my inability to provide gifts.

To my surprise, two or three presents had my name on the tags. That put me over the top, and I started to cry.

In one sack, a lone teddy bear peeked from between the other boxes, unwrapped and with no specified recipient.

Seriously? Such a cute little gift, but how would I divide one teddy bear among four children?

I didn't.

He became our family bear — Jeremiah — a reminder that God had good plans for us with a bright future. Many times over the years, I curled up with Jeremiah and cried myself to sleep, clinging to my faith that something better lay ahead.

Several years later, a series of events transformed my financial situation. For the first time in years, my bank account was in good shape as December approached. I looked forward to a splendid Christmas morning. It wasn't all about the presents, but for a change, I was able to show my girls love through the gifts I could give them that year. And it felt amazing. During the month, we made many trips to the mall and discount stores. I gave the girls money to spend on each other. Our excitement mounted as we all sneaked around.

My youngest daughter's eyes sparkled after one trip. "I got everyone a present, but I bought you two." With a hug, she skipped out of the room to finish her wrapping.

That year, putting up the tree and decorations brought with it the joy I remembered from childhood. After stopping at stores on my way home from work and hiding gifts in my bedroom, my heart soared. I wrapped and put little packages under the tree, watching the girls do the same.

We adopted a family from an angel tree at church. After selecting gifts, we went to deliver them, leaving everything unwrapped and providing tape and paper so the mother could enjoy being part of it all. Our home wasn't extravagant, but my girls saw another family with even less than what we had—an experience that left them sobered and grateful.

With less than a week to go, my daughters and I planned one last trip to the mall, including dinner at a place I loved from work but we rarely visited as a family. I couldn't wait.

During the day, I talked with one of my team members. With a recent move, this single mom had spent her last money on bedding sets for her two girls. "I gave them the choice of that or Christmas presents." She smiled. "They won't have presents under the tree, but they're happy."

My spirits plummeted as I remembered the year when I faced a Christmas morning without gifts for my children. This young mother worked so hard to provide for her daughters. Time simply ran out before another payday.

At dinner that night, I shared the story and then threw out an idea.

"I planned to spend a little more money on all of you tonight. I can do that, or I can use the money to buy gifts for this family."

None of my daughters hesitated, responding with a resounding yes. One of them said, "We have so many gifts already. Let's spend the rest of our money on them." The mental image of two small girls waking to an empty tree bothered them.

In that moment, I fought back my tears. My girls got it! They wanted to give, not receive. This was the best Christmas gift I could ever have.

We had so much fun at the mall that night, finding amazing gifts for kids we didn't know. We included multiple presents for the mother as well. Later, I tucked my girls into bed, even the seventeen-year-old, making sure to express my pride in their selflessness.

Before bed, I sat in front of my computer and typed out the story of our own adoption several years earlier when we needed it most. I assured my friend that her circumstances would change for the better just as mine had after that Christmas when we received the donated gifts. I told her how my girls couldn't stand the thought of her girls not getting gifts on Christmas morning. And I told her that one day their turn would come, and they could do the same for another family.

The next morning, I got to work early to sneak in the sacks of gifts and leave them on her desk. I didn't want accolades for what we did. A smart lady, she figured it out although she never got a confession out of me. After our holiday break from work, this sweet woman told me she read the letter to her daughters on Christmas morning because she wanted them to know why we chose to help.

Both of us moved on to different jobs and seldom saw each other. Several years later, I passed her in a hallway. "I finally got to pay it forward," she told me with an enormous smile. Enough said.

— Lisa Bell —

26

James

For it is in giving that we receive.
~Saint Francis

As a teenager, I helped my family with monthly church services at a local convalescent hospital. It was not a pleasant place. The cries of loneliness and confusion and the pungent aromas hit me hard each time I walked through the doors. But I felt a strange compulsion to be there, and I always left feeling blessed.

One Sunday, I saw a gentleman in the common area whom I didn't recognize. I knelt beside his wheelchair, and as I opened the hymnal to the first song, I introduced myself. He didn't respond, and a voice behind me said, "His name is James. He hasn't spoken since he arrived, and he never has any visitors." I turned to see one of the nurses who sometimes attended the services. Looking back to James, I asked, "Would you like to sing with me?" There was no sign of recognition, but I started singing anyway. Between each song, I would touch his hand and talk to him.

I do not know why I felt so drawn to James, but month after month I sought him out as soon as we arrived. There was still nothing but a dull stare in his eyes, and the only sound from his mouth was his slow, steady breathing.

As Christmas drew near, I told my parents that I wanted to use my allowance to purchase a gift for James, and they suggested that I talk to the staff on our next visit. I found the nurse who had told me about James and asked for her opinion. She thought for a moment and said, "Socks seem to disappear around here, but they would have to be white so we can write his name on them."

It didn't seem like much, but the Sunday before Christmas, I carried a brightly wrapped box full of plain white socks to the convalescent home. I found James and brought him to the common area. I got on my knees in front of his wheelchair and placed the box in his lap. Looking into his eyes, I said, "Merry Christmas, James. I have a little gift for you."

I knew that he couldn't open the package, so I removed the wrapping for him. As I lifted the lid from the box, I said, "It's not much, but I hope you like it." I looked up into James's eyes just as a tear escaped its silent prison. I reached over and touched his gnarled hands, and my own eyes swelled with emotion when he spoke two simple words, "Thank you." I looked over at the nurses who had been watching our exchange, and their eyes were wide with surprise. Almost in a reverent whisper, one of them said, "Those are the only words we have ever heard him say."

I had glanced away from James for just a moment, but when my eyes again rested on his, the vacant look had returned. We never heard him speak again. More than forty years have passed, but I remember James and his gift to me to this very day.

— Sandy Lynn Moffett —

27

Dear Santa

How wonderful it is that nobody need wait a single
moment before starting to improve the world.
~Anne Frank

Dear Santa, do you remember me?
Every Christmas, you put presents under my tree.
But this year, I want to try something new.
Can you help me? The work will surely take two.
You see, I have everything I need,
food on the table, and a loving family.
I've got lights in the windows,
and stockings row by row,
and a colourful wreath on my door.
That's all that a child wishes for.
Your gifts will do me no good,
so I ask if you possibly could,
give it to the hospital instead,
where the children lie sick in bed.
While we celebrate with everyone in our home,
they stay in their rooms, all alone.
Give them a tree, and presents, or more,
something you can't buy from a store.
Help them recover and dry their tears.
Sing a soft lullaby in their eager ears.
Give them a dance, put a smile on their face.

Tell them a joke, bring them laughter to replace,
the pain that they suffer, with joy in its place.
Offer them everything in your red sack,
and as you go, don't forget to look back.
Watch as they sleep with joy in their hearts,
dreaming of angels that lie afar.
And while you give my toys to others to play,
I think I may be happiest on Christmas Day.

—Victoria Hathfield—

Chicken Soup for the Soul

Lunches for Christmas

*Christmas is not as much about opening our presents
as opening our hearts.*
~Janice Maeditere

"I have no idea of what to get you for Christmas this year," my husband Larry lamented in early December.

My lips turned up in a rueful smile. "Same goes for me in finding something for you."

Though we knew that Christmas was not about presents, we still liked to remember each other with small gifts and we had reached the stage in our lives when we didn't need more things. In fact, we were actively downsizing, cleaning out and getting rid of unneeded and unwanted "stuff."

Then an article on the Internet caught my attention. It was about schools having to turn away needy children from receiving lunches because the children were in arrears in paying for their meals.

I shared the article with Larry. "Let's each give money to the school lunch program for our Christmas presents to each other," I said. "We'll pay for children who can't afford lunch."

Larry smiled widely. "That's a great idea. It's a way of paying it forward."

Many years ago, when our children were small, we went through a hard time when Larry was unemployed. We lived on rice and beans and a whole lot of faith. Finally, we had to humble ourselves and ask for help. It wasn't easy for either of us as we had been brought up on principles of self-reliance.

Now that we were in comfortable circumstances, we wanted to give back.

I visited our local elementary school, the same one our five children had attended years ago, and explained that we would like to pay for lunches for children who couldn't afford them.

The secretary at the front desk looked first surprised and then pleased. She directed me to the cafeteria to talk with the coordinator there.

The lady in charge accepted our gift of cash with effusive thanks. "This will make a big difference to so many children," she said. "Thank you. Over and over, thank you."

There weren't as many presents under the tree that year, but it was one of our best Christmases ever.

— Jane McBride —

29

My Black Friday Lesson

The Christmas spirit whispers softly in my ear
to be of good cheer.
~Richelle E. Goodrich, Being Bold

I had never participated in the Black Friday phenomenon. I was always recovering from hosting our big Thanksgiving dinner. But one year there was a sale on an item that I badly wanted to get my husband for Christmas.

And so it was that I arose at 4 a.m., donned yoga pants and an oversized sweatshirt, threw my hair into a ponytail, and set off into the cold November pre-dawn on my quest. I was sure that this most special gift would be worth the effort — and cause a declaration of undying love.

When I arrived at the store I was stunned by the full parking lot. I had to park a quarter-mile away. Once inside, I was greeted by what I would call, at best, "organized chaos." Wooden pallets stood stacked to unsafe heights in overly crowded aisles. Crowds of frighteningly determined shoppers surrounded pallets that were still shrink-wrapped, hands firmly placed upon coveted treasures that would not be available for purchase for several hours. Families scurried about — parents with overflowing shopping carts accompanied by children in pajamas. Groups of teenagers carrying energy drinks happily roamed as if this mayhem was the social event of the season.

Not only was I unable to locate the precious gold at the end of my personal rainbow, but even if I had found it, I would not have had a prayer of getting near it without GPS and two really large bodyguards.

I hiked the quarter-mile back to my car (fulfilling the cardio portion of my day) and proceeded to another store, where I was greeted by an almost identical scene. I actually witnessed a woman arguing with an armed security guard over her place in line. Now, I had always thought that "They who wear small artillery automatically win the debate," but no, apparently there were customers desperate enough to do battle over line placement anyway.

I left.

I drove around looking for the now-impossible Christmas gift at other stores. As I continued to find long lines of people outside the stores, I realized that despite my valiant efforts, I was not going to return home with my precious gift. All of my wee-hour efforts had been for naught.

And then I remembered…

My daughter Kendall was starting her career in fashion at that time, and that included preparing for and working on Black Friday. Kendall was due to arrive at her store at 6:30 a.m. While I would be heading home to climb back into pajamas with a hot, soothing cup of sanity and the TV remote, she would be on her feet for the next fourteen hours.

I hurriedly drove to a coffee house and purchased the largest latte I've ever seen, along with Kendall's favorite pastry. I drove to her store where there, too, a throng of people who had been sitting in the cold for hours awaited the store's opening.

I parked and waited.

When Kendall pulled into the parking lot, I jumped out of my car and hid behind another parked car, praying that no one whose name began with the word "Officer" caught a peculiar-looking, pony-tailed blonde skulking behind a parked car with a gigantic latte, while simultaneously stalking a young woman.

Kendall emerged from her car and strode purposefully toward her store. I was immediately struck by her beauty at that early hour — hair softly coaxed into chocolate-brown waves, gorgeous smoky-eyed make-up, bright red lipstick that popped against porcelain skin. She was the personification of "street chic" in a black mini dress, a red scarf that perfectly matched the lipstick, black tights and high-heeled ankle boots.

Quickly, I fell into step alongside and intentionally bumped into her.

Not immediately realizing with whom she had gently collided, Kendall started to politely say, "Excuse me, I'm sor…." Then, realizing who had bumped her, she finished the sentence with an expletive, presumably because she hadn't seen her mother awake at that hour since a long-ago vacation in Las Vegas. I quickly gave her the latte and the pastry, kissed her on the cheek and wished her a good day. The smile that crossed her grateful face made the fruitless odyssey preceding that moment fade into nothingness.

As I made my way home through the now-sunlit streets, I felt just as good as if I had successfully found that precious gift. No holiday magic comes from a store, no matter the gift or the deal-busting, door-smashing, ceiling-caving sale price that comes with it.

It really is about the little things. It's about putting a smile on the face of someone who badly needs to smile. It's about lifting a spirit that may be bruised. It's about putting spare change into a charity collection instead of the glove compartment. It's about something as simple as a surprise latte and a kiss on the cheek.

I have reverted to what works for me — spending the day after Thanksgiving curled up in a warm bed with hot coffee and a purring cat.

— Carole Brody Fleet —

Chapter 4

Through the Eyes of a Child

Caroling My Cart Out

The best way to spread Christmas cheer
is singing loud for all to hear.
~Will Ferrell, Elf

One hour. Two stores. Three children. Four days until Christmas.

Somehow, in all my efforts to make this holiday season less stressful than the ones before, I had neglected to stock up on groceries over the weekend. I had missed my chance at every mom's dream: grocery shopping alone.

So here I was, scurrying across the parking lot with my two-year-old in one arm, my five-year-old tugging at the other, and my seven-year-old asking how long this would take. Too long, Buddy, too long.

We had already been in the first store for twice as long as planned, and I had considered that the "quick" stop. I reviewed my to-do list. There was no way to fit in everything before Christmas.

We entered the store and grabbed a cart. I plunked one kid in the front and another in the back. I sized up my oldest's legs and decided to let him walk. I checked my watch.

As we careened down the aisles, I fired a volley of instructions over the kids' heads. "Don't touch that." "Stop running." "Stay in the cart." "Hurry up." "We're going to be late."

I flung sugar and chocolate chips into the back of the cart, narrowly missing the child sitting there. I wedged apples and oranges next to the toddler in the front. I sent my oldest to grab sour cream while I balanced milk cartons on the bottom of the cart and questioned whether the pantry at home held everything I needed to make green-bean casserole.

Then — somewhere around aisle 9 — my five-year-old daughter started singing.

Her brothers recognized their favorite carol and enthusiastically chimed in. They knew all the words to all the verses, though the two-year-old stopped every couple of lines to ask: "What next?"

Shoppers stared at the cacophonous cart with arms and legs flailing in all directions. I ducked my head. The kids got louder. "Hark! The Herald Angels Sing" gave way to "Joy to the World" and then "We Three Kings." When they finished that one, the kids started over.

More shoppers noticed us. I rolled my eyes. The singing continued.

A few aisles later, I glimpsed the joy on my children's faces. They didn't care whether all the cookies got baked or all the presents got wrapped. Nothing compared to the fun of singing at the top of their lungs in the middle of the grocery store.

"Joy to the world, the Lord is come! Let earth receive her king." ("What next?") "Let every heart prepare him room. And heav'n and nature sing." ("What next?") "And heav'n and nature sing. And heav'n and heav'n and nature sing."

I realized the shoppers around me weren't scowling. Their faces melted into smiles. I slowed the cart and smiled back.

We hadn't gone caroling this year anyway. The neighbors weren't home. They were here, rushing through their last-minute lists. I hummed along with the kids.

"You guys sound great," I found myself saying. I meandered down one aisle after another, enjoying the voices of my shopping companions.

A young lady waved as we passed. "If anyone wasn't in the holiday spirit, they should be now," she said.

We went through the checkout line, and the cashier grinned. The kids sang along to the metronome of the barcode scanner. A gentleman hobbled over to the cart and handed each of my little carolers a dollar bill. "Singing that good deserves to be paid," he said. Three voices thanked him and launched into the third verse of "We Three Kings."

As we strolled out the automatic doors, my son tugged at my hand. "I wasn't doing it for money, Mom," he said. "I was doing it because I wanted people to know about Jesus."

I stood still and looked into his eyes.

"I know, Buddy," I said.

My little guy just opened his mouth wider and continued belting out carols to everyone we spotted in the parking lot.

And me?

I joined him.

— Melissa Cutrera —

31

Chicken Soup
for the Soul

My First Christmas

*The bond that links your true family
is not one of blood, but of respect
and joy in each other's life.*
~Richard Bach

During the Thanksgiving and Christmas seasons each year, the baby stores always carry little infant shirts emblazoned with "Baby's First Thanksgiving" or "Baby's First Christmas." For me, though, that first Christmas didn't take place until I was seven years old!

I had been half-orphaned when I was only five after my birth mother died from complications of alcoholism. I had lots of memories from before she died but nothing very pleasant. No birthdays, Christmases, or other holidays. After her death, I was shifted from family member to family member before my birth father took me to Tehachapi, California, to live with him and my brother who was seven years older than me.

Quickly, I became familiar with the town, the people, and the businesses. I knew no strangers. I learned all kinds of bad habits, but I didn't realize at that time how bad they were.

Not only was I becoming more of a wild child, but something bad happened to me one night that made my birth father decide he couldn't care for me. Then he talked about me to a guy he met — a long-haul trucker from Oklahoma. The trucker and his wife had wanted children but never conceived. The more the trucker heard about my story, the more interested he became. He asked my birth father what he would think about a couple from Oklahoma City adopting his daughter. My birth father said if it was a good home, he would consider it.

The trucker called his wife in Oklahoma City and asked her what she thought about adopting a half-orphaned seven-year-old girl. Her reply? "Well, we won't have to change diapers!"

That was the beginning of the rest of my life. I came to Oklahoma City in August 1954, settled into school, and made lots of new friends. Adoption papers were signed, and I didn't even hesitate for a moment when the judge asked if this was all okay with me.

My new mom had a lot of work to do with me regarding boundaries. I had to learn not to speak to strangers, leave the yard without permission, or jump on the furniture, just to name a few.

The months went by, and soon it was December. It was no big deal for me since my life had never changed during the holiday season. But I was in for a big surprise! This was my mom and dad's first Christmas as parents.

Daddy had to wake me up that first Christmas morning, as Santa had never been able to find me before so I didn't know to be excited about Christmas morning. Under the tree, I discovered the greatest assortment of presents. There was a doll, doll bed, doll stroller, toy operator switchboard, and so many other fun things to keep me entertained for hours. I was so excited I didn't even want to eat — a very unusual thing for me.

Later Christmases would bring many other fun things a little girl wouldn't have thought to ask for, like a BB gun! I think my dad was the parent who chose most of the gifts for me. One year, he wanted to get me a train set, and another year, a pool table. I think Mom must have felt like she was taking care of two children when it was Christmas.

It wasn't the idea of Christmas, Santa Claus, or presents that made my life with my parents so special. It was the love I had never known before. It was the feeling of being safe, wanted, and secure just where I was, with them. Even though they have passed on now, those memories continue to make every Christmas particularly special for me, a little girl who had no idea what she was missing.

—Judy Allen Kemp—

32

Feels Like Christmas

*Each day of our lives we make deposits in the memory
banks of our children.*
~Charles R. Swindoll, The Strong Family

"Let's put the poinsettias on each side of the fireplace," I instructed my nine-year-old, Ryan.

He carefully placed his red tin-foiled pot down near his stocking below the mantel and asked, "Mom, how come Santa never leaves any mud or snow by the fireplace?"

"He's got all kinds of magic. If he can fly all over the world in one night, he can certainly keep things tidy," I replied.

"How does he make that flight anyway? Does he have some sort of time travel continuum device, like the Flux Capacitor from *Back to the Future*?"

"Wow, he might!" I exclaimed. "I know it's hard to understand, but I believe in things that I can't explain. Miracles, coincidences and the good will of Santa are real. Shall we go make some hot chocolate? We have whipped cream," I said, swiftly changing the subject.

We were entering a new era in Ryan's boyhood, and his seven-year-old brother, Leo, was never far behind him. The magic of childhood, especially at Christmas, filled my spirit with hope and my heart with joy. I adored watching my children's faces light up as they approached Santa to sit on his lap. Letters of love and gratitude were crayoned and sent off to Santa's workshop, and sugar cookies were decorated with care. We cuddled under fleece blankets and watched Christmas specials, and then thanked God for Santa during bedtime prayers. Those precious moments warmed my soul like the flames from our cozy fireplace.

One night as we sipped wine by the fire and wrapped gifts, I told my husband that Ryan was growing up and was full of questions. My husband hugged me and said, "If he asks me, I'm telling him that there's no better feeling than having faith." That's how I made my peace with what I thought would be my son's last magic Christmas.

Then came the spring of 2020. As we set up distance-learning stations, purchased facemasks and wondered when we would be able to hug grandparents again due to the coronavirus outbreak, my sadness over Ryan growing up seemed trivial.

My older son and I watched my seven-year-old perform his spring concert chorus song wearing his pajamas in his bedroom. He sang it to me as a Mother's Day gift.

"This is a love song to the earth, a diamond in the universe," he sang with pride.

Then came the chorus, which he sang with gusto.

"Heaven's poetry to us. Keep it saaaaafe 'cause it's our world."

He was smiling and using dramatic arm gestures now. He took an operatic bow. Wild mom-clapping ensued.

"I wish I could sing this with my friends at the spring concert, but I'm glad I can perform for you, Mom. I wouldn't rock out as much on the school stage," he explained with honesty.

I beamed, glad that he could find a silver lining to missing out on his spring concert as we quarantined at home.

"It's hard to be home from school and away from your friends. Do you feel lonely or sad? Are you worried about the virus?" I asked.

"I wish people weren't sick and I miss my friends, but I actually kind of like this. It feels like Christmas," he said, smiling.

"It does! I love quarantine," agreed Ryan.

"What do you mean?" I asked.

"We're all home together, not in a rush. We make pancakes and play Chinese Checkers," said Ryan.

"Yeah, and we make cards to thank the front-line workers, just like we send cards at Christmas," agreed Leo.

"And when Nicky's birthday party was canceled we got to secretly drop off his gift at his front door. It made me think of Santa sneaking gifts under the tree," said Ryan.

"And for Owen's birthday, we all drove by his house and honked our horns and sang 'Happy Birthday!' Instead of Christmas carols at church with bells, we sing in driveways and honk horns," he said with a smile.

"Plus, we keep baking cookies!" Leo added.

"You know how we read *'Twas the Night Before Christmas* by the fire? Well, I think of that when we listen to Mrs. Dean reading *Harry Potter* to the class on Zoom. We all listen to it together by the fire, just like at Christmas," Ryan said, smiling.

I was relieved to hear their take on the situation. We live in Westchester County, New York, which was ground zero for the virus. I thought they might have had anxiety, but they were already seeing the silver linings.

"I didn't think of it like that, you guys. What an awesome perspective. I was worried you might be feeling sad or scared. Do you have any feelings that have been tougher to deal with?" I asked.

"I wish this wasn't happening, but at Christmas we pray for those who are less fortunate than us, and now we pray for everyone affected by the virus. We donate toys at Christmas, but now we donate money to food banks. That's the best we can do," said Ryan.

"Are you worried?" I asked.

"A little, but I know everything will be okay," he said.

"How do you know?"

"I just do. I have faith. It's like Santa. I don't know how this will work, but I know it will. Peace on earth and all that, right, Mom?"

Leo sprang to his feet and, with dramatic flair, raised his arms and face to the heavens and belted "Joyful all ye nations riiiise," shaking his head in his best opera voice!

Not only did I laugh, but I learned what Christmas meant to my boys. It stood for treasured family time and united communities, threaded with love and generosity. Christmas is a home that cocoons us in safety and warmth, where we find solace in each other's good company. The Christmas spirit was carrying my children through an international crisis. It nourished them with resilience and optimism.

Discovering what Christmas meant to them was the best Mother's Day gift I could have received. As I write this in May, there is even a surprise snow squall outside! I wasn't expecting to feel overcome with the Christmas Spirit in the spring during a pandemic, but it traveled through time and space to this moment... It must have been that Flux Capacitor from *Back to the Future*. Thanks, Santa.

— Kelly Bakshi —

33

Where Does Santa Live?

Never ever doubt magic. The purest honest thoughts
come from children. Ask any child if they believe in magic,
and they will tell you the truth.
~Scott Dixon

I t was the end of October when my mom moved us from Communist Czechoslovakia to America to live with her parents — our grandparents. My brother was almost eleven, and I was eight. By November, we were enrolled in school, neither of us knowing more than five words of English. Very soon, I was speaking enough English to be understood — albeit with a heavy accent.

My brother, on the other hand, because he was older, or maybe because he was a boy, was more interested in kicking a ball than he was in learning.

I also had the advantage of having my cousin Millie in my class. She was my age and the best translator, helper and friend. By December, I was writing compositions in English.

My teacher had assigned the class homework, which was to write a story about Christmas. Of course, Santa Claus was a key player in my story, although in my home country he was called *Mikuláš*.

I wrote about the wonder of coming to a country where we were free to go to church on Christmas or anytime. This was not something we could do in the old country. I wrote about the joy of having uncles, aunts, cousins and neighbors in the U.S. whom we could trust. We had left very few relatives back home. But as skillful as I was in picking up English, it was very difficult for me to understand how Santa Claus or *Mikuláš* could travel from one part of the world to another in two days, from Christmas Eve to Christmas Day.

I asked my mother, "Where does *Mikuláš* live? How does he get here so quickly?" I asked Cousin Millie, and I asked my teacher the same question. "Where does Santa live?" The answer I got was always the same: "The North Pole." It still made no sense. It had taken us over a week to get to America, traveling by train, plane and ship. How could Santa get from one part of this vast world so far away so quickly — and in a sleigh, no less? One day, I asked my grandpa, Dedecko.

"Dedecko, I know Cousin Margie lives in Hoboken, Cousin Adele lives in Brooklyn, and we live in Astoria. Where exactly does Santa Claus live?"

My grandfather was a kindhearted soul, almost like Santa himself. He had come to the U.S. as a young man. Nevertheless, he still had a very heavy Czechoslovakian accent, like I did.

He said to me, "Come here, my child. Sit vit me. I vill explain eet to you."

I climbed onto his lap, and he said, "Evka, Santa lives een yo heart."

When I wrote my composition, I wrote what I heard my Dedecko say:

"For my first Christmas in America, my cousin who lives in Hoboken is coming, my cousin who lives in Brooklyn is coming, and so is Santa Claus, who lives in Yohart."

Whether Santa lives in "Your heart" or "Yohart," it makes no difference. As long as we believe in the magic of Christmas, he lives in us all.

— Eva Carter —

34

The Tale of Suzie Stretch

A characteristic of the normal child
is she doesn't act that way very often.
~Author Unknown

When I was four years old, the television commercials during the Christmas season were all about this grand and glorious doll named Suzie Stretch. The concept behind the Suzie Stretch doll was that she would be "just my size"!

Not only could I strap her feet onto mine and twirl around the room with a life-sized doll attached to me, but Suzie Stretch could also change the expressions on her face, which consisted of pulling her little bonnet back over her head and revealing a face that had eyes closed for bedtime snuggling.

Nothing could have been better than a doll my size, with "strappable" feet and a face that could change from smiling to sleeping! I begged for that doll. I pleaded for that doll. I asked Santa in the mall for that doll. I sent a letter to the North Pole about that doll.

On my little table on Christmas Eve, so as not to take any chances, I left cookies, red-velvet cake, ice-cream cake, and Dr. Pepper for Santa. I also wrote him a thank-you note in advance. I left snacks for Rudolph and the rest of the reindeer team, and I even wrote a note to Mrs. Claus giving her some of my mama's best recipes.

I had covered every base. So, when Christmas morning came and I raced down the hall, I wasn't surprised to find Suzie Stretch waiting for me under the Christmas tree. I paid no attention to any other gifts. I grabbed that doll, strapped her to my feet, and went twirling around the living room.

That is… until I looked into the face of Suzie Stretch. Her big, glaring eyes met mine. Her big, floppy mass of yellow hair flung itself in my face, and then… yes, then, my dad said, "Here, let's turn her face over." And, with one fell swoop, Dad changed that doll's face to the "sleeping side." Still attached to my feet, and nose-to-nose with me, her face on the "sleeping side" was more fearsome than anything I had ever seen in my life. To me, she looked just like she was dead.

I stopped twirling, threw that doll to the floor, and started to run — forgetting that she was still attached to my feet. So, as I ran, Suzie Stretch followed behind me. I thought she was chasing me. You should have seen my moves! I twisted and turned while leaping in the air. I ran to the right and bolted to the left. I kicked. I jumped. And I screamed! Still, Suzie Stretch hung onto my feet.

Finally, when Dad caught me, and Mom unhooked the doll, the Christmas drama was over. Well, sort of. For weeks after that, when I was drifting off to sleep in my bed, I would yell suddenly, "Mommy! You did get rid of Suzie Stretch, didn't you?"

So, I suppose Suzie Stretch taught me that "everything that glitters isn't gold," or, quite possibly, that Christmas toy marketing campaigns should be taken with a grain of salt and a healthy dose of child psychology. Or maybe what I really learned from Suzie Stretch was just to roll with the quirky, unexpected things that happen around our Christmas trees. Down the road, those will be the memories we treasure the most.

— Anna Elizabeth Gant —

35

A Guilty Christmas

Christmas isn't about candy canes or lights all aglow,
it's the hearts that we touch, and the care that we show.
~Mickey's Once Upon a Christmas

D ecember had been filled with hours of baking and holiday crafts. We had hung lights and decorations. Now it
was Christmas Eve and the children were bouncing with
excitement for the next morning.

My husband and I smiled, but those smiles hid our guilt. He
never said anything, but he didn't have to. Our family had struggled
financially. We'd cut back on family vacations and extra expenditures,
but we were still behind. It was hard not to feel like a failure when we
couldn't give our children the things they deserved.

We saw other families purchase electronics, phones and other
expensive gifts during shopping trips. I, on the other hand, had intentionally not attended Christmas parties because I didn't want to be
embarrassed by our low-quality gifts. I cried when I was alone so
my husband would not see the tears and think this was his fault. I
wondered how many times he had felt the same way.

We put the children to bed that night and read aloud 'Twas the
Night Before Christmas as we always did before they fell asleep. As we
were headed to bed ourselves, we heard a soft knock on the door. I
looked out the window as my husband stood near. It was late, and I
was a little nervous as I opened the door. A thin layer of snow blanketed
the ground. Tiny, delicate snowflakes were floating down and landing

gently. The air was crisp, and the moon shone down, illuminating the trees. The holiday lights created a colorful display. I didn't see anything right away, so I stepped out onto the porch.

Leaning up against our car were two child-sized sleds. My hands met my mouth, and tears instantly spilled from my eyes. We walked out to investigate, and as I picked up one of the sleds, my husband grabbed my hand. I turned to look at him. His cheeks and nose were rosy from the cold. His blue eyes were cheerful. We were both in pajamas and slippers.

At first, I was confused as he guided me to the top of the hill in our back yard. He carefully placed the child's sled down on the snow and gestured for me to sit. When I didn't, he sat down, pulled me onto his lap, and then down we flew. We hit the bottom of the hill laughing. In the distance, we heard someone singing, "I believe there are angels among us…" As they continued, more and more people chimed in. It sounded like a choir. My husband started to sing along loudly, so I did, too. Then, out of nowhere, our neighbors did. I saw tears glisten in my husband's eyes.

My husband's gaze left mine and looked past me. I turned to see what had caught his attention. Our two young children stood at the doorway of our home. They were half sleepy with smiles on their faces. They had boots on and coats over their pajamas. They raced to us and took turns sledding down the hill. Laughter echoed in the dark. After we made it back to the house, we were frozen. I heated up some hot chocolate and made toast. For the first time that season, true laughter filled our home as we shared stories and jokes. We tucked the children in again, and we all went to bed a little more cheerful.

The next morning, our tree felt bare. The guilt that had vanished was now creeping back in. The little money we spent on gifts just didn't go very far, and our Christmas felt like it was over in moments. I started to feel down when my kids vanished into their rooms.

They reemerged and begged my husband and me to go sledding with them again. I couldn't say no. It was the least I could give them since I hadn't been able to buy them much. As we headed out the door, my son hugged me and said, "This is the best Christmas ever."

His words sent me spinning. I realized in that moment that the gifts never mattered. My kids never needed gifts. They never complained about the gifts they received or the lack of gifts. All they wanted was for us to play together.

When I gave them my time, they felt more loved than if I had lavished them with gifts. Since then, we have made it a tradition to go sledding every Christmas.

— Alisha Isaacson —

36

The Big Coat Present

Christmas is the keeping-place
for memories of our innocence.
~Joan Mills

I was eight years old when I stood outside that store window with my father while the snow dusted our shoulders with soft white powder. It was dusk, and it was hard to see what my dad was looking at in the window. But then I saw it — a long blue coat.

A shiver ran down my spine.

Every Christmas, there was one special secret that my older brothers and sister were allowed to know. I had never been old enough to be trusted with it. I wondered if the time for that had finally come. Here. In the snow at dusk.

Knowing this secret was the true badge of honor and maturity in our family. Dad was a big, strong man, but he was also very gentle and kind. Every year, he would decide on a big gift for Mom. And every year, the kids who were old enough to know the secret would be told what that gift would be.

One year, it was a beautiful bathrobe. Dad had built a large wooden box and put the bathrobe in it so that Mom couldn't possibly guess what was in there.

Another year, he gave her a sewing machine. Mom loved to sew and was good at it, and that present had made her clap her hands and smile from ear-to-ear.

As the snow continued to fall this night, my father kept looking into the store window at that long blue wool coat. When I lifted my eyes, I saw a smile on his face I had never seen before.

"That's what I'm getting your mother for Christmas this year," he whispered, with a finger to his lips. "But you must not tell. You're old enough now to keep my Christmas secret."

I jumped up and down. My heart raced, and I clapped my mittened hands together, making a muffled sound while snowflakes danced on us.

"I won't tell!" I whispered back, promising with all my heart. And I meant it. I meant it more sincerely than anything I had ever promised before in my whole life.

Time stood still that winter night. We stood together in front of that store and felt the warmth of a shared secret. It was the most wonderful moment of my life.

Dad bought the coat. He took it home, wrapped it in beautiful paper and placed the package gently under the tree. It was, without a doubt, the prettiest present under the tree that year. And I knew what was in it! I felt so proud.

Christmas was a big event in our house, the most important day of the year. Presents were everywhere. We were not a rich family, but my parents always bought so many presents that they overflowed the living room and were lined up on top of the refrigerator in the kitchen! And every year, the big day was capped off by Dad giving Mom his secret present.

On Christmas Eve, there was nothing better than lying on the floor under the lit tree and looking at all those presents. Christmas carols played softly in the background.

This Christmas Eve, my brother Carl and I were lying on the floor in the living room under the lights of the tree. Rod and Shirl, my older siblings, sat across the room. They were teenagers and trying to act cool. Mom and Dad were in the kitchen, talking quietly at the table. I was filled with joy because I knew what was in that magnificently wrapped box for my mother.

All of a sudden, without thinking, I reached out just to touch the bright red bow on Mom's package. Before I knew it, Carl sat up quickly and shouted out loud: "Dad! Patty's touching Mom's big coat present!"

The silence that followed seemed to last forever.

I scooted back, away from the presents. My heart was racing and breaking at the same time. Rod and Shirl drew in big breaths and waited to see what would happen next. The Christmas secret was out. And it was my fault! It was my very first year of being allowed to know the secret, and I had ruined everything.

When Dad stood up, we all watched him, our mouths open, our eyes huge, having no clue what would happen next. But all he said was, "Do you want your big coat present now?"

Mom smiled up at him. He walked into the living room and bent down to pick up the present. He didn't get mad or seem upset at all. He just smiled and walked back to Mom, sitting there in the kitchen, and handed her the big package. She opened it happily, and then looked up and said, "This is wonderful because now I'll have a beautiful new coat to wear to Midnight Mass."

I have never forgotten that moment. We were all very relieved.

That night happened over sixty years ago. No one in the family ever forgot it. To this day, the biggest present given to anyone in our family is called "The Big Coat Present."

Even if it's not a coat. No matter what it is, the biggest and best and most secret present given in the family is called The Big Coat Present. And it will always be.

— Pat Dickinson —

37

Chicken Soup for the Soul

The Puzzle

Christmas is the season of joy, of holiday greetings
exchanged, of gift-giving, and of families united.
~Norman Vincent Peale

I remember pouting when I first caught wind that Uncle Stan and Aunt Grace were coming to spend Christmas with us. I was thirteen years old, and the last thing I wanted was to share the most special season of the year with two old people I barely knew.

Worse yet, my parents announced that Uncle Stan and Aunt Grace would be using my bedroom for the holidays, and I'd be sleeping on a cot in the storage room. I tried to protest, but my complaints fell on deaf ears.

"I'll freeze to death in there," I warned, reminding them how ice formed on top of the water pails the previous winter when the heater gave out.

"Don't be silly," Dad said, playfully cuffing the back of my head. "I'll bring in some old horse blankets from the stable for you to burrow under…" he joked, heading outdoors to do his morning chores. Mom continued to strip my bed while I sulked, having to move my clothes from the closet to make room for theirs.

"You remember visiting Uncle Stan and Aunt Grace at their place when you were a little younger, don't you, Lizzy?" Mom questioned, fussing with the new flannelette bedsheets she had bought especially for them.

"Sort of…" I nodded, faintly remembering a fairytale cottage by a river. There lived a tall man who called me "Pipsqueak" and a short, round woman who smothered me with hugs.

"I wonder if they'll bring me a present," I pondered aloud, trying, as Mom had suggested, to look on the bright side.

"Lizzy!" Mom scolded, shaking her head in disgust. "You know darn well Christmas is not about getting gifts. But," she added, "Speaking of gifts, you will have to buy your aunt and uncle something nice to put under the tree."

"Like what?" I questioned, rattling the few coins that were left over in my piggy bank after purchasing my gifts for Mom and Dad. I shuddered at the thought of having to spend my remaining savings on a gift that I feared would be impossible to find.

On our last trip into Huntsville before Christmas, Dad parked on Main Street not far from the grocery store as he and Mom had some last-minute shopping to do while I headed downtown, agreeing to meet them back at the truck in two hours. I didn't have a watch, but Mom reminded me to keep an eye on the Town Hall tower clock.

I shopped and shopped but found nothing suitable or affordable. Glancing at the clock, I knew time was running out. I had almost given up hope when I saw a sign in the window of Eaton's Department Store announcing a "clearance sale" on games and puzzles.

Suddenly, a light bulb went on in my head. Why not? I pondered the notion, worried my parents might think I was choosing Uncle Stan and Aunt Grace a gift I was hankering for myself. But the more I thought about it, the better I liked the idea — all because of something I remembered seeing at their house when I was little.

Filled with new hope, on a special mission, I rushed into Eaton's and made my way to the clearance tables where I eagerly rummaged through the items.

And then, lo and behold, there it was! It was the perfect gift and totally within my budget. In fact, I had enough money left over to pay the cashier for a square of wrapping paper and a pretty red bow.

Christmas came in a flurry, bringing Uncle Stan and Aunt Grace with it. Our small house was filled with laughter and excited chatter. Even though Uncle Stan still called me Pipsqueak and Aunt Grace couldn't get enough hugs, just seeing how much Mom and Dad enjoyed their company made me happy, too.

On Christmas Day, when we exchanged gifts, I learned one of life's most valuable lessons. Regardless of how much I loved the beautiful handmade gifts Uncle Stan and Aunt Grace had made for me — a hardwood rolling pin with my name, Lizzy, engraved onto the handle, wrapped up in a pretty lace-trimmed gingham apron — I received just as much joy, if not more so, in giving them my gift in return.

As Uncle Stan and Aunt Grace opened their present from me and discovered a 1,000-piece jigsaw puzzle that had on its lid a picture of a beautiful little cottage sitting on the banks of a river, their faces beamed.

"Oh, my goodness," praised Aunt Grace. "It's beautiful, Lizzy. It looks just like our place, doesn't it, Stan?"

"Right down to the Muskoka chairs on the veranda…" he said, pointing at the picture on the box.

Mom and Dad took their turns admiring the puzzle, and we all agreed that it surely did look a lot like Uncle Stan and Aunt Grace's home on the river.

"We love jigsaw puzzles," Aunt Grace sang, smothering me in hugs.

"We surely do, Pipsqueak!" Uncle Stan winked.

"I know!" I smiled proudly, telling them how I remembered seeing an unfinished puzzle on the table in their sunroom and several more framed ones hanging on the wall.

After the turkey dinner was over, we all huddled around the kitchen table in front of the woodstove and began working on the puzzle.

As our busy fingers fluttered over the colourful pieces, my aunt and uncle and mom and dad started swapping stories about their younger days. These were tales that I had never heard before.

Most of the stories were heartwarming. Others were amusing. And a few were sad. But I was captivated by every word. By the time the evening was over, I was happy that Uncle Stan and Aunt Grace had come for the holidays. In fact, I coaxed them to stay long enough to finish the puzzle.

And to this very day, that is one of my most cherished childhood memories of Christmas.

—Linda Gabris—

38

I Saw Santa!

May you never be too grown up to search the skies
on Christmas Eve.
~Author Unknown

Once upon a time in a town not far from Pittsburgh, there lived a family of five: a mother, a father, a big sister, a middle sister, and a little brother. It was in this town in the year of 1987 that something amazing happened. Something so amazing that it never happened before this night and has never happened since.

It was a Sunday night, and as was the weekly tradition in this house, each child was to bathe and get into pajamas before watching TV in the living room. The big sister and middle sister had finished their showers, put on their pajamas, and were playing in the living room while watching TV. The little brother had just showered and was wandering around in his yellow undies.

For reasons unknown (perhaps the sound of boot steps, the jangling of bells, or the scent of Christmas cookies), the little brother went to the back door just off the living room. And then the middle sister recalls that she and her big sister heard their little brother's tiny feet running from the back door to the living room, yelling, "I saw Santa! I saw Santa!"

"What?" cried the sisters. They ran to the back door looking for signs of Santa or his reindeer. They pressed their noses to the cold, frosty glass but didn't see anything. No Santa, no reindeer, no boot prints.

Was he there? Had he left? Did their little brother really see Santa?

They questioned their little brother repeatedly, who told them, "Yes, yes, I saw Santa!" With this amount of excitement, big sister and middle sister could only trust their little brother had indeed seen Santa Claus on their back porch. While disappointed they had not seen the man in red themselves, they were just as excited as their little brother who had seen him. They talked about it for days and days. They talked about it the next year, the year after that, and every year after.

As they got older, they began to question their parents. Who did little brother see at the back door that year? Was it a figment of his imagination? Had a friend dressed up as a shopping mall Santa to visit? Was it their father playing a trick on them? Their parents never wavered from the story that little brother indeed had seen Santa Claus that cold winter's night.

It wasn't until twenty or so years later that the middle sister asked the mother who their little brother really saw at the back door. Offhand, the mother said, "We told you years ago that was your dad."

"What?" said the middle sister. "You never told us that."

"I thought I did," said the mother.

The mystery of the little brother seeing Santa Claus was solved. It was their father, secretly dressed as Santa, as he often did for holiday gatherings. And, just like that, the magic was gone. And the decades-long mystery was solved.

Or was it?

While it certainly startled the middle sister to hear the answer after wondering for years and years, she realized something else. It didn't matter whether she knew who was at the back door that night or not. She had lived the magic of Christmas for more than twenty years with her siblings — reminiscing about that night.

Each Christmas, the story was retold, sometimes with details changed, and disagreements about what really happened. But did finding out the truth steal the magic of Christmas? Of course not, realized the middle sister. The magic of Christmas was planted well before 1987 in the hearts of children (and adults) all over the world.

The magic of Christmas wasn't just a Santa sighting. It was the love between the family members, the Christmas traditions they cultivated, and the friends and family they shared it with. It was the retelling of the Santa sighting with laughter and love. It was the magic of Christmas that the mother and father had created the night they chose to do something very special for their kids — but more so for keeping that magic secret for so long.

— Beth A. Wagner —

39

The Big, Yellow Turkey

*It wouldn't be Thanksgiving without
a little emotional scarring.*
~From the television show Friends

It was Thanksgiving Day, and the three of us cousins were downstairs at my grandparents' house watching *Sesame Street*, mostly to appease my youngest cousin, who was three years old. I was the oldest of the bunch and busied myself with my Ninja Turtle action figures on the fireplace bricks and getting into mischief with my grandparents' treadmill. My youngest cousin enjoyed singing and dancing along with Big Bird and Elmo, while her older sister played contentedly with her pink and purple My Little Ponies.

My mother came down the stairs to check on us. I quickly kicked up into a handstand against the wall to distract my mom so she would think I was practicing gymnastics and not getting into any trouble with the treadmill.

"Gwen, you really should not be doing handstands in a dress," my mother commented as she took her first glance around the corner of the stairwell, witnessing my feet above my head.

"It's okay. I put shorts on underneath," I replied matter-of-factly, as if this was normal with wearing dresses. For me, it was; getting me into a dress was like pulling teeth for my poor mother. I had complied for the holiday but only half-heartedly. Nothing fun ever happened while wearing a dress.

"Would any of you like to come upstairs and help set the table?" my mother inquired. The middle cousin was intrigued and nodded with enthusiasm. She ran toward the stairs and made her way up to the top to help in the kitchen. I shook my head, while my younger cousin finished an enthusiastic rendition of the alphabet song along with her favorite *Sesame Street* characters.

"Alright, Gwen, will you keep an eye on your little cousin until dinner is ready?"

"Uh-huh," I replied, as I took her hands in mine and began dancing with her to show that I meant it.

"Okay, then. It won't be long until dinner is ready, so start cleaning up down here."

"Okay, Mom!" I began gathering up my action figures but then remembered where I was with the treadmill. I kept an eye on my younger cousin while I went to find every pillow I could in the downstairs of my grandparents' home. I had just laid the very last pillow in the pile against the wall directly behind the treadmill when my grandmother called gently down the stairs.

"Dinner is ready!"

I rolled my eyes, looking longingly at the pile of pillows and thinking there would definitely be time later, maybe after dinner and before dessert. I turned off Big Bird and Elmo, and helped guide my little cousin up the stairs to eat.

The smell of green-bean casserole and sweet potatoes wafted in the air as we made our way up the stairs. My mouth began to water. Everyone was getting situated in the kitchen, but it still seemed like there was a lot to do, so I ran out onto the deck to join my grandfather as he finished up with the turkey.

"Hiya, Gwen, what do you say? Want to take a look at the turkey for me and tell me if you think she's ready to serve?" my grandfather lovingly inquired, as he took the lid off the smoker grill he had built himself, just for cooking turkeys at Thanksgiving.

"Yes, please!" I rubbed my hands together excitedly, eyeing the golden-brown bird up on the grill pan hungrily. This was the best part of any meal; my grandfather's smoked turkey was so moist and delicious. I looked forward to it every year. As I got older, it became a beloved ritual to get up early in the morning and hang out with my grandfather on the deck, or in the garage depending on the weather, as we chatted and tended to the smoking turkey.

My grandfather cut into the breast of the turkey, handing me a little piece of white meat to sample. He held a piece in his hand, and we taste-tested our pieces at the same time.

"Mmm, mmm! What do you say, Gwen? Is it good and ready?"

"Mmmm, it is a tasty turkey!" I smiled, as I rubbed my hand over my belly to give my approval for serving.

"I think we did a fine job here," my grandfather whistled. He put the turkey onto the pan to carry into the kitchen. I tagged along behind him and then helped open the deck door. There were smiles all around as he entered. Making quite the entrance, he exclaimed, "Here's Big Bird!"

Immediately, there was a shrill scream and hysterical crying. The youngest cousin took what my grandfather said to heart and screamed, "I don't want to eat Big Bird!" She sobbed uncontrollably.

The rest of us did all we could to console her and contain our laughter. We could not quite convince her that it was not actually Big Bird, with whom she had just spent time singing and dancing. She continued to look for traces of yellow feathers around the house just to be sure. She refused to eat Thanksgiving turkey for many years after that, and her antics are still recounted each and every year at our Thanksgiving table. When she got old enough, my grandfather started a new tradition, carrying in the turkey every year with the same announcement: "Here's Big Bird!"

— Gwen Cooper —

Gratitude & Grace

Remembering

Christmas is a day of meaning and traditions,
a special day spent in the warm circle
of family and friends.
~Margaret Thatcher

I t was a blistering cold Christmas Day. Everyone in the house was still asleep and I was alone with a very warm, fulfilling cup of dark coffee. For a moment, the world and everything in it was perfect.

This was an important day. It was the first time in many years that all my children made it home for Christmas. I walked from room to room and peeked in on their overgrown bodies that were once so small, now spread across king-sized beds with their feet dangling off. Once upon a time, they were up before the sun on Christmas morning, running to the tree to see what awaited them. Now, I was the one who was nervous and excited.

You see, I am a single mother of six kids. We grew up together. I was seventeen when I had my first child. She is now twenty-five. Her brothers are twenty-four, twenty-one, eighteen, and seventeen, and her baby sister is thirteen.

We grew up in financial turmoil. During the most crucial years, we lived in project housing. It was heartbreaking and difficult. I always did what I could, but sometimes that just wasn't enough.

Most Christmases, I had to rely on help from the Toys for Tots program. The program was such a blessing for our family, but as a mother it hurt to not be able to go and buy special gifts for my children. One Christmas, when my two oldest boys were eight and eleven, as I began to wrap their donated toys, I sat there and cried, thinking, "All these gifts that someone else picked out for my boys, and I couldn't afford to buy even one that was actually from me."

As I sat there, I wondered what I could buy with five dollars. I took my five dollars to Walmart, but all I could find were sets of marbles for eighty-eight cents each. So, I bought them. I wrapped them, and for that moment I felt better. The next morning, as they opened their gifts, they loved them all except for the marbles. I recall one of them saying, "Marbles, Mom? Really?" They kinda laughed it off and tossed them to the side. I retreated to my bathroom and quietly cried. I decided right then and there that I wasn't going to cry. Why should I? So, I went back out, and we all laughed off the marbles.

Every single year after that, I bought them a pack of marbles for Christmas. Time went on, and life got better. They went off to college on scholarships; one played college sports. I became a homeowner. Life was good, but I still continued to buy marbles. Every year, they would laugh. Every year, they expected them. Every year, they would ask, "Which gift is the marbles?" Every year, it was a thing.

On Christmas Day 2017, as I drank my coffee, I couldn't help but think about their gifts under the tree. I gave them marbles once again, but this time I placed them in a glass jar and enclosed a letter to each of them explaining the story of how the marbles came about. I asked them to display their marbles somewhere to always remind them of where they came from and how far we've come. I watched as they read their letters and tears streamed down their faces. I closed my letter with these life truths:

1) Be transparent
2) Stay well-rounded
3) Stay grounded
4) Always know who's in your circle
5) Always keep your shooter close
6) Don't let life make you lose your marbles

The hugs I got that Christmas were the best and most beautiful hugs I have ever gotten. Life had come full circle — just like a perfectly round marble.

— Cass Wingood —

The Nutcracker's Reluctant Fan

Sisters and brothers just happen, we don't get to choose them,
but they become one of our most cherished relationships.
~Wes Adamson

I saw The National Ballet of Canada perform *The Nutcracker* for the first time at age five. I eagerly anticipated watching my sister's performance as a mouse. She wore a head-to-toe costume, which meant I could only speculate as to which of the seven onstage mice she was. But the buzz surrounding her ballet debut carried me through the show, and I happily congratulated her on a job well done afterward. I would have preferred playing with my Thomas the Tank Engine that day, but I didn't mind going.

Then I saw the show roughly twenty-nine more times.

At some point in their lives, all three of my sisters moonlighted as very talented ballerinas, each of them performing in *The Nutcracker* numerous times over the past fifteen years.

I watched my sisters go through the ballet's natural role progression over many years: mouse to lamb, lamb to rat, rat to dog, and so on. I always felt proud when they were onstage, but as soon as they retreated to the wings, I used everything in my power to will the curtains shut.

As I saw the show more, my problems with its story and dancing became unavoidable. The music put me to sleep, I found the choreography repetitive, and even at a young age I could recognize

Gratitude & Grace | 121

the ballet's plot holes. Why were there dancing unicorns in a frozen Russian forest? How did the two lead children get to meet the Sugar Plum Fairy, the most valued person in the kingdom, without so much as making an appointment? And what on earth is so interesting about a wooden toy that cracks nuts?

By the time I was thirteen, I outright dreaded *The Nutcracker*. Once my third sister joined the show as I neared eighteen, I felt as though I'd seen the show an infinite amount of times. Apparently, I wasn't alone in this feeling as I asked my mom to guess how many times I'd seen the show, and she earnestly responded, "Sixty."

When I came home for the holidays this past winter, I expected to fall into what had become my usual routine: attend *The Nutcracker*, cheer for my sister, zone out for everything else. My days at home passed, and there was no mention of the show, so I finally asked what was going on. My mom said that my sister was in an "in-between year," waiting to become tall enough for her next role.

The last emotion I expected to feel from this news was sadness. But I couldn't help but mourn the absence of this yearly tradition, and I yearned to put a finger on the reason why I missed it so much. I wasn't a secret ballet aficionado, and the emotional absence didn't feel like nostalgia. I realized that while I didn't miss *The Nutcracker* itself, I did miss my yearly ritual of openly supporting my sisters.

The thing that kept me going back to the show year after year was the after-show moment when my family and I would pick up my sisters from backstage. We'd shower them with praise and flowers, and it was heartwarming to see how proud they were of themselves. The fact I didn't enjoy the show outside of their performances almost added to my fulfillment, since I'd made some sort of sacrifice — doing something I didn't enjoy — to support my sisters.

Once I'd figured this out, my whole attitude toward *The Nutcracker* seemed silly. Yes, I'd obviously overreacted by loathing it, but I'd also gotten into channeling all the praise I had for my sisters into feedback for their ballet performances.

I didn't need to wait for my sisters to hop off stage to tell them they were doing a great job — I could do it whenever I wanted.

For the rest of my time at home, I made sure to tell my sisters each and every time they impressed me. I commended one for her wildly impressive gender-studies essay and told the other how much her math skills had grown since I'd last helped her with her homework.

I'm embarrassed I hadn't adopted this strategy earlier, and I wish I'd avoided falling into a pattern of saving my praise for them for select December nights. I don't regret my *Nutcracker* experiences so long as my sisters are able to look back and see how proud I am of them, and how proud I've always been.

—Josh Granovsky—

42

The Angel's Voice

It is Christmas in the heart that puts
Christmas in the air.
~W.T. Ellis

Music has always been an integral part of my family. As a little girl, I remember my mother singing with the choir, her clear soprano blending with the others in praise. As I grew older, she and I would sing while we did the dishes or hung clothes on the line. When my brother Dean was born, he was also a musical soul, and he learned to play guitar as well as sing. In good times and in bad, there was always music in our house. It shaped us, comforted us, and gave us an outlet for feelings that might otherwise have gone unspoken.

After Dean became a father, we learned that his oldest son was on the autism spectrum. My nephew Dj did not handle social situations well, and sometimes even for him to speak aloud to more than just the family was a struggle. He worked very hard to overcome his fears, so much so that the year he was eight, he decided he wanted to be part of the Christmas music program at church with the other children in his Sunday school class. The part he had been offered was one that required him to sing a verse all on his own — a solo.

My brother carefully explained to him that to do this would mean that he would be singing in front of the whole congregation; there would be no one singing with him. Dj considered this very carefully. After a couple of days, he decided that he would accept the part. He explained to us that he believed he could do it because it was a very special occasion, and he would practice until he was as perfect as he could be. He said he knew his daddy would help him to be the best singer possible.

For over a month, he and his father practiced together. Every evening would find them locked away in the music room, my brother on guitar, and my nephew's small voice coming from somewhere deep down inside his little body. He gained confidence, and when the day of the concert arrived, he was certain all would go well. My brother waited backstage with him that night until it was almost time to go on. After giving Dj double thumbs-up, he came out to sit with the rest of the family to watch and take photos.

When it was finally time for Dj to sing, he and the line of angels filed out, with feathered wings perched on little shoulders and tinsel halos on tousled heads. They each stepped forward to sing their verses — until the time came for Dj to sing. The music played on, he heard his cue to sing, and he froze. His little face grew pale, and we could see the panic in his eyes as the silence grew. He seemed to get smaller as each note played out. The pianist started the intro again and played the cue, but still nothing came out. The entire congregation seemed to lean forward in anticipation. The silence seemed enormous.

The pianist started over again, and when the cue came, a low voice filled the air. It was my brother, singing the song in his son's place. Everyone turned to see who was singing, but my mother and I were fixed on the littlest angel on stage. With each word his father sang, Dj stood a little taller. The color came back to his face, and his eyes began to sparkle. He opened his mouth and began to sing along, his little voice growing stronger with each word. He finished his verses, stepped back into line, and the rest of the angels each took their turn. The show ended to thunderous applause, with the kids bowing dramatically, accepting their praise for a job well done.

From the back seat of the car on the way home that night, I looked at my family with new insight. My brother — this giant of a father, who had once been a goofy, tow-headed little monster who took every opportunity to prank me and torment me, but who also climbed into bed with me after having nightmares and cried if he couldn't follow me everywhere — had shown everyone what love was that Christmas Eve night.

His eyes met mine in the rearview mirror, and he reached a hand back between the seats to hold mine for a moment.

No words needed to be spoken. The understanding between us was louder than the voices of the choir that night.

— Cj Cole —

43

Rich Is Better

*Concentrate on counting your blessings, and you'll
have little time to count anything else.*
~Woodrow Kroll

The winter wind bit through my coat but didn't dampen my cheerfulness as I carried my four jars of home-canned tomatoes into the church basement. Excited to participate in feeding the less fortunate in our community at Christmas, I joined my Sunday school classmates as we boxed the goods for delivery.

That year, we went to Bobby's house. He was one grade ahead of me in school, but I never knew he was poor. When we took the box inside the small house, I saw bedrooms had been created by hanging sheets over ropes. Bobby came home while we were there, blushed, and disappeared behind a divider.

My heart ached for him. Even as a seven-year-old, I understood embarrassment. After we returned to the church, my teacher pulled me aside. I thought she was going to discuss Bobby's situation, but she didn't.

"Linda, we collected a lot of food this year. You have a large family. Why don't you take this extra box home with you?" She picked up the cardboard container, expecting me to accept the food.

"No. That's for poor people."

"All people need help at times," she said.

"Well, we don't." I pushed open the door and walked the three blocks to my house.

Were we poor? I began to look at our family with what I considered impartial, grown-up eyes and concluded that we were definitely poor.

My mother never suffered fools, and she didn't tolerate whining. After two days, she demanded to know why I'd been moping.

"We're poor."

"Who said that?" she demanded.

"Nobody said it. I figured it out." I couldn't look her in the eye. She'd been hiding this important truth from us.

"Why do you think we're poor?"

I listed reasons, becoming bolder as I elaborated on my realizations. "The church wanted to give us food. We don't have a car, only a pick-up, and we have to ride in the back when we go places. The women's missionary group offered to buy us shoes for this school year. And most of the clothes in my closet are hand-me-downs from a girl in my class. I never thought about it, but what if people are laughing about me wearing her clothes?"

"Are you done?"

I wracked my brain for other examples but came up with none.

My mother poured a cup of coffee and sat at the kitchen table, a rarity as she worked constantly. Maybe she hadn't known what people thought about us.

She stirred in a spoonful of sugar and sipped. "We are not poor. We are exceedingly rich."

This statement got my attention, and I grabbed a chair. "We are?"

"Do you have a healthy body? Can you run and play without any problem?"

I nodded. I was the fastest girl in our class.

"Do you have a good mind? Are you a good reader? Is there a library where you can learn about anything that interests you?"

I nodded again. My mother often reminded us that she only had an eighth-grade education, but she expected every one of her seven children to earn college degrees. I now felt embarrassed about bringing up the subject.

"Do you ever go to bed hungry?" She put down her cup. "I know you don't. We have a wonderful garden, and you eat well year-round. Canned food doesn't taste as good as home-grown. I should buy some tins just to prove it."

"But the rich people buy their food in cans," I protested.

"Because they don't have gardens. People in China don't get enough to eat. You do. And people in Africa don't have many clothes, hand-me-downs or not. Clothes aren't important. Consider the lilies of the field." She used that Bible reference when any of us complained about the clothes we wore.

"But people think we're poor."

"Well, they're wrong. You get to go to school and play, while some children in this world have to work. You live in America. You're free. You can go where you want to go, worship in any church you choose, and pursue any dream you can imagine. You are not poor! You're rich! I expect you to remember that every day of your life."

I never brought up the subject again.

Now that I'm older, I marvel at the riches we enjoyed, even on Christmases when there weren't many presents under the tree.

I've often heard the saying, "I've been rich, and I've been poor. Rich is better."

I know rich is better, for I'm an exceedingly wealthy woman.

— Linda Baten Johnson —

44

Babies' First Christmas

*When you look at your life, the greatest happinesses
are family happinesses.*
~Dr. Joyce Brothers

From the minute that second line showed up on the stick, I began dreaming of the little moments I'd share with my child, of the snapshots in time that would fill my memories and scrapbooks. Early days of snuggling on the couch. Drooly, toothless grins. First steps and favorite stuffed animals. Adorable outfits and funny faces.

And Christmas.

Christmas was "The Event" growing up, and I just knew my son was going to love the holiday magic as much as I did. As my belly got bigger, so did my plans. We'd bake Christmas cookies, sing carols, watch *A Charlie Brown Christmas*, and unwrap presents. He'd undoubtedly enjoy the wrapping paper more than the gifts, and my husband and I would laugh as we'd play in the mountains of wrapping paper. Baby's first Christmas was going to be the best day of our first year together.

Given that Reilly entered the world on January 11th, I had 348 days to dream before the big day.

As the days and milestones ticked by, my anticipation grew. He's smiling now — I can't wait to see the look on his face when he opens his gifts! He's crawling now — he's going to love barreling through the wrapping paper! He's standing on his own—how cute is he going to look standing in front of the Christmas tree in his footie pajamas?

I couldn't even wait until Thanksgiving before putting up the tree. After naptime on a day criminally early in November, I proudly escorted my son from his crib to the living room for his first glimpse of Christmas decorations. He pointed at the lights, giggled, and exclaimed his approval, clapping his chubby hands together.

I know he is going to love Christmas, I gleefully thought to myself.

Christmas Eve finally rolled around, and the plans were in full swing. Reilly, my husband, and I would sleep at my brother's house on Christmas Eve. Christmas morning would commence at my sister's house, with her husband, twenty-month-old and three-week-old babies, and our parents. We'd have a big breakfast, with fruit, muffins, a farmer's casserole, and our classic Christmas morning hot cocoa. With three young children on three different schedules, we'd decided to eschew a big Christmas dinner for appetizers and snacks throughout the day. The schedule was packed with presents, movies, crafts, and general yuletide merriment.

I barely slept that night, unable to contain my excitement. It was just before 7 a.m. when, through the wall, I heard my sister-in-law talking on the phone.

Finally! Someone's awake!

I tiptoed to the door to get myself ready before my son woke up so that we could get the party started as quickly as possible.

My brother met me outside the bathroom door.

"Merry Christmas!" I exclaimed with a bear hug, feeling five years old again.

"Merry Christmas!" he responded. "So, change of plans. Meg's water broke, so we're going to the hospital."

His words took a second to register. His wife was five weeks away from her scheduled C-section; she couldn't possibly be in labor.

Now somewhat of a childbirth veteran myself, I ventured into the master bedroom to assess the situation. When my sister-in-law's teary, panicked eyes locked onto mine, I knew, mama to mama, that this was not a drill.

Ready or not, we were going to need another "Baby's First Christmas" ornament for the tree.

The next few minutes were straight out of a sitcom, as my brother panicked that he hadn't yet gotten a memory card for his new camera. My sister-in-law tossed assorted items of clothing into a bag. My brother finally decided he didn't need to pack clothes — he just needed to go.

It wasn't until they backed the car out of the icy driveway that I remembered what day it was.

"Merry Christmas, buddy," I told my wide-eyed, confused son, who'd been watching the chaos unfold from the safety of his travel crib.

We eventually made it to my sister's house and tried to reclaim some normalcy. Christmas must go on! We dug into our breakfast while rehashing the morning's events. We videoed the kids' Christmas morning fun on our phones while anxiously awaiting texts from my brother.

At 10:38 a.m., as my son unwrapped a toy boat his grandparents had bought for him, little Avery was brought into the world via C-section and whisked away to the NICU.

Reilly loved every one of the gifts he received on his first Christmas. He drove his toy truck around the living room, pulled those adorable new outfits off their hangers, hugged his new teddy bear, and hammered away with his pretend tools. He climbed into the boxes, crinkled the wrapping paper, and rolled around amongst the bags. He gazed at the TV, totally enthralled, as Charlie Brown and his friends danced around their little tree. He gobbled down his first Christmas cookie.

He did everything I'd dreamed of and loved every second of his first Christmas. We snapped our way through every photo opportunity.

Yet, suddenly, it didn't matter in the slightest bit.

My baby's first Christmas wasn't about the wrapping paper, new traditions, or clothes and toys he'd outgrow in the blink of an eye. My baby's first Christmas wasn't about the gifts at all.

It was about my almost-one-year-old, happy, healthy baby boy, laughing his wonderful belly laugh as the dog tore past him and his Pop tickled him.

It was about my twenty-month-old, happy, healthy nephew, showing his baby sister his new car and sharing his toys with my son.

It was about my three-week-old, happy, healthy niece, cooing and smiling her sleepy smiles while nestled against her Nana's chest.

And it was about our Christmas surprise, tipping the scales at just over five pounds and nestled cozy and warm in a NICU incubator across town. It was about my beautiful, perfect, healthy, just-hours-old niece, wrapping her tiny fist around her daddy's finger, stealing her mommy's heart, and adding the final bow to the most wonderful day of the year.

It was the gifts of our precious babies that mattered the most on my baby's first Christmas — a day so special that his newest cousin just couldn't bear to miss it.

—Caitlin Q. Bailey O'Neill—

Fish Out of Water

Open your presents at Christmas time but be thankful
year round for the gifts you receive.
~Lorinda Ruth Lowen

I was gathering the ingredients for my husband's favorite dessert and talking to him. "I'll bake butterscotch squares while you're gone. On your way home, you'll pick up a pizza, right?" I was wearing my pajamas, ready for a night at home.

No response. Odd. I was sure he had been standing behind me a minute ago. I turned and immediately knew something was wrong. The grey-green pallor of his skin barely had time to register when it happened.

He fell straight back, stiff as a soldier. I screamed and dropped my wooden spoon, and then ran to him as fast as my open-backed slippers would take me. I was too late. As the back of his head hit the corner of a small Formica table, I screamed. I watched in horror as the furniture collapsed under the pressure, sending a ten-gallon aquarium crashing to the floor. Warm water rushed at my legs and feet, along with fish, fluorescent-green plants and a Davey Jones' Locker sign.

Numb with shock, I stared at my unconscious husband. Was he dead? I couldn't lose him. His head and shoulders lay in a puddle of water, on piles of shattered glass and iridescent stones.

With shaking hands, I punched in 911. Where did I live again? In the middle of stumbling through the emergency responder's questions, my husband opened his eyes. "Don't move! You'll cut yourself," I cried.

Baffled and confused, he was having no part of my instructions. I hung up with the dispatcher and helped him to a nearby kitchen chair. I ran my hand over the back of his head. No swelling. No gash. No blood. Miraculous.

"What happened?" he asked.

"You passed out and fell against the aquarium. An ambulance is on the way." I tried my best to comfort my husband, but he kept getting to his feet.

"Save the fish." His voice was frantic.

"Huh? Don't worry about the fish."

"No. I'm going to save them." He tried to get to his feet again. Seriously?

I offered a compromise. "Fine. I'll catch your fish if you promise to stay in that chair." I summoned my stern voice and pointed in a threatening manner. He finally backed down. As I sloshed around in ankle-deep water, dodging broken glass, the absurdity of the situation hit me. I bent over desperately trying to scoop up the flopping fish, and a thought ran through my brain. *I can't believe I'm fishing in my kitchen... and at a time like this.*

Mission accomplished. Goldie, Spot and Sparkles — yes, he named them — swam frantically around in my big yellow popcorn bowl. A plastic colander sat over the top — so they wouldn't jump out and make me start all over again. These were not normal-sized goldfish but fish that had been rescued from our backyard pond to save them from becoming fish-sickles (my husband's own words) during the winter months.

Check his blood sugar. I sloshed to the cupboard, found his glucometer and pricked his finger. Normal. I heard a whoop in the driveway, accompanied by bright red flashes on the foyer wall. Four paramedics hurried into the kitchen with their equipment. A quick medical assessment, and all results were normal. Strange but good.

They walked him to the ambulance, assuring me he was fine. I could meet them at the local emergency room in a few minutes. But I didn't change out of my wet clothes. Instead, I waded around my kitchen in a daze. The mess was not only external. I was a mess inside.

How would I possibly clean this up?

To complicate things, we had no family in the area. I phoned a young couple, friends from church. They assured me they would be right over. I picked up large shards of glass and dropped them in the garbage pail. I couldn't risk Faye and Ryan getting hurt while helping. I was thankful for my rubber-soled slippers.

Finally, I changed and drove myself to the hospital. My hands shook as I clutched the steering wheel. When I got to his cubicle, my husband was sitting up in bed, hooked up to a cardiac monitor. As soon as he saw me, heartfelt words tumbled over his lips. "I'm sorry for putting you through this."

The tender expression on his face made me want to break down and sob. At a time like this, he was worried about me? The doctor talked to us. All test results were normal. It could have been a faint, or it was possible that his heart had just stopped beating. Fear stabbed me in the chest. Had his heart stopped beating? If so, what made it re-start while he lay among the remnants of a broken fish aquarium?

We were free to go home.

After a simple supper of grilled-cheese sandwiches, we retired to bed. The next day would be our fortieth wedding anniversary. As I lay beside my husband that night, I placed my hand on his chest several times to make sure he was still breathing. The experience changed me. I felt like I'd been zapped with a reality stick.

Through it all, I saw the love of family, who were ready to drop everything they were doing and come help. Our oldest son, Tim, offered to drive two hours in dense fog the night of the accident to be with us. Our youngest son, Daniel, was nearing the end of a military training course, and he was nearby. He arrived the next day and stayed with us until just after Christmas. His presence was a source of strength.

All four children, their spouses, and seven grandchildren joined us thirteen days later. It was one of the most memorable Christmas Days I have ever experienced. The cause of the frightening medical episode was unknown, but what it exposed was my new knowledge: I knew without a doubt that I had received a precious Christmas gift that year. My husband was still with me. I would go forward and cherish each day, not sweat the small stuff, and love like there were no more tomorrows.

—LD Stauth—

Christmas in the NICU

This is the message of Christmas: We are never alone.
~Taylor Caldwell

The toy bin is turned over on the floor. Toys are scattered across the living room, but on this occasion I'm not fixating on how long it will take to clean up. Instead, one singular toy has my attention. It's a six-inch Cookie Monster doll, whose belly lights up when pressed.

A few yards away, under our glowing Christmas tree, an assortment of gifts in shiny paper are ready for Christmas morning. Playing nearby are my three dark-haired children, still too young to understand the concepts of gifts and Christmas. But if they could comprehend, they would be shocked by the contrast between this holiday season and the previous one — the one where my sons' first gift in life was a Cookie Monster doll from a stranger. Two Cookie Monster dolls donated anonymously to premature twin brothers.

The day the dolls appeared, the boys were four weeks old. I entered their hospital room and found the dolls, still in their store packaging, sitting by the boys' incubators. There was no card or information, just these brilliant blue dolls with crazy eyes staring up at me.

At the time, I thought it was a sweet, albeit odd, gift. I couldn't fathom why someone would choose battery-operated Cookie Monster dolls for these tiny, immobile babies. I refused to acknowledge we would spend Christmas in the NICU, or that the holiday season was passing almost unnoticed.

Over Thanksgiving, while I was in the hospital on bed rest trying not to go into pre-term labor, my husband had taken our toddler and bought a real Christmas tree. He said it was important for her to have some amount of normalcy. She was eleven months old at the time. I understood the normalcy he sought was for himself. They decorated it together, and there it sat in our vacant living room.

In all the commotion that followed, that tree stood un-watered and unloved. By the time I came home from the hospital sans twins, hundreds of pine needles had covered the floor. By Christmas morning, entire limbs had collapsed, and only the lightest ornaments managed to still cling to the near-naked branches. It was a pathetic sight, a stark reminder that there would be no real celebrating this year.

Christmas morning, we packed up our daughter and drove to the hospital. Looking around that bare, sterile environment, I was thankful for those Cookie Monster dolls. A pop of color in the land of gray and white, they were the only gifts my sons received for Christmas at the hospital. The few presents we had bought them would remain unopened under a pile of pine needles on the living-room floor.

Around the start of the new year, when the boys were strong enough to come home, the dolls tagged along in a box, tossed into the toy bin and forgotten. Life, in general, was forgotten as we focused all our energy on the care of our two ailing babies.

Now, one year later, with Christmas fast approaching, the memories are resurfacing — the tubes, the blood draws, the tests, the PICC line, the blood transfusion. I remember it all — the smell of antibacterial scrub, the location of the bathroom across the hall, and the associated painful trek due to my fresh cesarean.

I remember glancing into neighboring rooms, observing the babies on ECMO, and speculating who would be released before us. One day, it hit me that not all the babies would make it out of the hospital. I fervently prayed that mine would.

I avoided gazing into the rooms after that.

Now I sit in the comfort of my warm home admiring that Cookie

Monster with my three children playing at my feet. I think about the stranger who donated them. Someone knew it would be many months, but one day my sons would find joy in pressing Cookie Monster's belly and watching it glow.

I scoop up the little doll and apply a kiss to its head before passing it to my son. I watch as my son bites its ear and then drops it, keener to play with a piece of junk mail accidentally dropped on the floor. I retrieve the doll and sit with it on the couch, stroking its fuzzy blue hair. Perhaps this donation was not just for my sons. Perhaps my generous and wise donor knew there is nothing a parent needs more than hope for the future, hope for the day when a baby is capable of playing with a doll.

—Kristin Baldwin Homsi—

47

The Dollhouse

*That's the thing with handmade items. They still have
the person's mark on them, and when you hold them,
you feel less alone.*
~Aimee Bender, The Color Master: Stories

It was Christmas Eve, and my mother had spent all day enclosed in the laundry room. Everyone in my family knew she was working on a "special" Christmas present for Molly. I had been banned from the basement for weeks.

I was nine. More than anything, I wanted a ten-speed Schwinn bike. As the youngest of five children, I rarely received new items. I was convinced that I was going to get a brand-new bicycle this Christmas — the kind with curved handlebars. I was finally going to be cool.

It didn't dawn on me that bicycles usually come assembled, that whatever my mother might be doing behind those closed doors for weeks and months on end couldn't possibly involve a bicycle. As all children do, I saw and heard only the pieces that would fit the story I was telling myself: *I am going to get a new bike.*

Would it be blue like my neighborhood friend's? Maybe shiny and red like the one at the store? Or perhaps it would have a sparkle finish. I went to bed in my blue one-piece pajamas and lay awake most of the night with visions of wheelies dancing in my head.

I woke up Christmas morning bursting with excitement. I bounded out of bed, woke my older siblings, and even briefly considered the

Gratitude & Grace | 141

weather. How was I going to ride a bike through the Minnesota snow? I shrugged and yanked my boots out of the closet.

When I reached the bottom stair, I stopped. I saw my father with his Polaroid camera aimed and readied. I felt everyone's eyes upon me in eager anticipation of my reaction. But as I searched and searched the living room, I saw no sign of a ten-speed bicycle — or any bicycle at all. And then my gaze settled on the unwrapped gift placed under the Christmas tree with a giant red bow: a dollhouse.

A dollhouse.

In an instant, I understood. There was no bike, no shiny vehicle with which I would speed down Pinehurst Avenue. I would need to backpedal on my confident assertions that I was receiving a "brand-new bike" this year. My dreams of keeping up with my siblings in their neighborhood exploits and adventures sank, as did my heart.

I fought back tears. Blessedly, I was able to feign happiness and gratitude. The Polaroid photo from that morning shows me looking thrilled.

A tomboy by nature, I was slow to warm to the dollhouse, but eventually I did. My friend and I spent lots of time in craft stores, tapping our imaginations and our mothers' wallets to indulge our creativity. I wrote stories about the dolls; my friend rearranged the furniture. Our mothers sewed miniature drapes, davenport coverings, and bedspreads.

Quarantine 2020. My daughter is too grown-up for the dollhouse now; today was the day to brush off the dust, wipe it down, and store it away for future grandchildren. I lifted the heavy front cover off the dollhouse… and inhaled my heart.

There, on the inside, was my mom.

The painstaking detail, the cross-stitched doll-sized towels, the needlepointed wall hangings, the framed face of me at nine years old in the doll's bedroom. The Lilliputian-sized cereal boxes and novels and cans of vegetables. The piano with tiny sheet music of the real pieces that I once played. The shingles on the rooftop—each one glued on meticulously.

My mother had spent hours, weeks, and months creating something this special for her youngest child, the one who usually got the hand-me-downs. This was a gift of her soul, one that was opened in 1980, but not fully unwrapped until 2020.

— Molly Mulrooney Wade —

48

The 250 Christmas Presents

Those who we have loved never really leave us.
They live on forever in our hearts,
and cast their radiant light onto every shadow.
~Sylvana Rossetti

What kind of man takes on the job of giving the eulogy for a woman he's never even met? The kind of man who is called on by the kind of family that rarely goes to church — that's what kind.

He came to my parents' home and gathered us in the living room. He asked the basics, getting a sense of my mother in only the most obvious ways. I sat on the couch and tried to answer the man; he was only doing his job. He had been sent here to learn about a woman he would never meet and offer a summary of her entire life while standing at the front of a funeral home.

I could have written and said a million things about my mother. I should have. But, of course, then, I couldn't bear to do it. But who was this man in tan slacks and short sleeves, the owner of the big-and-tall shop in town? His long fingers took notes about my mother while his jacket hung nearly to the floor off the back of the rocking chair. He was a one-time visitor doing a job that I should have been doing. Asking and asking, and kind, so kind.

Sitting on the couch, I worked hard to like him. We answered his questions: blue eyes, 1947, Newberry High School. It was like Mad Libs: *The Young and the Restless*, bologna sandwiches, three daughters.

The questions droned on. He seemed to have an endless supply. Finally, he asked about our holiday traditions.

"Did Judy celebrate Christmas?" he asked.

The question was no sooner out of his mouth than my father's answer came thundering out of his: "Darn right, she did!"

The formal mood in the room stood on its tiptoes and waited. The tall, lanky man wrote nothing on this clipboard, unsure if this was going to be the beginning or the end.

"Presents," I said, trying to smooth things over. "She always went overboard on the presents."

"Yes, oh sure, absolutely," my sisters murmured.

My dad stiffened on the couch next to me, and I knew what was coming. It was like December 25th, and he'd just stepped into the living room and spotted how many gifts my mother had bought us all.

"So many presents," my father said, "it about broke me!" His voice boomed into the room, across the beige carpeting and slicing along the wooden blinds hanging behind our visitor's chair.

And with that, my father forgot his grief — his manners, too — and went into a full-on rant to the tall and lanky man.

"I'd bet there were 250 presents under that tree," Dad bellowed, leaning forward. "Who needs that many presents? Tell me, who?"

Even our last Christmas together, three weeks ago, had been huge. My mother had given her thirty-something daughters her checkbook and a long list. She had orchestrated a massive gifting like every other year, even if she hadn't had the actual pleasure of doing so herself.

My father was beside himself. Of course, I realized now, he hadn't had the heart to complain about it this year, the last year. Instead, it was a pretty, ribbon-wrapped bomb sitting inside him on the plaid couch.

And with one little flicker, the fuse was lit. He went on a jolly rage.

I didn't stop him. What a pleasure it was to hear him complain about our mother once more.

I started countering his points. "Over 250 gifts? I'd say 125, tops."

"Two of everything? Try three, one for each daughter," he said.

"And the year of the Barbie Doll campers? Santa did good work that year."

Now, I appreciated the tall and lanky man. He'd poked and prodded until he'd found a thread to pull at. What would be more telling about a woman and her family than to get her husband to go off on a well-practiced rant? We all played our parts, agreeing and denying at regularly scheduled intervals.

"Identical sweaters, same style, but," my father looked sideways at me in accusation, "different colors."

"One blue, one white," I said, conceding the point.

And the gift wrap and boxes and bows.

"I couldn't see the dining-room table for the month of December," my father said, pointing at the table in the other room, currently bare.

The moment almost derailed us, our eyes and hearts traveling to the table no longer holding our mother's meals.

But my father turned to the most pressing issue of all: coupons vs. costs.

"How much do you really save if you have to drive to town for ten dollars off a sweater?" he asked.

My father answered like he always did: before anyone else could.

"Nothing, once you figure twenty miles on the car and five dollars in gas!"

Tall and Lanky had quit writing, but he had started smiling. My father was enjoying himself; we all were.

"What about the time she bought two red turtlenecks for me and didn't remember until I unwrapped them both?" I asked.

"See?" my father bellowed to the man, who had one leg bent, ankle propped up on the other knee, his head thrown back laughing.

"But," I cut my father off, finally coming to my mother's defense, "what about the time Mom bought you a snowmobile for Christmas?"

"Speaking of which," my father replied joyously, "you should have seen the bills! She didn't care!"

And so it was that the tall and lanky guy delivered a perfect eulogy a month after our last Christmas with her. The story he played up the most was the one about 250 presents under the tree. ("Barry's number, not mine," he said.) We laughed even as we cried. And, in the end, he gave us the gift that we needed most that year. He'd worked through the grief, sifting and sifting, until the joy of our mother surfaced again.

— Kandace Chapple —

My Best Mistake

Christmas is the season for kindling the fire
of hospitality in the hall, the genial flame
of charity in the heart.
~Washington Irving

"It's the most wonderful time of the year," my seven-year-old son, Nathan, sang with a huge grin. I sighed. I love Christmas. I do. It's wonderful and cozy and brings families together. It's a chance to show the people we love how we really feel about them.

But it's also busy, bordering on chaotic. My to-do list is longer during the month of December than at any other time of the year.

But I really do love Christmas.

One evening in early December, I flopped down on the couch next to my husband, Eric. I'd spent all day decorating the house for the season, and I was tired.

"The tree looks great, honey," Eric said.

"Thanks. It's a shame it will only be up for three weeks before I have to spend another whole day taking it all down again." I shrugged. "It's pretty, but sometimes I wonder if it's worth all the effort."

He smirked. "I told you last year that it's okay with me if we don't decorate. I know it's a lot of work."

I looked around the house, loving the cozy feel the decorations provided. "I can't stop decorating for Christmas," I said. "Think of how upset the kids would be."

His smirk grew bigger. "Oh, yes, it's all for the kids."

I nudged him with my elbow. "Okay, I admit it. I love it, too."

But the next day, I was not loving it quite as much. I had a long list of other Christmas-related tasks, and nothing was going right. The previous week, I'd sent my kids' wish lists to my mom, my mother-in-law, and my former mother-in-law, who was still very much a part of our family. I'd been careful to monitor Nathan's lists to ensure that he didn't ask more than one grandma for the same toy. I'd told him to make three separate lists, one for each grandma. He'd done a great job creating the lists with about the same number of toys on each list but no duplicate items. He brought them to me, clearly excited about his carefully crafted lists.

I set them by the computer. "I'll send them to your grandmas tomorrow morning," I told him. The next morning, I scanned the three lists into the computer. And then I e-mailed the exact same list to each grandma. (I don't know how it happened except to say it was early, and I hadn't had coffee yet.)

Worse still, I didn't realize the mistake until the grandmas started texting me pictures of the toys they'd purchased. Three *Star Wars* light sabers — even in the same color. Three identical *Star Wars* Lego sets. Three of the same video game. Three of everything he'd ask for on one list. And nothing on the other two lists.

And it was all my fault.

"I was so careful," I moaned to Eric. "How can I tell the grandmas that two of them have to return all of the toys they just bought? And how do I choose which two to tell?"

"I'm sorry, honey," he said. "But I'm sure they'll understand. Mistakes happen."

"What mistake?" Nathan said.

I didn't realize he was listening to our conversation. I sighed and explained the situation. "I'm really sorry, Bud," I said. "I goofed, but I'm going to talk to the grandmas and try to fix it."

His shoulders slumped with disappointment. But an hour later, he came back, wearing a determined look on his face. "Mom, don't talk to the grandmas," he said. "The number of toys on just one of my lists is more than some kids get. I don't need all those toys."

"But the grandmas already bought them," I said. "So, if I don't call them, you'll have three of the exact same toy."

He nodded. "I know. That's why I'm going to give away the other two to kids who don't get much for Christmas."

Tears flooded my eyes. My silly mistake had turned into a proud parenting moment.

We talked to the grandmas, who all agreed that Nathan's selfless decision should be commended. The grandmas kindly understood that I'd sent the lists before being properly caffeinated.

It's true that Christmas is the busiest time of the year. But no doubt, it's also the best — especially when our kids remind us that it's not about the decorations we put up, the gifts we receive, or even the food we enjoy. It's about loving one another. It's about putting others ahead of ourselves.

Christmas is about giving to others to show them they are important to us.

Even when the giver is a seven-year-old boy and the gift is a *Star Wars* light saber.

And the recipient is another child. A stranger whose only gift this Christmas might be that duplicate toy.

It was the best mistake I ever made.

— Diane Stark —

The Dinner Guest

If you really are thankful, what do you do? You share.
~W. Clement Stone

I nervously checked my cluttered kitchen that Thanksgiving morning. My turkey was stuffed and roasting in the oven, while vegetables simmered on the stove top. Fresh apple pie filled the house with an aroma that tempted my youngest son to linger close by my side, just in case I needed someone to help with tasting.

"What in the world was I thinking?" I muttered as I sent my boys to tidy the stray toys that had found their way into the living room. Meanwhile, their father went out into the cool November air to pick up our dinner guest, Joann. I had run into the elderly widow at the grocery store in the frozen-foods aisle the week before and spoken to her. She told me that since she was alone for the holiday, she was choosing a frozen turkey dinner with bigger portions so she could share with the fuzzy yellow cat that was her companion. My heart ached at her loneliness, and I invited her to come to my home to share the meal with my family.

Now that the day had come, I was filled with nervous dread. My cooking was good enough for my little family, but what if she found it unacceptable? I was a young mother of two lively boys, and our conversation consisted of baseball and video games most of the time. What would we talk about, and how would I entertain her? The answer came to mind so suddenly that it seemed inspired. I knew exactly how to fill the time! I would let my children decorate the Christmas tree while Joann was at our home. Surely, their excitement and joy would cheer her.

The dinner went better than I anticipated, and compliments about the best stuffing she had ever been served eased my worries. The lack of decorum of brothers tossing dinner rolls across the table to each other brought a glare from me, but my guest merely laughed at their antics. As I cleared the table, my husband went to the attic and returned with boxes of colorful ornaments, ropes of glittering garland, and the artificial tree that was folded carefully into its cardboard container.

I watched the animated faces of my children as they told Joann about presents, Santa, and all the toys they were hoping they would find on Christmas morning. I also saw the smiles each tale brought to her wrinkled face. Her eyes glittered nearly as much as theirs as the dreams of gifts grew more and more grand with each story.

As the evening ended, my husband warmed the car to drive her home. I pulled a plate from my shelf and filled it with leftovers for Joann, enough that even her kitty could enjoy a meal. Her bent frame came near, and her wrinkled hands grasped mine. She gently kissed my cheek and whispered, "Thank you for having me."

The years that followed brought Joann to our Thanksgiving table many times, and we always pulled out the Christmas tree decorations to finish the celebration. Most years, Joann brought a cherished ornament of her own to add to its branches. We talked about a time when she was very young and the only gifts she received were fruit and candies. Sometimes, she reminisced about raising her own son just after the war and struggling to buy a few meager toys for his Christmas gifts. I treasured her tales of a life much slower and simpler than the hectic pace of mine.

Over time, her gait slowed, and the year came that we had to build a makeshift ramp to bring her wheelchair into our house. Finally, her weakened body was no longer able to make the trip, so I brought the turkey dinner to her. My boys missed her that year, but the tinseled tree still went up that evening.

The guest I had so reluctantly welcomed that first year somehow became a dear friend, and my attempt to entertain her had become our family's holiday tradition. Joann had gained a little companionship, but my own life was enriched by knowing her. I had learned a valuable lesson through a simple act of sharing a meal: Kindness is a gift that gives both directions.

Many years have passed since those days. My sons are now grown. I miss the days when dinner rolls flew across my table and discussion centered around what Santa might bring. My dear friend Joann has been in heaven for several years now, but the memory of her gentle wisdom and faith has remained with our family. This year, like every one that will follow, when we gather at my table for Thanksgiving, it will be a time of love, fellowship, and an occasional guest. Then someone will remind me with a smile that it is time to put up the Christmas tree.

— Cyndi Bowen —

Doing Dishes

When all the dust is settled and all the crowds
are gone, the things that matter are faith,
family, and friends.
~Barbara Bush

I survey the pile of dirty dishes filling the sink, trailing across the counter, spilling onto the stove, seeming to reproduce exponentially. With no working dishwasher other than my two hands, the task is daunting. Thank goodness we'd had leftovers the night before. No big pots and pans to scrub, just plates, glasses and silverware... tons of silverware. How can nine people, three of them children, use every knife, fork and spoon I own?

While I wait for hot water to fill the sink, I pick up a glass jammed into one corner of the counter. I study it. My eight-year-old grandson beamed last night when I handed it to him, milk sloshing over the rim. Shaped like a football, that glass has become his special glass every time he visits. I smile at his smile.

Still grumbling, though now somewhat subdued, I think back to how I was left with this mountain of dishes. This was what my family calls a "Birthday Weekend." We observe birthdays as long and as hard as we can. It's pure luck my birthday falls during the holiday season, wedged equidistant between Thanksgiving and Christmas. Sometimes, birthday "weekends" can last a full seven or eight days. Friday night was a birthday party for me, which included hosting thirteen people — nine family and four friends. My friends brought mounds of mashed sweet potatoes and a ham casserole, while my two daughters brought homemade rolls and a pot of delicious pinto beans. I supplied grilled chicken, gravy, and mincemeat pie.

My family returned last night, Saturday, to enjoy a leftover feast. Instead of cooking something new, we simply reheated — for the nine of us.

After dinner and with darkness threatening, the out-of-town daughter and son-in-law announced they had to leave. "Sorry about the dishes, Mom, but we've got a long drive ahead and, you know, the kids… school… work…" There was a hug with a whispered birthday wish for me. *Okay*, I thought. *Maybe I won't be left all alone.* I turned to my other daughter, who, with amazingly perfect timing, announced, "Didn't realize the time. Tomorrow's an early day. Gotta go." I think I heard a mumbled "Sorry" trailing after her. *Next time I see her, I'd better get a nice, long hug.* The door closed, and she and her husband drove off before I could hand her a dishtowel.

My husband, no stranger to hot water and dirty dishes, is recovering from slicing his hands while repairing a water heater. He reminds me his doctor gave strict instructions to "keep your hands dry." And besides, he shrugs, no gloves fit his big, bandaged hand.

Which left… me.

Now with the water nice and frothy and up to the brim, I plunge my hands into the warmth and bring up a tiny spoon, still encrusted with applesauce. I smile as I recall the eleven-month-old eating it with wild abandon.

I pick up a plate. Remnants of grilled chicken cling to the rim. The fragrance lingers. I smile. My husband cooked the chicken using one of those big-as-a-small-house grills, one he even polishes on occasion. He took great pride in doing the chicken just right.

A bowl with bits of lettuce stuck like glue to the side reminds me that my younger daughter's trying to eat healthy. It's a battle she wins at times, but when the craving for pasta at Olive Garden takes over, she succumbs. We've had countless discussions about food, weight and desires. I wash away the lettuce and piece of cabbage and wish she still lived at home. Even though she's set up her own house across town, I miss her.

My older daughter lives in the south-central part of the state, over sixty miles away, so I don't see her all that often. Busy with three active boys, her life is one of naps, diapers, homework and cooking. I remember her struggling to cut meat for the four-year-old, pick up the sippy cup thrown by the baby for the hundredth time, and correct the eight-year-old's table manners while attempting to eat her own supper.

Then it hits me. Standing with a spoon in my hand, tears run down my cheeks. Every dish, spoon and glass bring back memories. Good memories. My two daughters, now grown, get along better than they ever did as children. Their discussions range from current fashions to the best way to freeze blueberries to efficient vacuuming techniques. My sons-in-law now engage in long discussions over politics, educational reform and gaming strategies. They've become friends over the years. And the three grandsons seem to be perfectly at ease here in our house. The two oldest, as usual, wanted their bikes brought out of the garage to ride in last night's waning light. They whined when their dad nixed the idea. The baby, having taken his first steps mere days before, delighted us when he erupted with bursts of giggles at the feel of soft carpet under his foot instead of the usual hard vinyl.

It all floods back to me. My husband and I did the same thing at this same table not too many years ago — pick up sippy cups, correct table manners, listen to tiny, excited voices talk about Christmas. I sniff back a tear and pick up another fork, another memory.

Before I know it, the dishes are done, and the counter, stove and sink are empty once more.

Empty. But I'm not empty. My life isn't empty. It's full of happy, healthy adult children and blossoming grandchildren. My life is full.

And I thank the dishes for reminding me.

— Melody S. Groves —

Chapter

6

Homemade Holidays

52

Chicken Soup
for the *Soul*

Merry Christmas, Marines

Bake the world a better place.
~Author Unknown

S till dripping sweat, I had just completed my usual post-run stretch. Today's run had been on the northern half of Perimeter Road in a slight drizzle—typical December weather on Okinawa. Plus, there hadn't been much to see in the way of scenery—just a tall fence with barbed wire on top.

I walked into the Operations Building, looking forward to a hot shower, a cold lunch, and completing the second half of my workday.

As I plodded up the stairs, I met my Staff Sergeant coming down. As we passed, he asked, "How was the run, sir?"

"Great. Did I miss anything big?"

"No, sir," he replied. "I put your mail on your desk."

"Thanks, Staff Sergeant."

"Yes, sir."

I continued upstairs, using the railing more than I desired to pull up my tired body. "Whew." I exhaled again at the top of the stairs.

Then I pushed through the double doors and maneuvered my way between men and women in camouflage uniforms to arrive at my desk.

"Oh, what is this?"

I plucked a box from my desk blotter. Wrapped in brown paper from a grocery-store bag, the box must've weighed ten pounds. The first thing I did was check the return address. It was from "Mom Scanlan."

I smiled. My mother never used "Mrs. John T. Scanlan." Likewise, she never used "Dorothy Scanlan."

"Well, a shower can just wait," I declared. Reaching into my desk drawer, I pulled out a pair of scissors as I sat down. Then I cut into the brown paper and cardboard.

Layered on top were peanut-butter Kisses individually packaged in plastic wrap. Alright! What better place to put a Hershey's chocolate Kiss than in the center of a peanut-butter cookie?

Then I dug down to the next layer, made up of chocolate crinkles—also individually wrapped. Woo-hoo! They consisted of chocolate cookie dough rolled in powdered sugar and baked into a chewy perfection.

Lastly, the bottom layer was made up of Christmas sugar cookies with colored icing atop the shapes of Santa Claus, angels, reindeer, and bells. I had grown up on Mom's sugar cookies.

I looked around to see if anyone had noticed. Nope. So, I grabbed a peanut-butter Kiss and a chocolate crinkle and stashed them in my top desk drawer.

Then I stood erect and beckoned, "Hey, Marines!"

Every head in the office swiveled to look at me.

"Have some Christmas cookies, courtesy of Mom Scanlan."

Instantly, my desk was overrun with young enlisted men and women who were probably spending their first Christmas away from home.

"Thank you, sir."

"Thank you, sir."

"Thank you, sir."

Seconds later, I was left with an empty cardboard box.

A tear welled in the corner of my eye, which I quickly wiped away. These were eighteen- and nineteen-year-old kids, spending Christmas on Okinawa, and I had just made their day.

I mumbled, "Merry Christmas, Marines."

—John M. Scanlan—

53

Christmas with a New Family

I don't remember who said this, but there really are
places in the heart you don't even know exist
until you love a child.
~Anne Lamott

When I married my husband, we blended our families and I got a new twelve-year-old daughter. She came to live with us and my eight-year-old daughter. When Christmastime came, I started hearing a certain phrase: "We used to…"

"We used to make sugar cookies for Christmas and decorate them," my husband said to me. So, I made sugar-cookie dough — the kind you stick in the fridge for hours and then come back to roll out and shape. I botched it. It got warm beneath my rolling pin and stuck to everything. My husband tried to comfort me by saying, "I remember when we tried to make them for the first time. We screwed it up, too." I started to feel jealous.

"We used to make breakfast pizza and cheesy potatoes for Christmas morning," he said to me on a walk through the grocery store. My throat tightened. I felt like a replacement — a stand-in for some once-upon-a-time that I had nothing to do with.

At home, I put the groceries in the fridge and heard the intro of yet another anecdote beginning with, "We used to…" He started to say it, but I didn't let him finish.

"If you're trying to recreate something you had with someone else, then why am I here?" I asked. I wanted to create new, different memories with the man I loved and our blended family. The last thing I wanted to bring into our home were traditions of some other marriage that ended badly.

He stopped unpacking a grocery sack and looked at me. "I hope you understand that all of this isn't for me."

The knot inside me unclenched. In his face, I saw the worry that only a father could carry. This wasn't about what he needed for his holiday. How could I have missed that?

Later, I retrieved the Christmas decorations from the basement. "I love ornaments," the twelve-year-old said to me.

Smiling, she reached into the plastic tub, looked over the decorations and pulled them out one at a time. There were crocheted ornaments and wall hangings that my mother had made when I was a child. I even had the crocheted stocking that Mom had made. Ornaments I had made in school were in there as well as my eight-year-old's baby ornaments and more decorations from her craft days at school.

I watched my twelve-year-old grow quiet and her excitement vanish. In this tub of decorations, she didn't exist. Her childhood ornaments and holiday memories were someplace else. I didn't have to say the words. Every item in the box screamed, "We used to… without you."

"Great," she said. "So, everyone's going to have stuff to put up except me."

She started to walk away.

"Wait a minute," I said. Then I shouted to my husband, who was in the other room, "We're going to the store!" We got in the car and I wanted to say something. My face was pinched, and I was mad. What was I doing? I had no idea. All I could see was my husband's worried face and hear his repeated attempts to save the pleasant scraps from his past for his little girl — *our* little girl — the now silent, angry girl in my passenger seat. We arrived at the supermarket. I turned off the engine.

"Listen," I said with a heavy sigh. "I can't bring back the past or duplicate your traditions. I can't go get your ornaments. I wish that I could, but I can't."

She looked out the windshield and didn't blink. It wasn't like I was telling her something she didn't already know.

"Here's what I can do," I said. "I can promise you that we'll create new traditions together." She looked at me doubtfully. "Let's go," I said.

We got out of the car, and I took her to the seasonal department of the supermarket. "Pick out some ornaments, whichever ones you want," I said. She looked at me, and I knew it wasn't the same, but we had to start somewhere. She went up and down the aisle and settled on a multi-pack of blue and silver ornaments of varying shapes and sizes.

At home, I opened my sewing machine. I sewed everyone a stocking to hang over the fireplace. The twelve-year-old's stocking had penguins on it, the eight-year-old's stocking was adorned with cookies, and my husband's stocking featured bears.

While my mom was visiting, we made salt-dough ornaments, which are made like cookies. Once they were baked and painted, they would keep forever thanks to the salt. Well, the ones the dog didn't eat off the tree would keep forever....

Then, the twelve-year-old and I went to a local paint-and-bake ceramic studio. We painted Christmas ornaments for a family gift.

Each year since then, I've made the girls a Christmas ornament with their name and year on it. Some are cross-stitched, and some are painted.

"For how long will I get these ornaments?" the older one once asked.

"Until you have babies," I told her. "Then I'll make the ornaments for my grandchildren."

"I might never have kids then," she said, and I laughed.

Last year, I cross-stitched an extra ornament for my now eighteen-year-old. It had the year of her birth on it along with her name. I gave it to her privately on Christmas Eve. "Every baby deserves a first Christmas ornament," I told her. If I could've turned back time and made her mine from day one, I would have.

I've also mastered the sugar cookies in my own way. A friend gave me a recipe that doesn't require the dough to be refrigerated. This works for me. I make cookies with the girls every year. I also make cheesy potatoes. Turns out, they're really good.

— Bonnie Jean Feldkamp —

54

Mom's Handmade Masterpieces

From home to home, and heart to heart,
from one place to another, the warmth and
joy of Christmas brings us closer to each other.
~Emily Matthews

"What bright idea do you think Mom has for us this Christmas?" I said to my brother Mike, as we waited in the living room for Mom to return with our handmade gifts.

I was making a pun about Mom's "bright idea." Last year, Mom had fashioned lamps out of tree limbs that were two feet tall, and she did all the sawing, drilling and wiring herself. We had each received one to take home.

Mom's lamp constantly needed repairs. The bright light and shade leaned from side to side, and then from front to back. It looked like I was sending out a nightly distress signal.

But Mike and I never told Mom about the faulty fixtures on the lamps.

Mike had a house in Missouri near Mom; I had moved to Indiana. Mom lived alone; Dad had passed away many years ago. When others would have retired, she still worked as a custodian at the local school. We all admired her giving spirit, as well as her cooking and gardening skills. Her personality was fun-loving and creative, which made for some interesting handmade gifts. We didn't want to hurt her feelings or discourage those projects.

Ten years ago, Mom's handmade Christmas tradition began. After all the gifts had been unwrapped, Mom said, "I have made something for each of you." She disappeared to the back bedroom. Mike and I looked at each other, not knowing what to expect. Mom reappeared with an unwrapped gift and handed it to Mike. Then she went back to retrieve mine.

Mike held up the mystery item for me to see. It was a blue-jean rug. Mom laid an identical, hefty rug on my lap. She was beaming from ear to ear as she explained the details of the entire three-month project — buying blue jeans from yard sales, cutting, braiding and stitching.

After Christmas, I packed the rug in my car for the return trip home. I noticed an unpleasant odor coming from the back seat. At the first rest stop, I pinpointed the smell; it was the blue-jean rug. When I arrived at my house, I unpacked the rug and placed it outdoors. It remained there as a door mat until the stitching gave out.

I didn't tell Mom or Mike how I was using the rug. But during the next visit to my brother's house, I did some blue-jean rug sleuthing. Mike had placed the rug in his garage under his dog's bed. That worked out fine because Mom loved that dog.

Every Christmas since, after unwrapping our other gifts, Mom has had a handmade item to give us. There have been quilts, embroidered tablecloths, and throw pillows. She made us latch-hook wall hangings with our likenesses, using our high-school graduation pictures, despite Mike and I being in our fifties at the time. Since Mom visited Mike regularly, his wall hanging was on display in his home. I kept mine in a drawer, ready to be hung up when Mom decided to travel to my house.

Four Christmases ago, Mom learned how to use a band saw. That's when she began to make wooden gifts, including the lamps. She made picture frames with unique items glued to the wood. They fell off before February. She made bird feeders and birdhouses that turned out to not be weatherproof.

This Christmas, Mike and I weren't sure what to expect. We had already unwrapped all the other gifts, and Mom had left the room. Mike and I looked at each other, trying to prepare ourselves for what this handmade item would be.

Mom returned with not two items but three. This time, she had wrapped the handmade gifts, too. She said, "Two of these are yours, and the other one is mine. This project took a year to make."

As we unwrapped the gifts, I slowed down and let Mike reveal his first. It was a wooden shadow box with a glass front. I couldn't tell what was inside, so I quickly unwrapped mine. As the wrapping came off, I noticed baby clothes—a faded green coat and bonnet set with matching felt shoes. Mounted inside my shadow box was a black-and-white photograph of me at eighteen months old, wearing the identical outfit.

I finally turned my attention to my brother's shadow box. Inside were his baby clothes and a photograph of him wearing his outfit, at around the same age.

Mom said, "Now, I want you to see mine." She, too, unwrapped a shadow box. Inside were her two pairs of baby shoes—pink and brown—and a pair of hand-knit socks. In the background was a handmade white dress and a photo of Mom, at three years old, wearing that dress.

Mom told us that she had stored a few of our special baby clothes, just like her mom had done, intending to pass them along at just the right time.

I could have stared at our shadow boxes all day, but my vision was getting blurry through my tears. Our mom's gift of love was indestructible, timeless and meant to be treasured forever.

Mike and I looked at each other and smiled, thinking this certainly was the grand finale of Mom's handmade tradition.

I said, "This is the best Christmas gift you have ever made. There is no way to top this one."

"Oh, yes, there is," Mom said. "I already have an idea for next Christmas."

We couldn't wait.

— Glenda Ferguson —

55

A Labor of Love

Gratitude is the memory of the heart.
~Jean Baptiste Massieu

For most of my young life, the best part of Christmas was scrambling down the stairs in my pajamas to see the gifts under the Christmas tree. My sister and I had an unspoken agreement that whoever woke up first would wake the other sister up also. So we always arrived at the tree together. Mom and Dad arranged the gifts by name, so it was easy to find what we were looking for. The next part was the hardest — waiting for Mom and Dad to get up, then eat breakfast, and then finally open the presents.

Like most children, I didn't give much thought to where the gifts came from. I knew several of the tags would be labeled "From Santa." And there were always a few with tags labeled, "From Mom" or "From Dad." All of this made perfect sense to me.

One Christmas Eve I woke up after having only slept for a few hours. Unsure of the time, and seeing a light on in the family room, I sleepily found my way down the stairs to see what was going on. Turning the corner, I was surprised to find my dad sitting in the middle of the family room floor, surrounded by assorted large pieces of fabric, strange-shaped pieces of something that looked like foam, and a random collection of hand tools. But I soon realized my dad was even more surprised to see me. He quickly tried to cover up this odd collection of things, all while asking me, "What are you doing up at this time?" and telling me, "You need to go back to bed!"—all in one breath. Rubbing my eyes and turning around to head upstairs, I had this strange feeling that, while I wasn't really in trouble, something had not gone right.

The rest of the night's sleep erased that memory from my mind. Waking up early Christmas morning as usual, I ran down the stairs with my sister to see what was under the tree. Again, we waited for Mom and Dad to wake up so we could eat breakfast and open our gifts, some from Santa and some from Mom and Dad.

At this point in the story it is important to note this: My sister and I were huge Barbie doll fans. We had received several dolls by then—occasionally as a birthday gift, sometimes as a garage sale find. We even had a Barbie camper, complete with a plastic campfire, two plastic camp chairs, a sleeping bag and a plastic coffee pot that could sit on the campfire so our Barbie dolls could have hot coffee when they woke up in the morning. My parents let us set up most of the family room floor as our Barbie world—a house, a store, a school with paper and pencils that were way too large for our dolls, and the essential parking spot for the camper. Most of the time we could keep this set up for several days. It was a sisters' paradise!

On this Christmas morning, my sister and I opened a large wrapped box that contained something we had never seen before: Barbie furniture. A sectional couch complete with a triangle wedge piece that joined it in the middle was partner to two chairs and a large oval rug. The maroon-swirled soft fabric of the couch complemented the black-swirled soft fabric of the chairs and rug. Later that Christmas Day we excitedly set up our new Barbie living room, lining up our favorite dolls on the couch and in the chairs.

For the rest of Christmas break, my sister and I set up the best Barbie world ever! Our new living room furniture was placed front and center. A bedroom area to the left was outfitted with scraps of fabric serving as sleeping bags and blankets, along with a Barbie case that served as their closet. Some random toy kitchen frying pans and plastic food items identified the kitchen. The Barbie car was parked over by the TV stand (the garage), and the camper was on the other side of the room in case they wanted to go there on a trip. The story possibilities were endless!

At some point, possibly even a few years later, as I was pulling out the Barbie furniture to play with again, that foggy memory of surprising my dad late on a Christmas Eve came back to mind. I looked at that maroon-swirled soft fabric couch, turning it over for the first time to see how it was made. Beneath the fabric, visible through a tiny space, I could see a light green foam material. Turning over the black-swirled chairs, I saw the same green foam peeking through between staples and glue that secured the fabric in place. And in that moment, I grew up a little bit.

In that moment, as I held that furniture, I realized where it had come from. And I understood that not all gifts come from Santa, and not all gifts come from a store. Some gifts come from a labor of love. Some gifts are borne out of a desire to give your children more, even if the bank account won't allow it. Some gifts mean staying up late and making something from almost nothing — nothing more than foam and fabric and time and love.

At the beginning, I loved that furniture because it represented Christmas to me. Ultimately, I loved that furniture because it represented my parents' love for me. In fact, I still love that furniture. I have saved it for over forty years. My daughter, now a freshman in college, played with her Barbie dolls on this same living-room furniture. It is now safely stored away for my grandchildren to use someday. Remarkably, this handmade furniture has outlasted all the plastic Barbie toys of my childhood — just as the memories of that very special Christmas gift have stayed with me as well.

— Debbie Ashley —

56

The Belly-Dancing Christmas

You can't use up creativity. The more you use,
the more you have.
~Maya Angelou

A month before Christmas, I saw a flyer at a paint-your-own-pottery shop promoting a class where one could make a decorative clay tile. I decided to sign up, create a tile, frame it, and give it to my husband Steve as a Christmas gift. Little did I know then that the class would become a nagging mystery to my husband and, ultimately, make for what came to be known in our family as The Belly-Dancing Christmas.

That night, I told Steve that I had to be somewhere every Wednesday evening for the following four weeks. I explained that it was a surprise, and I couldn't tell him where I was going or what I was doing. While I was gone, he would be in charge of our two boys, Ross, four, and Jack, eleven. My announcement made Steve extremely curious.

He speculated about where I was going and what I was doing. Over lunch with a friend, he pondered aloud where I was headed each week and wondered why it was such a secret.

"Maybe she's taking belly-dancing lessons," the friend offered.

"I can only hope!" Steve replied.

That tongue-in-cheek conversation set in motion a Christmas like no other.

After his friend's conjecturing, Steve asked me the same question each week as I left for my date with a clay tile: "So, how are the belly-dancing lessons going?"

"Oh, we're learning hip gyrations tonight," I teased as I headed out the door.

"Ooh, I can't wait!"

Coincidentally, I had a writer friend, Caroline, who was a belly dancer in her single days. Since marrying and having three sons, she had hung up her hip scarf, so to speak, and had not danced in years. Yet, I remembered her writing in our writing group about her belly-dancing experiences. I ran into Caroline at a party and told her that Steve theorized I was taking belly-dancing lessons when I was actually creating an art project. I thought she would find it amusing since she was a belly-dancing alum. Caroline laughed and said, "I still have all my costumes."

That's when a light bulb went off over each of our heads.

"Could I borrow a costume?"

"Sure," Caroline said. "I have everything, even the finger cymbals."

"Perfect."

Fast forward to Christmas Day. All of our gifts around the tree had been opened, and our family room looked like an explosion of gift-wrap when I made an announcement: "There is one more gift that has not been opened."

My three males looked at me expectantly.

"It's for your father."

My sons stopped looking excited.

"But first, I must go upstairs."

I headed to the bedroom where I dressed in blue and gold sparkling harem pants and matching peasant top. My midriff was modestly bare. I felt like Barbara Eden in the old television sitcom *I Dream of Jeannie*. I slipped tiny cymbals onto my forefingers and thumbs, grabbed the tile wrapped in Christmas paper, and proceeded barefooted downstairs.

I danced into the family room with my arms held high, grasping the present in one hand and humming "The Streets of Cairo," known as the snake-charmer song: "Da, dee, daaa, da, da. Da, dee, daaa, dee, da, dee, da." I clanged the finger cymbals together and waved Steve's gift in the air. My men sat wide-eyed, with their mouths agape. I handed the package to Steve. "Here is your belly-dancing gift!"

Giggling, Ross ran to me and hugged my waist, while Steve laughed, ripped at the gift wrap and opened the box. When he saw the tile in its lovely walnut frame, he visibly melted.

"Oh, wow. This is neat."

"I made it."

"You made this?" Steve stared at the tile gleaming in glaze.

"Yep. Sorry, I wasn't taking belly-dancing lessons after all," I said. "I took a class where I hand-carved the tile, painted it, and put it in the frame."

Steve was truly impressed, although a smidge disappointed that belly dancing had only been a "cover-up."

From time to time for the remainder of that harem-scarem Christmas Day, my sons would imitate their mother performing hip shimmies dressed like Jasmine from Disney's *Aladdin*. They pulled up their shirts to expose their navels and danced around the house.

My sons are now grown men in their twenties, and the most quirky and laughable holiday memory of their childhoods is The Belly-Dancing Christmas.

—Angie Klink—

The Sweetest Memories

Christmas waves a magic wand over this world,
and behold, everything is softer and more beautiful.
~Norman Vincent Peale

The wind is howling outside. A mix of sleet and light snow whips through the trees in the back yard and begins to pile up on the deck in small, rounded mounds. Logs crackle in the fireplace, warming the living room and adding the sweet smell of burning hickory logs as Michael Bublé's Christmas album plays in the background.

I walk into my dining room to assess the task before me. The table is covered with a variety of nuts, baking chips, almond bark, flour, sugar, baking sheets, candy thermometers, storage containers and everything needed to create fourteen batches of homemade Christmas candy for family and friends. It's a big undertaking, but I've had years of practice.

As I slip my head through the strap of my red-and-white holiday apron, I can almost hear my mom say, "Donna, I found these in Kirksville, and I thought we needed to have matching aprons." I tie mine behind my back, while Mom's hangs on the hook in the laundry room.

I pull my trusty stainless-steel pot from under the cooktop. I've been making fudge in this pot for thirty-five years. I always start with marshmallow fudge. The recipe is pretty reliable, yielding a large sheet-cake pan of creamy chocolate goodness with just enough walnuts to add a little bit of crunch. I pour the ingredients into the pot, clasp the thermometer onto the side, and begin to stir until all the sugar dissolves. When the candy reaches 236 degrees, I drag the pot from the stove, add the final ingredients and pour it onto the baking sheet to cool.

As I carry the pan into the dining room, I picture Mom sitting at the table with a tiny paring knife, slicing through the fudge, stacking it in our separate Tupperware containers and explaining, "This is just the right size. No one really needs a big old glob of fudge." With a sigh, I wish she still had that job. I'm not as patient as Mom.

I add two logs to the fire, change over to a blended playlist of Christmas songs, and fire up the oven. Dribble bars — a forever favorite — are simple to make yet delicious. As I melt two sticks of butter in the oven, I remember how, in her later years, Mom preferred baking versus candy-making. Arthritis limited her ability to stand over the bubbling pots, but she could whip out pumpkin bread and pecan tarts from a more comfortable spot — her chair in the dining room. "Donna, don't forget to tap the tops of the loaves to make sure they're done," she'd call to me as the tangy aroma of poppy-seed bread wafted through the house. I always use a timer; my nose never developed the skills my mom had.

As I sort through the remaining recipes, I encounter my old nemesis… divinity. I have flashbacks of Mom and me taking turns frantically whipping the white syrupy liquid in an attempt to find the sweet spot between "loses its gloss" and being too dry. I decide life is too short to tackle this on my own. Justifying my cowardice, I tell myself Divinity isn't really that good anyway.

The sky darkens. The streetlight pops on as I wander over to the window to gaze outside. The snowflakes lazily drift through the beams of the corner streetlight. My feet ache, and my hands are sore from dipping pretzels and coconut balls, and the endless chopping of nuts and chocolate. For twenty-five years, this was a two-woman job. I will need tomorrow to finish it up on my own.

I clean the kitchen and put the remaining supplies in the cabinets. My corner of the leather couch is calling me. I turn off the overhead lights, slip off my shoes and relax in the soft lights emanating from our

Christmas tree in the corner. I think about family, traditions, and the future. As I rest my head on the sofa, I can still hear her whisper: "Let's get an early start tomorrow, Donna." These are the sweetest memories.

— Donna Womack —

58

A Changing Tradition

Creativity involves breaking out of expected patterns
in order to look at things in a different way.
~Edward de Bono

When I was a child, my parents gave a gummy-bear or chocolate Advent calendar to my sister and me every December first. Like good sisters, we'd alternate eating the treats on even and odd days.

Once I had a family of my own, my parents continued the tradition for my son. Each December morning, Gavin would race to the calendar and search for the next date so he could open the tiny door and find that day's sweet surprise. When he got older, though, he cared less about the sweets, and the calendar sat forgotten on the table.

One January as I lifted the half-open calendar from the table to discard it, I shook my head sadly. "I guess this is an end to a tradition," I said.

"We can do better than this. He doesn't even like sweets all that much," my husband Daniel mentioned as he took the calendar from me and pried open a forgotten door.

"What do you mean?" I questioned, not sure what he was suggesting.

Dan tasted a piece of the abandoned chocolate. "Ewwww... Have you tried this?"

I nibbled from the same piece. It certainly was not the chocolate

I'd grown up on. It was terrible. "I had no idea," I said as I spit the remaining piece into a napkin.

His eyebrow raised, and he grinned. I swear I could hear the cranks turning in his mind. I'd issued a challenge he was more than ready to accept.

The first Advent calendar he created for our son was filled with generic LEGO-style men we'd inexpensively purchased on eBay. Each little figure was placed in the nook of a shadow box and numbered. Then the top of the box was covered in wrapping paper.

Our son Gavin was seven then and loved this Advent calendar. He spent hours building his little block men and playing with them. We counted it as a success.

The next year, my husband took apart a block kit and gave him a few pieces each day. Gavin had to try to figure out what it was. He didn't get the instructions until the last day.

Another year, he gave him cards for his favorite game, one card a day.

My husband had as much fun putting together the calendar as my son did in receiving it, and I was happy to see the countdown tradition continue.

Our daughter was only one when she got her first Advent calendar. And the tradition continued through the years for Gavin.

"Don't you think you're getting too old for this?" Dan teased one day as Gavin shot out of bed his senior year of high school. Before our son even went to the bathroom, he rushed over to his Advent calendar to see what surprise it held. His little sister in footie pajamas followed her big brother eagerly.

My son laughed. "Never," he replied.

"He'll be thirty and expect his Advent calendar," I told my husband jokingly.

"You and Dad did this for me, and I look forward to doing it for my children just like this. There is so much about Christmas I don't like," my son confided, listing all the commercialism, hype and stress of the holiday season. "But this is so personal. It means a lot to me."

Up until that point, I had no idea how much this tradition had meant to him or how much it improved his feelings about the holidays.

Over the years, I started making Advent calendars for the family, too. I began collecting little treasures in July — special crystals, miniature village pieces, oysters with pearls hidden inside, geodes, and other bits and pieces. The children and my husband had a miniature tree they decorated with their calendar goodies, and each day they waited to open that day's treasure together.

Our tradition has caught on so much that when I made Advent calendars for my sister, brother-in-law and parents, everyone was thrilled. What had begun as a thirty-second solitary event for one child had turned into an inclusive tradition for our extended family.

— Nicole Ann Rook McAlister —

59

Kiss the Cook

Trapped by reality, freed by imagination.
~Nicolas Manetta

"How are we ever going to buy Christmas gifts this year?" I asked, with tears in my eyes.

Mark, my husband of ten years, cupped my face in his hands and silently mouthed the words, "We're not."

It was our first Christmas back in the States after spending six years in Italy where our older son was born. We returned just in time for our second son to be born in Walnut Creek, California. Afterward, our little family settled in Brentwood and rented from my parents. We lived on a pauper's income that year — $900 a month, which had to cover rent, health insurance, food, gas, and utilities.

I planted zucchini in the back yard. After three months, we had what we called "zucchini world": zucchini bread, zucchini soup, and zucchini pasta for three "square" meals a day. Mark rode his bike to work, and I homeschooled our older son, Jeremy, so we only needed to use the car for shopping and going to church.

It would be a slim Christmas, and I was overwhelmed with things to do. Mark's family celebrated Christmas in a big way. There were so many gifts under the tree that they spilled out into the entryway and dining room. My family was more modest with gift-giving; it wasn't a priority.

After ten years of marriage, I had come to dislike Christmas because it was always the same story. "What are we going to buy your family for Christmas?" I'd ask. It was stressful to worry about stretching our budget to accommodate their kind of Christmas.

That night, after I got the boys to bed, I went through all my cross-stitch materials and found the perfect pattern. There were two hearts, one on each side, with the words "Kiss the Cook" in the middle. It could be framed in an embroidery hoop with a ruffle made from material or lace. I would need to make ten hoops in all. It was already the middle of October, so I had a little over two months to complete the task. Thankfully, I had enough fabric in my stash to match the colors in everyone's kitchen. And, of course, I'd make zucchini bread to go along with it.

The only time I had to work on the gifts was after the boys went to bed. I made sure everything was done during the day, including lesson plans for Jeremy, dishes washed, and laundry folded and put away. If I worked a few hours every night, I'd have them finished by Christmas Eve.

What I hadn't planned on was both boys getting sick with earaches and strep throat, which meant doctor visits and medicine. When one got better, the other one got worse. It was a vicious cycle. At 3:00 one Saturday morning in late November, I realized that the "Kiss the Cook" project might have to be abandoned, and zucchini bread might have to suffice. I knew my family wouldn't mind, but Mark's family was a different story. I simply couldn't arrive empty-handed on Christmas Eve for the big Italian tradition of eating dinner, opening gifts, and attending Mass.

I persevered, even though I barely slept during the last week leading up to Christmas. On the eve of Christmas Eve, I stayed up all night finishing up the ruffles that adorned each hoop, wrapped them in boxes, and added zucchini bread in red and green bags.

As Mark loaded up the "sleigh" with the kids and gifts, I made sure that I had extra zucchini bread — with the recipe written on the front — just in case I had forgotten someone. The drive across the Bay Bridge to Mark's childhood home in San Mateo was bumper-to-bumper. But all was forgotten when we pulled into the driveway and smelled the makings of a Pombo Family Christmas. It was all fish, of course, starting with shrimp cocktail, oysters on the half-shell, crab cioppino soup, crab and prawns. Mark's mom made sure she put in her order at Petrini's Italian Market months in advance to ensure everything was the very best.

When I saw all the gifts under the tree and spilling into the entryway, I started to panic. What if my best wasn't good enough? Maybe we could leave right after dinner and spare the disappointment on everyone's faces.

Too late.

After dinner, we all gathered in the living room, and the gift-giving began in a time-honored tradition: reading out the name (to and from) and waiting until that person opened the gift and said "thank you" before going on to the next person. It went on for hours. Since I placed our gifts near the wall, away from the tree, maybe ours would be overlooked.

No such luck.

"To Mom and Dad — Love Connie, Mark and Boys!" Dad Pombo read aloud from the gift tag. Mom Pombo smiled warmly and asked, "What have we here?"

I glanced over at Mark, with my heart racing, and gave him a weak smile as all eyes were on Mom Pombo.

I wrapped Mom and Dad's gift in the nicest paper I could find with a handmade card. It was the boys' handprints sprinkled with red and green glitter. And I made Mom's hoop in blue — to match her kitchen colors. I grabbed Mark's hand and squeezed tightly as Mom opened the box and peeled away the tissue paper. Mom clutched her hand over her heart, with tears filling her eyes, as she held up "Kiss the Cook."

"You made this?" she asked tentatively.

I nodded my head and felt a sense of relief wash over me. Mom Pombo got up from her chair, walked across the living room, and kissed me on the cheek. "I know exactly where I'm going to put this," she said, as her face filled with a bright smile. When she got back to her chair, she carefully put "Kiss the Cook" back in the box — as if it was a piece of fine china. My heart swelled as I wiped away tears.

I hardly noticed the stack of cashmere sweaters, pearls, and glass figurines next to her.

Years after that first Christmas back in the States — even after we moved to Pennsylvania — I enjoyed coming back to Mom Pombo's kitchen and seeing "Kiss the Cook" over the stove where she attached blue ribbons with a gold fork and spoon on either side. It was the only decoration in her kitchen, and it stayed there for three more decades until we kissed the "cook" goodbye.

— Connie K. Pombo —

60

The Wreath

Memories are timeless treasures of heart.
~Author Unknown

During the early hours of a cold winter morning, my six-year-old son crept into my bed and cuddled next to me. He fell asleep within minutes; I could feel his warm breath on my neck as I drifted back to sleep. A couple of hours later, my ten-year-old daughter crawled into bed and snuggled next to me, too. This was a regular occurrence whenever my husband was away on a long business trip.

Both children slept until about seven. I was awake by then, and as the sun peeked through the bedroom window drapes, I watched them slowly stir, yawning and stretching before they opened their eyes. Andrew was the first to speak. After giving me a good-morning kiss, he asked what I had planned for the day. Michelle blinked, rubbed her eyes, sat straight up in bed and said, "Morning, Mom. What are we going to do today?"

It was the first weekend in December. We were spending it without my husband. After finishing his meetings in Germany, he was spending the weekend with his parents in Scotland before returning home.

I pulled my children toward me, and I reminded them both about the pinecones we had collected during some of our trips the previous year. We had dried out the pinecones and put them in a basket on a shelf in the storage room. Having previously purchased a wreath form and other craft items, I suggested we make a Christmas wreath out of the pinecones after we had breakfast.

We made pancakes and talked about what we needed to make the wreath. It took us a while to gather all the craft supplies from the storage room. By then, it was time for a quick lunch. Afterward, we finally started to work on the wreath.

I laid a large piece of cardboard on the kitchen floor and put the Styrofoam wreath form in the center. Michelle and Andrew started sorting the pinecones into piles of various sizes. They had selected twenty cones to be painted white, to give the wreath a "snow effect." We spread out a piece of plastic on the garage floor for spray-painting the pinecones. Using a canister of white paint, I sprayed them and Michelle sprinkled silver glitter on them. Then we glued the pinecones to the wreath, finishing it with artificial holly sprigs and a tartan bow.

The whole process took hours and the children were very excited about their beautiful creation. We all agreed that, for the first year, we would hang the wreath inside the front door instead of outside.

Every year, when I take the large pinecone wreath out of storage, my mind wanders back to the day my children made it more than thirty years ago. Although the bow has been replaced numerous times, and a few pinecones have been glued back in place over the years, I continue to display the wreath on the outside of our front door. It's a treasured reminder of a day when our children experienced the joy of creativity and a job well done.

— Kathy Dickie —

61

Chicken Soup *for the* Soul

Menorah Memories

The darkness of the whole world cannot swallow
the glowing of a candle.
~Robert Altinger

My mom had a classic brass U-shaped menorah that looked as if it had been plucked straight out of the Old World, while my dad's menorah was rectangular and gold-plated in a sleek, art-deco style. We alternated between the two from one year to the next until I added a third menorah into the mix.

I was in pre-kindergarten at the YMHA (the Young Men's Hebrew Association). We had already made dreidels, and with plenty of clay left over, we made menorahs. I remember the rest of the kids built up towering branches, but I went in a different direction. I crafted an oval-shaped bowl with nine indents for the candles. Hanukkah lasts for eight nights, one additional candle lit every night, and the ninth candle is called the shamash, or "helper," that lights the rest.

There were a lot of tears when our menorahs came out of the kiln. Many of my classmates' more ambitious menorahs had fractured in the heat, but mine was perfect. Granted, my parents were a little confused by the design, and I had to explain where to put the candles, but they appreciated my creativity.

That Hanukkah, we used my menorah for the first time. Unlike with my parents' menorahs, the wax didn't drip over the side. Rather, it melted into a colorful puddle. We didn't want to chisel it out because we were afraid we might strike too hard and break the menorah. So, we decided it would be smarter to leave it be and simply melt new candles on top of the old wax. It took forty-four candles to make it through the eight nights, so by the time we reached the last night, the wax was about to spill over the side. The twisting strands of reds, yellows, blues and whites all melted and swirled together so that it looked like a giant, old-fashioned lollipop.

We agreed that my menorah had done its job and earned its retirement. My family has acquired a whole host of menorahs since then — glass ones, plastic ones — but my little clay menorah will always shine brightest in my memory.

— Maxwell Bauman —

Holiday Hijinks

How Embarrassing

The rate at which a person can mature is directly
proportional to the embarrassment he can tolerate.
~Douglas Engelbart

My parents were ancient. I loved them both dearly, but as a thirteen-year-old, I was convinced the physical side of their relationship had dwindled to nothing more than the occasional handholding they engaged in while sitting on the sofa.

My sister, Vicki, who was my elder by three years, believed differently. My parents had been married for more than twenty years when Vicki dreamed up the "perfect" Christmas gifts for my parents.

Every year, she and I would pool our allowance money as well as whatever my sister had made from her after-school job, and we'd go shopping for their presents. This year, though, Vicki was secretive, insisting on shopping by herself. I protested, but my sister was very persuasive, bribing me with a week's worth of her lunch desserts.

Having school and friends to occupy me, I didn't press her too hard as to what she'd bought for our joint gift — until a week before Christmas Eve. That's when she told me what she'd bought: "A lacy negligee for Mom and silk pajamas for Dad."

"Eew! Why did you do that? Take them back!"

My sister grinned. "Absolutely not. It won't be long before I'm at college, and you're always out with your friends. Mom and Dad need to rediscover romance." She shrugged. "Besides, they may not even wear them."

I clung to her last comment as if it were a raft in a raging river. "Okay, but promise me we'll give them the presents here instead of in front of everybody." *Everybody* meant my aunt and her strait-laced husband, my bachelor uncle, my cousins, and my grandmother.

Vicki shrugged. "Yeah. Okay."

Unwilling to let it go, I persisted. "Promise?"

She sighed, obviously impatient with her little sister. "I said yes." With a put-upon air, she pushed me out of her bedroom. "Now, go away. I have to study."

Christmas morning came, and as usual my dad roused us with, "Are you gonna sleep all day?"

In our bathrobes, my sister and I gathered around the artificial tree my mother had insisted upon. I scanned the presents, but I didn't see the two boxes for my parents. Could Vicki have thought better of it and returned the gifts? My hopes were dashed when Vicki said, "Mom, where are the boxes I put on the kitchen counter?"

"Oh, your aunt came over yesterday to pick up the presents for your cousins. She probably took them by mistake. That's okay. We'll just open them there."

My sister's horrified look probably matched mine. This was a disaster! They couldn't open those presents in front of our relatives. My parents would ground Vicki and me for life.

When it was almost time to leave for my aunt's house, Vicki grabbed my arm and pulled me into the bathroom. "It's gonna be okay. I'll ask Aunt Angie to give me back the presents."

Not good enough. "What if she won't?"

With the confidence Vicki always showed, she assured me that she'd handle it.

A wave of relief washed over me. For the first time since those X-rated gifts had gone to my aunt's house, I looked forward to Christmas afternoon. I'd be able to enjoy the wonderful only-at-Christmas dishes that'd surely be at my aunt's house, and I could practice my coolness in front of my cousins. After all, Vicki assured me she'd take care of the gift mix-up, and I believed her.

I shouldn't have.

The gift distribution was the same as every year. My aunt handed out one present at a time, and everyone watched as the recipient opened it. It was a nice idea, except for this time. One of the vice-filled boxes was the first my aunt picked up. Making matters worse, her eyesight wasn't what it once was. She misread the tag and handed my father the gift intended for my mother.

Before my sister or I could grab the misdirected present, my father ripped off the wrapping paper and opened the box. First, his face turned the color of a poinsettia. He shook his head. "Whoa!" was the only word he could manage.

"That was supposed to be for Mom!" Vicki yelled.

My conservative uncle looked away and cleared his throat.

My grandmother yelled, "What is it?"

"Hold it up." That command came from one of my snickering cousins.

"Let me see it." My mother grabbed the skimpy, diaphanous night-gown from Dad's hands. The color of her face matched Dad's, and she quickly buried the negligee under some discarded wrapping paper.

My aunt grabbed another gift from the pile and just glanced at the tag. "Mary, here's one more from your kids."

My mother gave Vicki and me what we called "the look," which fit different occasions but always meant we were in trouble. She checked the tag and handed the box to my father. "This one's yours."

He warily opened the gift and then chuckled, holding up a pair of men's silky red-and-black pajamas, complete with a dragon on the back.

My bachelor uncle whistled. "Ben, you're gonna be dressed to kill for bed." My grandmother slapped him on the arm for that comment.

I was terrified my parents were going to kill Vicki and me for those presents. That is, until my dad laughed and winked at my mother.

To my amazement, she blushed and giggled like a teenager on her first date. All was right with my world. I wasn't going to die on Christmas Eve. Relief fanned my appetite, and I grabbed three cookies, gobbling them down.

Two evenings later, my sister had a date, and I was going to hang out at a friend's house. Neither of my parents fussed at us about being home early.

The next morning, I discovered the boxes with the negligee and the dragon pajamas were empty. No wonder Mom and Dad didn't mind us being gone! At the time, I pushed it out of my mind. It wasn't something a teenager wanted to think about regarding her parents.

Now, the same age my parents were then, I realize they weren't ancient. And I'm glad Vicki and I brought a bit of excitement into their romantic lives.

— Carole Fowkes —

63

Christmas, Censored

Next to a circus there ain't nothing that packs up and
tears out faster than the Christmas spirit.
~Frank McKinney Hubbard

The one present I'd always wanted was a dollhouse — one of those huge, old-fashioned affairs with multiple levels, tiny furniture, and real lighting.

On my tenth Christmas, I got one. "Really?! Santa brought it!" I squealed as I ripped off the wrapping paper. I was thrilled, bouncing about the house like a kangaroo.

"Calm down, love," my mother said. "It's not ready yet. Daddy still has to assemble it."

That didn't matter. I was excited just to have it.

My father laughed at my obvious joy. "Want me to start putting it together right now?" At my exuberant nod, he ushered me from the kitchen. "Wait in the living room. Let it be a surprise."

"Don't forget these."

When my mother tried to hand over the instructions, he scoffed. "'The Destructions'? Bah! It'll be easy enough without them. Don't need all that jargon."

And with a dismissive wave, he shut the door.

He did that a lot — never liked to use the directions. He said it made things unnecessarily complicated.

I listened at the door for what seemed like hours, hearing hammering, the buzz of a screwdriver, the tinkle of nails... I was waiting on tenterhooks for him to finish assembling the kit.

Then, finally, the door opened.

His grin was huge. "Want to see it?"

I didn't need to be asked twice.

It was magnificent. Bigger than I was. Still plain wood, unpainted, but I could already envision the interior, how I could decorate it, and where I would place my dolls.

"What do you think?" my father asked. "It's coming along nicely, isn't it?"

It was. However, something looked not quite right. It took a moment to spot it.

"Daddy, why are the doors on the ceiling?"

He'd fitted the slats wrong — upside down.

My father gawped. Behind him, my mother pressed her lips together, as if trying to suppress laughter.

Squeezing his eyes shut, my father rubbed his forehead.

"Leave the room, please."

I did, quietly. My mother placed "The Destructions" on the floor beside him before retreating and shutting the door. Even through the wood, I could hear him, though.

That was the Christmas I learnt my first curse word.

— Nemma Wollenfang —

Drawing Names

Families are like fudge... mostly sweet with a few nuts.
~Author Unknown

Holidays were always memorable for my two sisters and me, filled with laughter, love, and my mom's wonderful, home-cooked meals. As the years went by, our family grew to include husbands, children, and grandchildren. The Christmas tree seemed to shrink as the mountain of presents expanded.

One year, during the recession, my sisters, our parents, and I were discussing how we were going to buy Christmas presents for everyone in the family. Mom spoke up. "Say, I know we've never done it before, but why don't we draw names at Thanksgiving for the gifts for the adults? We could still buy a little gift for each of the kids. And you know kids, the more gifts they have under the tree, the more excited they are. It would be something different and a whole lot easier on everyone's purse strings."

My eldest sister Donnis pointed out, "Lots of families draw names, and it seems to work great for them."

"Let's do it!" I said. Everyone agreed.

On Thanksgiving Day, after another tableful of scrumptious food had all but disappeared, Mom looked around and said, "Alright everyone, before any of you disappear, let's have a name-drawing for Christmas gifts, and then we'll eat dessert!"

As we looked for pen and paper in the kitchen to begin the task of drawing names, my husband Don appeared in the doorway. "Let me help. I'd like to practice my penmanship and write the names on the slips of paper," he said with a grin on his face.

Don sat down at the breakfast table and tore a strip of paper for each person. As he began to write names on the strips, Don looked at us and said, "You ladies go back to the living room now and relax. I've got this under control." That sounded good to us!

After a few minutes, with no sign of Don, I called to him from the living room. "Are you just about finished? We're waiting for the drawing — and the dessert!"

He answered, "Yes, I'm almost done. I just need to double-check the strips to make sure I didn't forget anyone."

A minute later, Don appeared from the kitchen with a big yellow Pyrex bowl in his hands. He announced with a big smile on his face, "Okay, everyone, I've printed all the names in big letters to make sure they're legible. Just don't tell each other whose name you've drawn because it needs to be a complete surprise on Christmas Day." With that said, each person drew out a slip of paper and held the name close so no one would see whose name they had drawn.

After the drawing was over, my sisters and I followed Mom back to the kitchen to help fix dessert plates for everyone. As we were cutting the pie and cake, Donnis whispered, "Whose name did you get?" The girl never could keep a secret if she tried!

I whispered back, "I drew Don's name, but I need to trade with you because I shouldn't be buying a present for my own husband!"

She looked at me, laughed, and said, "There must be a mistake because I got Don's name, too!"

At that point, I became very suspicious of what Don might have done.

I asked my sister Junie whose name she had drawn, but she didn't want to tell me.

"It's supposed to be a secret!" she said.

"Junie," I said, "there is something fishy about the drawing because Donnis and I both drew Don's name."

"Me, too!" Junie said with astonishment.

At that point, Mom exclaimed, "Oh, that big stinker! He wrote his own name on all the drawing slips!"

We were all laughing as we brought the dessert into the dining room. Mom began to tell everyone in the living room, "Guess what? Would you believe that we have a prankster in our midst? Luckily, we caught him just in the nick of time!"

Mom said, "Don, would you like to tell everyone what you did?" Don, of course, was red-faced and couldn't talk because he was doubled over with laughter.

Mom continued, "Don wrote his own name on all the slips!"

When he had recovered a little from laughing, Don admitted, "I thought for sure I would get away with that. I wanted to watch everyone's face as I opened *all* the presents on Christmas Day!"

While laughing, Dad asked Don, "You really didn't think you'd get away with that, did you?"

"No, not really, but it was sure fun to try!" Don said.

It didn't take Mom long to assign the task of writing out new drawing slips to my sister Donnis, which she quickly completed. The drawing went off without a hitch.

That was the one and only name-drawing our family ever had. We never did make it a tradition.

— Sheryl K. James —

65

The Convert

There's a little bit of fruitcake left in every one of us.
~Jimmy Buffett

People have been trying to convert me for a long time. I think it officially started during my rebellious teens when a best friend insisted, "Just try it. You might like it!" I told her to quit being so annoying. She backed off. People were always trying to convert me, especially during the Christmas season.

I'm talking about fruitcake — that terrible concoction of suspicious, rubbery green-and-red fruit blobs held together in a loaf of tasteless, dreadful dough.

There is just something about the word "fruitcake" that causes people to either smile or smirk. Johnny Carson proclaimed, "There is only one fruitcake in the entire world, and people keep sending it to each other." The great humorist Erma Bombeck wrote, "A fruitcake weighs more than the stove it was cooked in!" I think she also said a fruitcake makes a dandy doorstop. Erma and Johnny were my kind of people.

My husband, a certified member of F.A.A. (Fruitcake Addicts Anonymous), never met a fruitcake he didn't like. He always needed to know there was one lurking in our freezer. Fortunately, for the sake of our happy marriage, he never tried to convert me.

In 1997, we received a fruitcake from friends, but we already had two, so I put that one in the freezer and forgot about it — until two years later when we were going to visit my daughter Rocki and her husband Glen. Rocki (bless her heart) also hates fruitcake. Like mother, like daughter. I waited until the right moment and buried that fruitcake in the bottom of their freezer, still bearing its 1997 label. One day Rocki would find it and be horrified.

For the record, we always played pranks on one another, especially during the years we lived near them in Los Angeles. Because Glen took such pride in their large and pristine lawn, we bought out the plastic flamingos from Kmart one day and planted them all over their lawn when they weren't home.

Part of the game was to never be around for the discovery, so we flamingoed their lawn and escaped. Then we forgot all about the flamingos. Six months later, we returned from a vacation, tired and ready for bed. Our dog-sitter failed to mention there had been "visitors." We walked into our bedroom, and found a flock of pink plastic flamingos propped against the pillows. We were both reminded of the horse-head scene in *The Godfather*. About that time, we decided to get out of town and move to Oregon.

Rocki and Glen came to visit us in 2006 in our new Oregon coast home. Two years later, while cleaning out our garage freezer, we found that fruitcake dated 1997.

The fruitcake stayed put until the year 2012 when we drove down to Los Angeles for the summer wedding of our granddaughter, Autumn. I gift-wrapped over the original wrap and tossed the ancient fruitcake into my suitcase. During the two days we spent with Rocki and Glen before the wedding, we waited for them to leave the house. Once again, we hurried to their freezer and buried the fruitcake under the frozen vegetables.

One night, months after returning from the wedding, we received this phone call from Rocki: "Last night, we had a dinner party," she said in a stern tone, "and ended up with extra guests." We were both listening on the speakerphone and wondering where she was headed. "I did not have enough dessert for everyone," she said. "Then I remembered seeing what I assumed was a loaf of my mother-in-law's delicious chocolate chip–zucchini bread in the freezer."

"I unwrapped that thing," Rocki continued, "and can't believe you guys pulled it off again!" My husband and I smiled and gave each other a thumbs-up.

That last episode happened in the spring of 2013. Since then, several Christmases have come and gone, along with the changes that life hands all of us.

I am now a widow, and one of the things I miss the most, other than my husband, is playing pranks on Rocki and Glen.

Since the arrival of COVID-19 and the challenge of being quarantined, there are so many uncertainties with the Christmas season ahead. Will I have to pull off a socially distanced prank? Will I be able to? You know, there's an alternate definition of the word "fruitcake" if you look it up: "an eccentric or crazy person."

I think I'll figure something out. Maybe I'm a convert after all!

— Bobbie Jensen Lippman —

66

Anti-Santa

Your children get only one childhood.
Make it memorable.
~Regina Brett

I t was my husband Fred's fault really. I never would have thought of doing something like this before I met him.

Fred never just wraps gifts; he likes to add things to packages to weigh them down or make them rattle. He is particularly good at wrapping gifts in such a way that the receiver has no clue what the gift is — even something that would otherwise be obvious, such as a book.

I am usually not as clever as him when it comes to wrapping. With so many gifts to wrap and other things to do at Christmas, I do not have time to be clever. But I do have my moments. One such time was the Christmas of 2006, the year our kids — fourteen-year-old Ashleigh and twelve-year-old Christian — asked for a new game system.

We always stressed the true meaning of Christmas with our kids. It is a time for giving not getting. And often giving is much more fun.

That year, they made out their Christmas wish lists, knowing as always that they would not necessarily get everything they asked for.

Dominating the top of each of their short Christmas 2006 wish lists was a GameCube. *Typical,* I thought. *The older the kids get, the shorter and more expensive their lists get.*

"I don't know about that, guys," I said, shaking my head slightly. "That might not be in the budget this year."

Ashleigh shrugged. "We can always hope."

True! Christmas is not only a time for giving; it is also a time for hope and believing, even when the odds are against you.

"The kids would really like a GameCube this year," I told Fred as we were getting ready for bed that night.

"Yeah, I know," he said with a sigh. "What about GameStop? They might have a used one."

"Couldn't hurt to check," I agreed.

The next day, I stopped by the local GameStop. The small store was well-stocked with all the latest game systems and games for every age from toddlers to adults. There were games based on movies, TV shows, monsters, war, space and even children's toys. Things have come a long way since the days of Atari.

I asked the young salesclerk if they had any used GameCubes for sale.

"I think so. Let me check." He disappeared into the backroom and returned carrying the cube-shaped game system, complete with the wires and controller, all wrapped in plastic.

This was the first time I had ever seen one. I had thought that they were small, hand-held things until Ashleigh informed me that they hooked up to the TV. Duh!

"Do you know why it was returned?" I asked, looking it over.

"Well, these have been around for a few years," the clerk said. "People like to upgrade when new systems come out."

I smirked. Our kids are so far behind the times. What horrible parents we are!

"How much is it?"

He scanned the bar code. "Fifty dollars."

Perfect! Well within the budget. I set it on the counter. "Do you have a box? This is a Christmas gift."

He called to the manager in the back of the store. "Hey, do you know if we have an extra GameCube box?"

A few minutes later, the manager brought up a folded-up white box with the words "GameCube" written across it in bold black letters.

"Thanks. Just go ahead and put it in the bag. I can box it up when

I get home." I also bought each of the kids a game. After all, what good is a new game system without any games? I just had to make sure that they open the GameCube first, or it would ruin the surprise.

Smiling, I carried the bag out to the car and set it beside me in the passenger's seat. I loved it when I could get gifts that people really wanted. They were going to be ecstatic.

I glanced at the bag. The empty GameCube box gave me an idea—worthy of my gift-wrapping guru husband. This Christmas was going to be the most memorable one yet!

If I'd had my car windows down, the other drivers would have heard me laughing hysterically. Yes, giving is definitely as much fun as getting—and sometimes even more fun!

Later that evening, I told Fred my idea.

"Oh, that's good," he said. "Maybe Anti-Santa can have a part in this, too."

Like many families, Santa Claus is a part of our holiday tradition. When they were small, we often reminded Ashleigh and Christian that Santa would come and bring them new toys if they were good. If they were naughty, then Anti-Santa would take away their toys and leave sticks, rotten potatoes, and underwear.

As Christmas drew closer, the kids continued to talk about the GameCube and how awesome it would be to get one.

"I wouldn't count on it this year," I told them. Meanwhile, a gift-wrapped box labeled with their names and a mysterious black plastic bag lay hidden in my office. It was difficult to keep a straight face.

On Christmas Eve, I returned from church around midnight. The kids were in their beds, with visions, I was sure, of GameCubes rather than sugar plums dancing in their heads.

"Did you get it hidden?" I asked Fred.

He held up the empty black bag and grinned. "Yep, we're all set. And I put the box under the tree, behind all the other presents."

The next morning, we plugged in the tree lights and gave the kids the okay to come downstairs.

Each of them eyed the pile of presents, especially the large box tucked behind the tree against the wall. Anticipation clearly showed in their faces, and we could see them thinking, *Is that a GameCube?*

Per our family tradition, we each opened the contents of our stockings first. Then the gifts were handed out. No opening until everyone had one. A barrage of excited oohs, aahs, thank-yous and laughter filled the living room. Soon, the carpet was covered with brightly colored paper, ribbon, and bows. One gift remained under the tree: the large box.

Fred set the box between them. I stood by with the camera and bit my lip to keep from laughing.

Ashleigh and Christian looked at each other with hope-filled eyes and began to tear at the wrapping. In a manner of seconds, the box was uncovered.

"It's a GameCube, Chris!" Ashleigh exclaimed.

"All right!" Christian cried in excitement. "We got a GameCube!"

The box was torn open with the gusto of a pirate opening a newly discovered treasure chest. Tissue flew everywhere, and the kids pulled out… underwear!

Ashleigh uttered a four-letter word, which I would have reprimanded her for had I not been laughing so hard.

"Wait," Christian said. "What's this piece of paper?" He read the crudely written note out loud. "Ha! Anti-Santa has confiscated your gift. However, since you haven't been quite that bad, I am not able to take it permanently, only hide it. There is a separate clue for each of you in this box that will lead to more clues. But be warned: The final clue is torn in two — a portion for each of you — which means you will have to work together to find your gift."

They each found their clues and tore off through the house, going in opposite directions, searching frantically for more clues. Before long, they found the GameCube and games hidden in the dryer. It was quite a workout, but the things we treasure the most are the ones we work hardest for.

— Laura Moehrle —

67

Everyone's a Winner!

Christmas sweaters are only acceptable
as a cry for help.
~Andy Borowitz

E very October, my girlfriend and I go shopping for ugly Christmas sweaters at our local thrift stores. We have amassed quite a collection. Last year, I bought a few, not unattractive enough to win an ugly sweater contest but perfect to wear during the celebratory month of December. I like to show them off at my writing groups and social events. They seem to stimulate brain cells and inspire creative holiday stories. By purchasing them in discount stores, I can usually buy two or three for the price of one department-store sweater. Since they are hardly worn, they appear practically new.

If the sweaters have any sayings on them, that is a plus. I especially like the red sweater I have with a picture of the "Elf on the Shelf" hanging from inside the chimney by one arm saying, "Is it Christmas yet?" I guess the elf was tired of being pushed, shoved, and hidden all over the house for some little kid to find in the morning. Elves have feelings, too.

Another favorite of mine is a large white sheep, wrapped in Christmas lights, singing a battery-operated song, "Fleece Naavidad."

Last year, I found a great yuletide sweater depicting a scared cat hiding under the tree he knocked over. Sitting on his head was a silver-star tree topper. As soon as I saw it, I realized it had great potential to be a winning sweater and would wow my friends. I stitched a few holiday ornaments on the sweater to give it some extra pizzazz and bought a string of Dollar Store flashing lights and sewed them on the tree. It looked festive when I tried it on.

One day last December, I held an "Ugly, or Not So Ugly Christmas Sweater Day" during our weekly writing group. Ten members showed up wearing laughable sweaters, which they wrote about in a writing prompt. I wanted to know where they found their sweater, if they embellished it, and where they were going to wear it, other than at our writing group. Would they keep it or give it away to a thrift store after the holidays, so I could find and purchase it, and add it to my collection? As each member read their story and spun around modeling their personal sweater, we couldn't contain our laughter. I should have brought a gavel to silence the hysteria.

A smiling yellow "Happy Hannukkat" sweater with a picture of a cat wearing a yarmulke on its head got the biggest laugh, especially when the author wore a yarmulke while reading his story.

Mine was the most creative and the brightest. The ornaments and beads were dazzling and flashing. I had to turn off the blinding lights to concentrate on my writing.

It was a ten-way tie for the best sweater and first place. It seems we all voted for our own sweater. Isn't that how it's done today? Everyone's a winner and brings home a trophy. Even better than winning, everyone had fun and left with a holiday selfie, a gift they'll never forget.

— Irene Maran —

68

Mystery Wrapping Paper

Creativity is intelligence having fun.
~Albert Einstein

My children were quite young when they learned the age-old skill of shaking and assessing wrapped Christmas gifts to figure out what was inside! My three apples didn't fall far from the tree; I had done the same at their age! And now I understood how my mother felt, and I was incredibly irritated with the situation, especially when my kids were able to guess their exact gift long before Christmas morning arrived.

This situation just wouldn't do! Many hours of planning and shopping went into finding the perfect gifts for my beloved children. More importantly, I delighted in surprising them on Christmas morning, not a week earlier.

I began to wrack my brain for ways to fool my kids where their gifts were concerned. One year, I took all the toys out of the original boxes and repackaged them. This was more effective than leaving the gifts in their original boxes, but the kids still guessed a majority of their gifts prior to Christmas Day.

I needed a better plan, and it was hatched the next day as I stood in the store buying wrapping paper at the after-Christmas sale.

I would choose a single wrapping paper, preferably a paper that the child wouldn't expect to have their gifts wrapped in, and wrap all their presents in it without tagging the gifts!

This way, my kids would only see gifts wrapped in three neutral papers under the tree. They would have no clue which ones belonged to them!

In order to figure out what was in the boxes, they would first have to figure out which gifts were their own.

The day that my kids came home from school to find wrapped gifts under the tree, they squealed in delight. But then my sweet angels discovered that the gifts weren't tagged with names, and the papers they were wrapped in could be paper for anyone! No princess or car paper in sight. They were perplexed.

They asked how they were supposed to know which gifts were theirs, and I just smiled. "You'll know on Christmas morning!"

So, they shook all the gifts under the Christmas tree. Every single gift. They debated amongst themselves which gifts might be their own. They argued on the basis of what the paper looked like and what they thought might be in the box. However, it was much more difficult to determine what was in the box if they didn't know who the box belonged to.

They were frustrated. I was amused.

When Christmas morning arrived, they excitedly dumped out their stockings. They oohed and aahed over candy, cars, stickers, and soaps. As always, they seemed to enjoy their new electronic toothbrush most of all, clicking the button to make sure it actually worked before tossing it into their pile of stocking goodies.

Then, the moment of truth arrived! At the bottom of their beautifully embroidered stocking, they found a slip of wrapping paper that matched the paper that all their gifts were wrapped in. The mystery that had intrigued them for a couple of weeks was delightfully solved.

Since that Christmas morning, we have maintained our new tradition of untagged Christmas gifts. There have been years that the kids have guessed which paper was their own, but more often than not, at least one of them is thoroughly fooled!

I have occasionally thrown them a curveball, just to keep things fresh and new. One year, they thought that the paper was the identifying mark of whose gift was whose, as that was the status quo. However, on Christmas morning, they discovered that the bow was that year's identifying mark.

The kids are always excited to see which gifts belong to whom on Christmas morning. They're always gleeful when they know that they guessed correctly and generally surprised by what they find in their Christmas boxes.

Mystery wrapping paper ended up being the perfect Christmas solution for three nosy children and their surprise-loving mother.

— Shonda Holt —

69

Harebrained Christmas

Probably the reason we all go so haywire at
Christmas time with the endless unrestrained
and often silly buying of gifts is that we don't
quite know how to put our love into words.
~Harlan Miller

When I was a kid, I thought the word harebrained was spelled H-A-I-R, as if a person's hair indicated how crazy they might be. I was well into my twenties before I learned that the word came from the idea that someone could have a brain like a rabbit — zigzagging from one thing to the next with no apparent reason.

Everyone has that person in their family, and for me it is Aunt Dianna. She just so happens to have crazy hair — a fluff of cropped salt-and-pepper that always seems to be askew. Her hair is always in her eyes, sticking out to one side, or occasionally, standing straight up from her head. When I heard people use the word harebrained as a kid, it was often in reference to Aunt Dianna.

So, your hair grows out of your brain, I thought.

I also inferred the meaning because of the wacky, albeit fun adventures my aunt would take us on. We went to movies, mini-golf, bowling, and weekends away with zero notice. She would show up at our house, pack up my brother and me, and away we would go.

Sometimes, it was just us; other times, it was a whole gaggle of cousins. One fall day, she made us change into old plaid shirts and took us apple bobbing in her back yard.

There are eight cousins, and in addition to her adventures, she also got a reputation for her gift giving. One Christmas, she showed up late to our traditional family gathering on my uncle's Ozark farm. In her arms were boxes full of gifts wrapped in newspaper, and we were recruited to help unload the rest from her car. I must have been about nine years old, and I remember sneaking a peek at a couple of the labels as I carried one of the boxes into the house.

My name was on a long, tube-shaped box, and my cousin Renea's was on a square box, about ten inches across. I was perplexed because it was tradition for the girls to receive the same thing, and it didn't look possible. We often received earrings or jewelry, while the boys got matching toy tractors and farm collectibles. Further inspection revealed that all the boxes were mismatched sizes and shapes. One of my cousins began to brag as soon as the adults were out of earshot. "I got the biggest box, so it must be the best present!" We were all trying to figure out what Aunt Dianna could be up to.

We waited impatiently for dinner to end so we could open presents. When the time came, the adults joined us in the family room, and my aunt began passing out packages. She was grinning ear-to-ear and announced that the cousins were to open our presents all at once. My cousin continued to gloat that his present must be the best.

On her count of three, we tore into the gifts, and the shreds of paper flew about the room. I quickly realized that I would not be able to pry off the plastic end of the cardboard tube without help, so I found my dad and jumped up and down while I waited for him to slice through the shipping tape with his pocketknife.

Was it a poster of my favorite band? A new softball bat? Some sort of art easel? I had forgotten about everyone else in the room when he handed the tube back to me. I spun around to face the group as I ripped off the piece of plastic keeping me from knowing. I tipped the tube and out rolled four oranges, a pencil, and a deck of playing cards.

Confused, I looked into the darkness of the tube to check that everything had come out. I looked up to see similar looks of confusion around the room. It turned out, we had all gotten the same thing with one exception. Each of us had a different number of oranges used to fill the remaining space in whatever box we got. I fell over on the floor laughing when I realized my bragging cousin was now surrounded by a large pile of oranges.

A few Christmases had passed when we thought surely Aunt Dianna couldn't top the orange scheme. Then she showed up with a large black trash bag that she informed us contained a joint gift for all of us. This time, we gathered in the basement at my grandma's house while the adults finished putting out dinner upstairs. We wracked our brains to figure out what could be inside the bag. We tried to be patient, but my youngest cousin must have asked a dozen times during dessert if it was time for presents.

This time, Aunt Dianna waited for the finale, and after all the other gifts were opened, she picked up the bag and said, "Follow me!"

We marched behind her down the stairs to the basement, our parents and grandparents bringing up the rear. She put us to work moving the table and chairs in the main room, and once we had cleared an open space, she opened the bag to reveal a donkey piñata. My uncles helped to tie it up to the rafters in the unfinished basement ceiling, and Aunt Dianna had us draw numbers out of a hat to see who would go first.

The biggest, strongest boy drew the number one.

She giggled as she tied the blindfold around his head and spun him around before handing him the stick. I started to realize the rest of us might not get a swing at it.

He reached out tentatively and brushed the piñata, and then reared back like a baseball player hitting a homer and let it rip.

The papier-mâché flew into pieces, and we hit the deck as the shrapnel from inside started pinging through the air and bouncing off the walls and concrete floor. Mothers jumped to shield the younger children, and we all squealed as we tried to see what kind of loot was flying through the air and what the plastic packages were falling directly below. This piñata was not filled with the traditional Tootsie

Rolls, suckers, and bubblegum. No, it was filled with pennies and gooey, soft Twinkies. The chaos settled as the loose change came to rest on the floor, and we fell into fits of laughter as we tried to salvage the smashed, oozing Twinkies.

More than twenty years after the famous Twinkie and penny piñata incident, we still talk about it around the Christmas table. It turns out, harebrained schemes make for the best memories. As an adult, I have decided that it is a shame that a person with harebrained ideas is not as easy to find as a person with crazy hair. I think we could all use a few more people who think it's a good idea to put Twinkies in a piñata!

— Sasha Rives —

70

Going Crazy

Perhaps the best Yuletide decoration
is being wreathed in smiles.
~Author Unknown

My husband James bathed our toddlers and dressed them in their warm pajamas as if it were any regular night. I popped popcorn and poured hot cocoa into thermoses. We read bedtime stories, prayed, and tucked them into bed. Then we put on our Christmas pajamas and tiptoed downstairs, whispering and giggling, while we waited for both kids to quiet down but not quite fall asleep. Our first family tradition was about to begin.

We tiptoed up the stairs. I went into my son's room while James went into my daughter's.

"Wake up, Jon. We are going crazy!" His eyes widened as I bundled him in blankets and carried him to the car where I met James holding Catie. We buckled them into their car seats and handed them snacks and drinks. Questions abounded. I think James and I were more excited than the kids.

The snow fell as we backed out of the driveway. We turned on Christmas music and drove through the neighborhood looking at Christmas lights. I took a mental snapshot of that moment, my family laughing and singing all together.

Each year, we continued the tradition, both kids squealing with delight the night we would sneak upstairs and whisper, "We're going crazy!" In elementary school, cheers turned to groans when we succeeded in surprising them. They tried to come up with ways to not forget the following December. But James and I took great pleasure in picking a night they weren't expecting.

As they got older, it became more and more challenging. One year, I took the popcorn popper into the basement, so they wouldn't hear it. Another year, I was sick in bed all day with the flu but crawled out to catch them unaware. Then they became teenagers and started going to bed after us. Gone were the Christmas pajamas and sleepy dreams in their eyes, but the magic continued as we drove through the neighborhoods commenting on which light displays were our favorites.

Then, they got bigger still. They had jobs, classes, and friends. It seemed almost every night one of them was not home. James and I plotted, chose our route, and waited for the perfect night. As Christmas neared, we worried that this would be the year the magic of the Christmas lights would end.

A few days before Christmas, I was watching TV when Catie came home at 10:30 p.m. She popped into my room to tell me she was back and going to get something to eat. A few minutes later, I hear her hollering from the main level. "The toilet is overflowing. Come quickly, Mama!"

In my selfless and caring way, I promptly replied, "Get Dad!" She *insisted* she needed *me*. "Bring towels. Lots of towels!" I heard Jon calling for his dad. "Come quickly. There's water everywhere!"

I hurried downstairs but didn't see anyone in the bathroom. I heard the children hushing James as he asked, "Where's the overflowing toilet?"

Confused, I turned the corner. They handed me a bag of popcorn and a thermos of hot cocoa. "We're going crazy!" they both shouted.

They herded James and me out to my son's warmed-up car, blankets already in the back seat, route already planned on the GPS, and Christmas music playing. They sat in the front seat asking us which displays were our favorites. Roles reverse, and I realized just how grown-up my babies were.

Later that night, James and I began to plot how to outdo the kids the next Christmas. Catie was living in Germany but would arrive home in early December. We figured we had all month to surprise them after she got home and settled in.

My son's car was in the driveway when we pulled in around 9 p.m. from picking Catie up at the airport. She ran and hugged her brother. We stood around the foyer making small talk. Catie sat on the bench by me, Jon leaned back with one foot on the wall, and James sat on the stairs.

"I'm tired, but it's going to be a while before I get some sleep," Jon said.

"Why is that?" I wondered if he had to go to work this late at night.

"Because we are going crazy."

I sat silently as the words rushed over me. I rubbed both my kids' backs at the same time, trying to hide my big, ugly tears. They sent James and me upstairs to put on our pajamas. Popcorn, hot cocoa, and Christmas music waited for us in Jon's car. Catie brought up the route on her phone. As everyone chatted, I sat trying to absorb the night. The blur of houses, laughter, cool breezes, a warm drink, and my babies, together in one car. I could reach out and touch them at the same time.

Catie returned to Germany a few weeks later. The following December, I checked off squares on my calendar, counting down the days until I would see her again. The night before she was due home I was so excited that I wondered if I'd be able to sleep.

At 11 p.m., the doorbell rang.

Concerned, my husband and I headed downstairs and opened the door, wondering who would ring a doorbell that late. There stood my daughter. A day early. My beautiful and amazing children had planned that moment for months. Jon took off work, picked her up from the airport, and brought her home to surprise us. That night, I sat on my couch and hugged my babies into the early hours of the morning, thinking this was the best Christmas surprise ever.

The next night, Catie said, "Hey, Mom, so in Germany, we have this thing we do to unwind. We watch a TV show and then everyone runs upstairs and puts on pajamas. Then we watch another show before bed."

You'd think I would have caught on. Nope. I took my dear, sweet daughter at face value. After the first TV show, I hurried upstairs and put on my pajamas. The day had been full. It would feel good to unwind on the couch with James and Catie.

We started the second show. I heard some commotion in the kitchen. I turned to see someone standing in my kitchen. The lights were off, and he was wearing dark clothes. I was startled. James was startled. We'd locked the front door. There wasn't anyone in the house except the three of us.

From the shadows, the deep voice of my son said, "We're going crazy."

As James and I rode in the back seat sipping hot cocoa and munching on popcorn, I thought about how our children had surprised us twice in twenty-four hours. My heart swelled with love. I imagined this tradition continuing into the next generation, each of my children with their own children snuggled in the back seat, wide-eyed in wonder, going crazy for decades more.

— Nancy Beach —

Hung by the Chimney with Care

The stockings were hung by the chimney with care,
In hopes that St. Nicholas soon would be there.
~Clement Clarke Moore

My mother always made sure that walnuts, tangerines and chocolate were in the Christmas stockings for the six of us. They were a fond memory for me, so I continued the tradition when I grew up.

One year, I forgot that I had already put the chocolate in the stockings. On Christmas Eve, we were hosting our extended families' annual Christmas party, so I decided to hang the stockings on the mantel to make it look like a picture-perfect holiday. I had many compliments on my decorating and the food I served. We had a great family gathering with Christmas carols and a beautiful lit fireplace.

Christmas morning, after the excitement of the night before, the children and I settled down to a quite relaxing morning of juice and hot rolls. We lit the tree and candles and put on soft Christmas music. My daughter was eager to open her stocking and handed the other to her older brother. I was thinking what a picture-perfect holiday this was turning into when my son, lying on the couch with his hand deep into his stocking looking for a Christmas treasure, said, "Yuck!" He pulled out his hand quickly. Instead of a fun treasure, he came up with a handful of chocolate goo. His sister followed suit. "Oh, yucky!"

she said. "I have it, too!"

That lovely evening the night before? Yep, it appeared that all the chocolate had melted as the stockings were hung by the roaring fire. Tangerines, walnuts and small gifts were all nicely coated in chocolate.

"Mom," they said, rolling their eyes, "only you could do something like this."

That taught me not to try so hard to make everything "perfect."

— Sharon Harmon —

The Perfect Gift

72

A Priceless Nativity

Gratitude is the music of the heart, when its chords
are swept by the breeze of kindness.
~Author Unknown

A fresh pot of coffee percolated as a small group of women sat around a kitchen table, critiquing the abundant selection of holiday sweets provided by local churches. One of the women smiled as I entered the kitchen, and she offered suggestions on which after-dinner treats were tastiest. "The brownies from that one church were really good, but that red velvet cake over there..." She pointed at the counter. "Well, I thought it was a little dry."

Another woman bit into a cookie and wrinkled her nose at the mention of the cake. "I didn't care for it either."

It was all I could do not to laugh. The rest of the year, such treats rarely showed up at the homeless shelter where I volunteered. At Christmas, however, our cup was overflowing — and now the kitchen counters were too.

Occasionally, I was called on to serve as an "overnight hostess" at the local homeless shelter for women and children. My lofty title fooled no one. I lay on the office sofa bed at night, sleeping with one eye open and praying that no angry ex showed up demanding to see one of the residents, as happened occasionally.

One morning, before a fresh volunteer arrived and I could leave for my day job, I was surprised to learn that I wouldn't be able to get a shower that day. When I pulled aside the shower curtain in the office bathroom, I found the space filled to overflowing with children's toys, games, and dolls. Bicycles were already crammed into the small office along with countless gifts of toiletries for the women.

My town had always been a generous one, and I wasn't a bit surprised to find that they had, once again, outdone themselves at Christmas. And because I had grown so attached to this particular group of residents at the shelter, I couldn't have been happier.

A homeless shelter was an unusual place to make friends, but I had indeed made a few that fall. Some of them even corresponded with me by letter for a few years.

One stunningly beautiful woman was the single mother of twin girls, just trying to craft a better life for her daughters. Then there was the quiet-spoken wife who decided she'd been beaten one time too many and courageously decided she wanted more for herself. Another single mom was the quietest resident I met there, hardly ever speaking and rarely making eye contact with anyone. One night during a crafts session, however, she learned to use a crochet hook and a skein of yarn, and she became a crocheting machine who whipped out granny squares and pastel afghans like nobody's business. I like to imagine that when she eventually left the shelter, she opened a needlework design firm.

But the woman I remember most from that magical Christmas was a mom named Lynn. She was shy and a little aloof at first, so I'd made an effort to draw her out of her shell. Counselors were available to help these women rise above the circumstances that had led them to the shelter, so I always simply tried to be an encourager. Lynn said she felt guilty for having left an abusive husband, and I assured her that she had made a wise decision in getting her and her young daughter out of that danger zone.

That Christmas, between working and shopping and going to church Christmas parties and volunteering, I found the holidays arriving much faster than I'd expected. Before I knew it, I was at the shelter for my last volunteer shift before Christmas Day. The office was jam-packed with gifts, and I was thrilled that we had collected enough toys and treats that all the residents — especially the children — would have a magnificent Christmas.

I ate dinner and dessert with the women that night, led the evening devotional, and headed to the office and prepared to pull out the trusty sofa bed.

As often happened, a tap sounded at the door before I could lay my head down. Did somebody need a new toothbrush? Were they out of toothpaste? It was rare that I went to sleep without addressing some last-minute need.

To my surprise, Lynn stood there, quietly asking to come in. And in an act of generosity I've never quite gotten over, she handed me a small, wrapped box.

"What is this?" I was puzzled.

"It's for you. Take it!" she said.

My heart dropped. Please, Lord. Tell me this sweet woman at the homeless shelter didn't actually use some of her hard-earned money to buy me a gift.

"Oh, Lynn, you shouldn't have."

"Oh no, I had to get you something." Lynn's big brown eyes sparkled, and she was clearly eager to see me open her gift.

I quickly unwrapped the package and found a small glass nativity set from the local dollar store. A big yellow "$3" was imprinted right on the box, and I was more than a little humbled that a homeless woman had bought a gift for me. What was worse was that it had not even occurred to me to get her or any of the other ladies a personal gift.

"Oh, Lynn, it's beautiful," I said, admiring the glass figures in my hands.

Her smile was huge. "Merry Christmas!"

"And Merry Christmas to you." I gave her a hug, and we said good night.

Lynn clearly valued me and my volunteer work much more than she should have, and her friendship was an amazing gift that she had already given me.

It's been more than twenty years since I received that unforgettable Christmas gift at a homeless shelter. The women and children all moved on. The shelter itself has since closed.

And each Christmas, I reach for a tin that contains the most valuable nativity set I will ever own. Down on her luck, a young mother with no place of her own to lay her head — and where had I heard a story like that before? — gave me a sacrificial gift that became one of the loveliest Christmas decorations of all time.

As I ready my house for Christmas each year, I love rediscovering the pieces of the nativity from Lynn. I pray that she is well and happy and lavished with gifts at Christmas. By now, her daughter would be a young woman and perhaps a mother herself. I hope the little girl grew up to have a heart as big as her mom's.

Last Christmas, I was flipping through the pages of a twenty-something-year-old issue of the charming Victoria magazine and came upon an ad that nearly took my breath away. There, in a corner of the page, appeared an advertisement for a nativity set by a well-known crystal manufacturer. My dollar-store nativity set of twenty years ago was a fairly accurate imitation of that one.

I had to smile, for I know where to find a truly priceless nativity set.

And it isn't at any crystal company. It's in my home — and forever in my heart.

— Angela McRae —

73

Chicken Soup for the Soul

Love at Work

Character is the ability to carry out a good resolution
long after the excitement of the moment has passed.
~Cavett Robert

"For today's art class, you're making Christmas presents for your family," said Mrs. Jelsma, my fifth-grade teacher. My classmates quickly scrambled over to the arts-and-crafts table to collect paper, pens, colored pencils, markers, glue, glitter, and any supplies they would need for their projects.

I watched as each of them returned to their desks and went to work. Kelsey began cutting strips of paper to make a garland for her tree. Melinda was busy designing an ornament. Kelly was making a cardboard picture frame covered in red and green glitter.

I was stuck. I wasn't sure what to make. I sat there for a while, and then it came to me: I could create a poster for my dad. I grabbed what I would need: a large piece of paper, some crayons, and magic markers.

In big bubble letters, I wrote my heart's desire for my dad: "PLEASE STOP SMOKING!" In smaller print, I wrote the biggest concern of my life at age ten: "I'm afraid you're going to die."

There is nothing like the bluntness of a child who has not learned to filter her words and says — or writes — exactly what she feels.

I took my time coloring each bubble letter. It was plain and simple, but I hoped it would be enough for him to take my plea to heart.

I folded the poster in two and took special care to get it home that day. I got off the school bus, marched into the house and went immediately upstairs to where Mom kept the boxes and wrapping paper. I wrapped my poster, added a label, and placed it under the tree.

On Christmas morning my sister and I tore through our gifts eagerly. Finally, there was just one left. The poster I made for my dad was leaning against the wall, unnoticed. I handed it to him quietly, unsure what his reaction would be.

He kneeled on the floor, surrounded by opened presents, toys, and wrapping paper. He held the box in his hands, reading the label out loud: "To Daddy, Love Lori."

He gently shook the box, but it was as light as a feather. Slowly, he unwrapped his gift.

I held my breath as he read the words quietly to himself. I watched as a tear leaked out of his eye. My mom glanced over his shoulder, gasped and started to cry. My sister ran behind them both to see what all the fuss was about.

There wasn't a dry eye in our home that Christmas morning. Dad wrapped me in a hug and said, "Okay, Lori. Okay."

The tender moment passed, and we all got absorbed in the bustle of the day. I forgot about my poster as soon as I returned to school after winter break. It seemed as if everyone else had forgotten my gift as well. That was, until a beautiful summer day.

We were outside riding our bikes, my sister on her ten-speed and me on my little girl bike, wishing I had a grownup bike like she had. All of a sudden, from around the corner of the house, my dad appeared, pushing a brand-new, red-and-white ten-speed bicycle.

"Is that for me?" I squealed with delight.

"It sure is, kiddo. I took your Christmas gift to heart. Over the last six months, I saved all the money I would have spent each week on cigarettes. This is what I bought with the money I saved."

I jumped into his arms, nearly toppling him over. "Thank you, Daddy!"

I took off to show my friends my new bike, thankful for the practice I had riding my sister's ten-speed. But I was even more grateful that my dad had quit smoking.

It has been almost four decades. I'm proud of him and grateful for the many years that we've had together. I look forward to many more.

I'm also proud of my younger self for having the courage to ask my dad for what I wanted most: for him to quit an unhealthy habit. I'm grateful for the sparks this experience created in my own life as, to this day, I'm still riding my bike and writing about my heart's desires.

—Lori Ann King—

74

All I Want for Christmas

*Life is really simple, but we insist
on making it complicated.*
~Confucius

This year, Evan and Delaney asked the Santa Claus at the store to bring them smelly markers and "cat stuff." I quit worrying a long time ago about whether Santa (or anyone waiting behind us in line to visit him) would think we were a strange family. It's okay; I know we are.

I also know that Santa appreciated their modest, budget-friendly wish list because the days for simple requests are definitely numbered in our household. My children will soon ask for big-ticket items like expensive shoes, gaming systems, and tech gadgets that haven't even been invented yet. But not this year. This would be the Christmas of cat pillows, art supplies, and scented markers.

Sure, I could have worked with Santa to pull off an additional Christmas surprise—a larger gift for them to enjoy—but I just didn't feel like creating a want that wasn't there. It reminded me of a conversation I had with a young child years ago, before I had children of my own.

"Did you get everything you wanted for Christmas?" I asked him.

"Yes, I did! I even got things I didn't *know* I wanted!" he responded.

The child was excited and adorable, but I have remembered this line for years. This is what parents do. We let our children know what they should want. We put the ideas in their heads for things they should ask for, things they might enjoy. Most of the time, their actual wants are quite simple.

But not this year.

This year, with the exception of a few small surprises, Evan and Delaney received exactly what they asked for. And this year, coming downstairs to see what Santa brought was not the highlight of Christmas. The true magic appeared in all the little moments that followed.

Since Christmas morning, they have played together with every gift they received. Evan has helped Delaney create beaded necklaces and decoupage, and Delaney has worked with Evan on LEGO projects and complex art designs. And when they aren't playing with their actual toys, they are busy building things with the boxes the toys came in.

They have spent the most time with their beloved scented markers. Some nights, my husband and I have to take the markers away from them and force them to go to bed. Then, we check on them an hour later and find them asleep with a couple of markers under their pillows and blue-and-orange streaks below their noses. We are starting to think they have a marker problem.

This was truly one of our favorite Christmases, and the best part has been watching an incredible bond develop between my two children. They really are best friends. They want to be together constantly, and they make cards and gifts for each other when they must be apart.

Sure, they have their moments of friction like most siblings do. They argue and fight, but they also forgive. And then they return to playing. Their wants are simple: markers, a cardboard box, space to play, and each other.

The best things in life really are free, or easily purchased at a discount store. I'm glad Santa listened to my kids' simple requests last Christmas. I'm glad I did, too.

— Melissa Face —

75

The Little Blue Box

If I know what love is, it's because of you.
~Hermann Hesse

My mother was a magician—not the kind who pulls a rabbit out of a hat, but the kind who could always pull Christmas presents out of thin air for me when I was growing up. This was especially true the Christmas I was sixteen, when I knew we had even less money than usual.

I remember telling my mother that she and Daddy didn't have to get me many presents so that there would be enough money to buy things for my little brother, who was six years old. She smiled and said, "We'll see."

A few days before Christmas, my mother and I were walking down the sidewalk past the only jewelry store in the small town where she worked. As we passed the store, I slowed down to look at the display in the window. My eyes immediately fell on the most beautiful diamond ring I had ever seen. Seven round diamonds were clustered into a silver setting mounted high on a thin, sleek band. The light shining in the display made those diamonds sparkle like they were alive with fire. I stood there in silence. My mother stopped alongside me and followed my gaze.

"That really is beautiful, isn't it?" she asked.

I breathed in. "Oh, my goodness. Yes, it is!"

We were silent for a few seconds. Then Mother said, "Would you like to go inside and try on that ring?"

I looked up at her and answered, "Oh, no. Maybe someday, but not right now."

I knew all too well our financial situation. She smiled. "Well, what if there's not another day to do it? I say we go in and see what that ring looks like on your hand."

She opened the door to the jewelry store, and I quietly followed her inside. The man behind the counter greeted us warmly. He knew my mother because she had worked in that town for many years. Mother pointed out the ring in the window and asked him to let me try it on. He pulled the little blue box from the display and brought it to the counter. He reached for my right hand and gently slid the ring onto my finger.

The lights in the store made that ring sparkle and glow. I tilted my hand in different directions, captivated by the beauty of those diamonds. I looked at my mother and smiled. Her eyes puddled up with tears, and she smiled, too. "Looks like it was just made for you," she said. I took off the ring and handed it back to the jeweler. I thanked him for letting me try it on. My mother thanked him, too. We walked back out onto the busy sidewalk full of Christmas shoppers and went on our way.

On Christmas Eve, I busied myself with my little brother, enjoying his excitement over Santa's imminent arrival. We giggled the night away, sleeping in the same bed and listening for sleigh bells until we fell asleep. When he awoke, the whole house came alive as he raced to the Christmas tree to find his presents.

I was focused on my brother and didn't immediately look at my gifts. My mother eased up beside me and whispered, "Aren't you going to see what Santa brought you?" I smiled and looked at where my gifts lay. There, under the Christmas tree, were new jeans, sweaters, perfume, make-up, and one small blue box. I looked at that box. I had seen it before. I looked at my mother's face. She was smiling. I lifted the little box and, with trembling hands, raised its top. Inside was that beautiful diamond ring. My eyes filled with tears as I raced to my mother and threw my arms around her neck.

I whispered, "Mother, we can't afford this! Maybe some other time when things get better for us."

She held my face with both her hands, looked into my eyes, and said, "And what if there's not another time, little one? What if we just have right now?" I hugged her tightly as I felt my tears trickle onto her shoulder.

Forty-three years have come and gone since that Christmas morning. My mother passed away when she was still very young. Maybe she knew something.

That ring is still one of my most treasured possessions. And, when I look at it on my hand, I am always reminded of my mother's words, "What if we just have right now?"

—Lea Gillespie Gant—

The Hanukkah Story

Memory is a way of holding onto the things you love,
the things you are, the things you never want to lose.
~From the television show The Wonder Years

When my daughter, Rachel, was planning her wedding, she asked me to speak. I was honored, of course, and suggested that I tell one of several "Rachel stories" from her childhood. I mentioned a few, but she quickly rejected them. I guess she thought they were embarrassing, so I told her I would think of something else.

Of course, with Rachel, there is always plenty of material, so I really had everything I needed for my wedding speech. But the one childhood story I've always treasured above all the rest is one of those she refused to let me tell at her wedding. It's the Hanukkah story, a tale that has haunted Rachel ever since that fateful Hanukkah night.

Hanukkah, as some may know, is one of the best holidays in the world… if you are a kid! It's the absolute worst for adults because you must give each child a gift on each of the eight days of Hanukkah. That added up to eight gifts per child, or twenty-four in all for my three kids. Let me add that we celebrated Christmas as well, but that was much easier since the presents were purchased by my wife. Hanukkah was different. That was my responsibility. It was made more difficult by several factors.

First, I hate to shop. Second, I am really bad at it. I have a tendency to buy the first thing I see just so I can get out of whatever store I'm in.

And, finally, I'm utterly clueless when shopping, especially for a little girl. All these factors led to a certain amount of tension and drama on Hanukkah nights. The kids recognized that they weren't going to get a blockbuster gift every night, especially the first few nights, but it had to be something they liked. All the pressure was on me.

Not surprisingly, I made several missteps. One year, I was vilified for repurposing lint removers that I received as Christmas gifts from the laundry up the street from my office. The pens and little knickknacks I received from salespeople who stopped by my office every Christmas season didn't go over very well either. Nonetheless, I was able to manage fairly well, at least when Rachel was younger and didn't know any better. As she got older, the inevitable comparisons between the gifts she received and the gifts her two big brothers got started. She didn't want the same gifts they got, but she wanted something comparable; and, like any kid her age, she knew how to compare!

It all came to a head on Rachel's eighth Hanukkah. Her brother Lee opened his present first. It was a neat little toy, and he really liked it. Rachel's turn was next. Her gift was a word game on cards. She looked perplexed when she opened it, so I explained to her that it was fun and would help her learn spelling and vocabulary. I ended by saying it was "educational." As soon as I uttered the word "educational" I knew I had made a mistake. In that moment, her expression turned to one of pure, overwhelming grief. She ran out of the family room in tears.

I caught up with her in the living room. She was on our big, plush chair with tears streaming down her face. I sat beside her, picked her up and put her on my lap as she buried her head in my shoulder, sobbing uncontrollably. As gently as I could, I asked her what was wrong. She lifted her head and looked at me with pure disdain. It was then that I got "the speech." She stared at me with her most serious, grown-up expression, and in that moment, our ages flipped. She became the adult, earnestly and somewhat condescendingly explaining to me, as though I was a seven-year-old, what the problem was.

Through her tears, she explained that presents are supposed to be fun. She complained that Lee got a toy, but she got something educational instead of fun. Then she complained that I was always giving her things that were either educational or good for her. And, while she was on the subject, she mentioned that I was always making her eat healthy foods as well. She was especially aggrieved by my recent ban on sugary cereals.

According to Rachel, no other parent in the neighborhood treated their child so badly! As she laid out her case, she became more and more indignant — not just at the futility of trying to explain something so basic to a clueless adult, but even more so at the sheer injustice of it all. She was quickly losing her composure again but was nonetheless able to sum up the problem and the solution in two short sentences. She looked me straight in the eyes and spoke. Her exact words, said as seriously and earnestly as any seven-year-old ever could, and which I will never forget, were: "Wake up, Dad! The neighbors are eating Froot Loops!"

With that, overwhelmed yet again by the injustice of it all, she burst into tears for a second time. I held her head tightly against my shoulder so that she couldn't see that I was laughing, and we sat that way for a while — she trying to control her tears, and I trying to hide my laughter. When I was finally able to speak, I reassured her that I would do better next time. I still held her head on my shoulder, though, so she couldn't see my broad smile, which I was struggling to erase. Finally, we were both able to compose ourselves, and we went back into the family room to finish our Hanukkah celebration.

Over the next few days, I told my friends and family what Rachel had said. Of course, they all sided with her. Not only did several of them buy her Froot Loops, but a tradition was also started. On birthdays, Rachel got Froot Loops. When she was Bat Mitzvahed, she got Froot Loops. When she graduated from high school, she got Froot Loops. Rachel gratefully and with good humor accepted all these gifts, although I suspect she grew tired of the story after a while. That's probably another reason why she wouldn't let me tell it at her wedding.

However, the story has a life of its own. Even though I couldn't tell the Froot Loops story at Rachel's wedding, I have the satisfaction of knowing that it was told shortly thereafter, and by Rachel herself. I am just sorry I wasn't there to hear Rachel explain to her new husband why one of their wedding gifts was a box of Froot Loops!

—Rob Goldberg—

77

Chicken Soup for the Soul

The Christmas Birthday Gift

Like father, like son: every good tree makes good fruits.
~Author Unknown

When our family would gather on Christmas Eve, my presents to my adult sons, Morgan and Graham, had become all too predictable. I usually gave cash or gift cards, and they were received with appreciation but with no surprise and delight. But two years ago, I actually thought of a gift I was pretty sure would elicit the desired response from my older son, Morgan.

So, what was this amazing gift that was certain to delight my thirty-seven-year-old son? A new MacBook Pro? An iPad Air? A Ferrari, perhaps? Nope. It was a seven-inch-wide, four-inch-high, cylindrical, metallic cake stand. Not exactly what you were expecting? But this was no ordinary cake stand. This cake stand had a wind-up top that could rotate while playing a music-box version of the "Happy Birthday" tune. Still sounds rather lame, I know.

Maybe it might help for you to know that my mom owned an identical cake stand from the early 1950s, which she would bring out every time one of her grandchildren celebrated a birthday at my parents' house. And I remember how this little family tradition seemed especially fun for Morgan when he was very young.

He'd sit at the dining-room table in the dim light waiting patiently.

The birthday cake, aglow with candlelight, would be ushered into the room and set down on the cake stand in front of Morgan as the family gathered around. And this was not simply some bakery-bought dessert. This would usually be my mother's super-duper, homemade, chocolate brownie cake. Though it had the consistency and weight of a brick, it tasted like heaven.

And then, with a flip of the switch on the base of the stand, this chocolate-frosted taste sensation would slowly begin its rotation as Morgan's face, flickering in candlelight, would beam in response to the voices of those who loved him as we all sang "Happy Birthday" to the accompaniment of the cake stand.

Morgan would make his wish and blow out the candles. We'd all applaud and wait for the music to wind down before cutting into what would affectionately come to be known as Grandma's Brick Brownie.

My mom passed away when Morgan was fourteen years old, and the cake stand stopped working not long after, leaving it to become only a fond memory for him. But he wasn't alone. You see, that metallic cake stand was an equally nostalgic gadget for me. Along with the Brick Brownie, it was there for every birthday of mine as far back as I could remember. So, I totally got it when Morgan confided in me only a few years ago that he genuinely missed the musical rotating cake experience along with missing his grandma. The two would forever be linked together.

And then it dawned on me a few years ago, just before the holidays, that maybe one of those archaic contraptions could be found on eBay. Much to my surprise, a fully working model exactly like my mom's was available for an opening bid of a mere nineteen bucks. Immediately, I placed a bid on the cake stand, and then for the next few days I periodically checked back on eBay to find that my bid continued to remain the highest one. But with a couple of days remaining, I discovered the bid had gone up to twenty-five dollars. Apparently, there was another equally nostalgic person staring at his or her computer screen in Kalamazoo or somewhere, watching the same antique cake stand, hoping to deprive Morgan of the best present his dad had given him in years. I figured no one would dare pay more than fifty dollars, so I raised my bid to fifty-two. Take that, Kalamazoo!

The following day, I watched as the digital clock on the eBay auction site counted down toward the end of the listing. With fifteen seconds left, nothing had changed… But with six seconds remaining, it jumped to thirty-one bucks… then forty! Then as time ran out the bidding closed at fifty dollars. I had won the cake stand by only two dollars.

Though the cake stand hadn't come cheap or easy, the only thing on my mind after receiving it in the mail a few days later and wrapping it was imagining the surprise and delight on Morgan's face when he opened the gift on Christmas Eve. It would be priceless.

And so, Christmas Eve arrived, and our extended family gathered in our living room to munch on snacks and open presents as we listened to classic Christmas songs. With the warmth of a blazing fire, we started in on our gift exchange.

Aside from my wife, Susan, the only other person who knew about the cake stand gift was my other son, Graham, who promised to keep it a surprise. We were about halfway through opening the presents when Graham grabbed my gift for Morgan out from under the tree and handed it to him. "Here, I think you might like this one," he said.

Morgan ripped off the paper and popped open the box. He peered inside and then removed the gift wrapped in tissue paper. I was sitting on one side of him and his wife, Julie, on the other when he pulled the paper away to reveal the marvelous, metallic cake stand. I looked for the genuine look of surprise and delight on his face… and there it was. Success!

Smiling, Morgan turned to me and asked, "Did you get this on eBay?"

"Yeah… barely," I said. "I was winning it at a reasonable price until the last few seconds when some bozo bid it way up."

"To fifty-one dollars?" Morgan said, with a curious grin.

"Yeah, how did you know? Did Graham tell you?"

"No… I was the bozo." Morgan laughed. My first instinct was to laugh as well, but then I found myself holding back tears, aware of how much Morgan's gesture had touched my heart.

Only Graham had known that both Morgan and I were bidding on the same item.

So now for every birthday, we share the old cake stand and usually weigh it down with Grandma's Brick Brownie. And then, with the flip of a switch, our family sings "Happy Birthday" as the cake does its dance. You might think the only thing missing from the moment would be the presence of my mom, but our collective awareness of her absence only serves to make her all the more present in our hearts.

— Don Locke —

78

Chicken Soup for the Soul.

This Little Light of Mine

We should give as we would receive, cheerfully, quickly,
and without hesitation; for there is no grace in a
benefit that sticks to the fingers.
~Seneca

Joyce was the kind of person who was always trying to win a popularity contest. She would inquire, "How was your surgery?" and then ask the person beside you about her cat before you could murmur a two-word answer. Every year, she organized the book-club Christmas party, and every year I'd say to myself I wasn't going because Joyce would get so bossy about what everyone was supposed to bring, do, and discuss at the event.

One year, I was supposed to bring spinach soufflé. "Enough for ten people, and please use real butter," she'd dictated. "Let me know if you need my recipe." Before I could buy the ingredients (I didn't even know it called for butter), I was already thinking up an excuse for missing the next year's gathering.

So, I shouldn't have been surprised when she commandeered the gift exchange after we'd finished eating. It was that "Sneaky Santa" game where the recipients pick a number and then can choose a wrapped gift or "steal" one that's been opened. There are some variations that limit how many times a gift may be stolen, and I've seen some celebrants (after a few glasses of wine) get visibly combative when their beloved ceramic bell or snowman lamp is spirited away, and they're left with an ugly tree ornament or a million-calorie box of candy.

"It's all in good fun," Joyce said, explaining her unbendable rules. Like most people in our group, I'd spent a little over the ten-dollar limit and found a pretty foil bag for the bath-and-body ensemble I had painstakingly chosen, hoping they would go half-price after Christmas so I could buy one for myself.

Two newcomers, Marsha and Betty, somehow missed the announcement about bringing gifts for exchanging but agreed they were glad just to watch everyone open theirs.

"Oh, no," said General Joyce. "Everyone should participate." At that decree, she dashed out to her car to retrieve two small, cylindrical packages that she spaced among the assortment of gifts.

"Must be those votive candles," said Mrs. Aiken, slightly under her breath. "I saw them at Dollar Tree when I was buying Christmas cards."

She had brought a wrapped box about the size of a bath-and-body set, so I chose Mrs. Aiken's gift when my number came up. I was right! "Thank you!" I said to her, inhaling the vanilla scent.

My victory lasted less than a minute. Marsha's number was next, and she (who hadn't brought a gift at all) "Sneaky Santasized" it away. Betty, her partner in the mysterious gift boycott, had ended up with the bath set I brought, just a few sneaky moves before. So much for being content to watch everyone open their gifts.

When the sham was over, I stuffed Joyce's candle in a bag with my leftover spinach soufflé. Mrs. Aiken, who'd been stuck with the other candle, had been wrong. The price sticker revealed it had been purchased at another store — and it cost exactly $1.99 plus tax. Shameless Joyce, I couldn't help but notice, was going home with a set of thick holiday towels that I could have used in my bathroom.

I tried to console myself with its generous cinnamon scent as the days wore on. I could think of no one to insult with such an inconsequential item as a gift, even if it was guaranteed to burn for twelve hours as the label had indicated.

With too much time on my hands and no other parties to attend, I persisted in plotting my revenge against meddling Joyce, who was oblivious to the disparity in gifts that she had created by throwing in the two items she had in her car. I couldn't wait for next year. I would insist on having the party at my house and give out those cheap candles as table favors for everyone. Or maybe I'd wrap mine in a big, deceptive box and rig the gift exchange so Joyce would end up with her measly substitute gift. That would teach her to rob me so Marsha and Betty could feel better. Even sooner, I could tie a pink ribbon around it and give it to Joyce as a little Valentine's Day "thank you" for all the "great" work she did at the Christmas party.

Then the winter storm hit. The icy roads became impassable, and power outages were reported everywhere. When the lights began to flicker, I thought of my mother, who had always kept kerosene lanterns in the house for both decorative and practical purposes. I hated them because they were greasy and hard to clean. I thought of my mother-in-law, who always burned religious candles in the house at Christmastime. I liked how they smelled but worried about the hazard with animals in the house. Then I thought of the cinnamon candle hidden away in the closet.

I got that candle out and found myself comforted by its Christmasy smell. When the lights went out, I lit it. With the help of my standing make-up mirror behind it, the little flame illuminated my entire living room where I quietly sat with my cat and read our January book selection, Anthony Doerr's *All the Light We Cannot See*.

True to its promise, the little candle lasted the full twelve hours, just long enough for the power to come back. It was also just long enough for me to realize that, in spite of myself, Joyce had given me the perfect gift—just what I needed.

—Linda Maxwell—

79

Best Book Ever

The manner of giving is worth more than the gift.
~Pierre Corneille

The Christmas Day drive to the Amtrak station had already been tough. Heavy snow had plagued us from Wyoming to Denver, and we'd now have to run to catch our 9 p.m. train. I hoisted on the giant backpack that left my hands free for my three-year-old and five-year-old boys. And, like a momma turtle with two hatchlings in tow, we took off at a fast waddle.

It turned out the California Zephyr was also battling the weather as it crossed the Rocky Mountains, with multiple delays pushing our departure by hours. As the waiting dragged on, it became harder to occupy the little ones, who were up way past their bedtime.

We were making the trip to my sister's on a very tight budget and probably shouldn't have come, but it had been a lonely winter, and I was determined. I'd scraped together just enough, without a dime to spare. Subsequently, I found myself constantly saying "no" in the train station as the boys asked for activities we couldn't afford — video games, vending machines, the station restaurant. Zach, my older son, spent a considerable amount of time in the tiny gift shop, fingering the five dollars of vacation money his grandpa had given him.

Nearing midnight, I had exhausted my supply of games, songs and snacks, and began to fantasize about the quiet of the train. I had brought a thick novel from the library, and knowing the boys would fall asleep quickly, I couldn't wait to settle in for a peaceful read.

Immersing myself in a book that wasn't *Goodnight Moon* was a treat I'd been looking forward to for weeks.

Finally, they announced our train's arrival. I hurriedly gathered our things, unzipping a spot to tuck in Ziggy the Zebra, the Beanie Baby that had doubled as a soccer ball while we waited. That's when I noticed there was no novel. I searched frantically, my eyes stinging, dreading a twelve-hour train ride with little chance of sleep and nothing to do. I tried not to let the boys see my disappointment. I know it was a little thing, but that idea of wrapping myself in fiction had sustained me all evening. With no money to buy a book, I hefted on the backpack and turned for the boys' hands.

White-hot panic hit when I saw that Zach was not on the bench beside me. It only lasted a second, and I breathed again as I saw him coming out of the gift shop. The rebuke on the tip of my tongue stalled as I looked into his shining face, his hands mysteriously tucked behind his back. "Look what I got you, Mom," he said, pulling out a paperback book, the green cover of castles and woods inviting me in like a spell. All of his precious money spent on me. "Do you like it?" His proud grin took my breath away as I wrapped him and his brother in a tight squeeze. The gift of his kindness flooded my heart.

Twenty-five years later, I've still never received a better present. Unexpected and lifesaving, given with such selflessness, that gift told me a lot about the man my son would become. And that night on the train, snuggled in the darkness between my sleeping sons, lulled by a rhythmic cadence of clackety-clack, I'd never read a better book.

— Louisa Wilkinson —

80

Just Right

Christmas magic is silent. You don't hear it —
you feel it. You know it. You believe it.
~Kevin Alan Milne

I wrote out the letter in my best handwriting before walking to the post office with my mother to mail it.

Dear Santa,

Thank you once again for the Giant Book of Fairytales last year. It was smashing. I choose a different bedtime story every night.

We moved houses this summer, but Mummy says you'll know where to find us. Our new house doesn't have a chimney. I hope this isn't a problem.

This year I'd like a cat, please, but I don't know how you will deliver one. I am responsible and will feed and brush the cat every day. I promise.

I hope you and the workshop elves are all well.

Please give the reindeer a pat for me. I'll leave out carrots on Christmas Eve.

Love from Sue

On Christmas morning, I found an enormous, gaily wrapped box with my name on the label. I started to tear off the festive paper but remembered I'd told Santa I was a responsible girl, so I gently peeled away the wrapping, careful not to scare the cat inside.

When I lifted the flaps and peeked in, I found cat litter and a tray, along with boxes of dried and canned cat food. There was a food bowl and a water dish, both decorated with paw patterns, and a sparkly cat collar with a jingle bell. A stocking was filled with cat toys: things that rolled and clicked, and catnip-infused, neon-coloured feathers on elastic. There was even a grooming kit of a brush and claw clippers so I could be true to my word and brush the cat every day. Squished at the bottom lay a plush cat bed.

But there was no cat.

I started to cry. "Santa thought I wanted presents for a cat."

"Santa doesn't make mistakes," said Mommy. "Look. What's that envelope?"

The red envelope bearing my name lay hidden under wrapping paper.

Dear Sue,

> *I couldn't put your cat in my sack. He'd get scared and claw his way out.*
> *He is waiting for you at the shelter.*
> *You will recognise him.*
> *I am glad you are still enjoying your book.*
> *The elves and the reindeer say hello.*

Merry Christmas,
Santa Claus

I spent the day arranging and rearranging the bed and toys. My mother helped me clear a shelf in the larder for the cat food.

The next day, we visited the shelter. I thought that Santa must have been very busy with cat requests because there were lots of other children there, too.

Then I saw it. There were kittens galore, but an older striped cat cowered at the back of the enclosure, hissing at whoever approached. That cat looked like he might be the one I was supposed to recognise. I sat cross-legged in front of the open cage and waited patiently. He eventually limped out and climbed into my lap. He curled up, closed his orange eyes, and rumbled like a train.

"Thank you, Santa," I said over my new cat's purring head. "He's absolutely perfect."

— Sue Mitchell —

81

Papa, Perfume, and Me

*Love is the greatest gift that one generation
can leave to another.*
~Richard Garnett

"Make sure Papa finds me an atomizer this year," said Grandmama in her usual brisk way. I was home from college, and my grandfather and I were heading out on our annual Christmas shopping trip. My Christmas excursions with Papa began in childhood, when he and I made the twenty-minute drive to collect my great-grandmother to spend Christmas Eve at my grandparents' house. On the way, he pointed out any strange light in the sky that he thought might be Santa's sleigh.

When I grew older, Papa took me on his "Christmas visits," a round of calls to relatives by blood, marriage, and friendship that invariably ended with a cheerful wave and a parting wish: "Hope Santa Claus is good to you!" By the time I started high school, many of those relatives were gone, and our Christmas outing morphed into a shopping trip for Grandmama, one that inevitably ended with cholesterol-laden meals at a local cafeteria and a conspiratorial, "Don't tell your grandmother."

"What's an atomizer?" I asked Grandmama.

"A bottle for perfume," she said. "With a little ball on the end of a string. You squeeze the ball, and the perfume mists out. The one I've had forever has finally fallen apart, and I can't find a new one anywhere."

"So, you don't want an Estée Lauder Pleasures gift set this year?"

"Oh, no. I have years' worth of that stuff stockpiled."

There went Papa's go-to gift.

We went to the first mall, in our own county. We looked in all the department stores. We went to the second mall, in the county to the east. We went to the third mall, in the county to the west. *Sorry,* salespeople repeated. *No one buys atomizers anymore. They're so old-fashioned.*

This was before the rise of online shopping, so we'd have to find the atomizers in person or not at all. We ended up empty-handed over a late lunch at the cafeteria.

"We're close to the cemetery where Mom and Pap are buried," said Papa, scraping cake crumbs and chocolate icing from his plate. "I know it's getting late, but do you mind if we make a stop?"

"I'd like that," I agreed, licking the last of my ice cream from the spoon.

We got out of the car and stood before my great-grandparents' headstone. Papa's father had died when I was very young, but I remembered the warm day in the spring of my fifth-grade year when we buried his mother, the woman we'd chauffeured together all those Christmas Eves. Earlier that year, on another spring day, we'd buried Papa's only sibling, my Uncle Jack.

Now, the sky was gray and white, and the air was cold and soft, with the chilly humidity of a Southern winter. The wind ruffled the petals of red and white poinsettias on the graves and rustled the brittle, faded grass.

"You know," said Papa, after a while, "sometimes, I look around, and I realize I'm all alone here."

I slipped my arm into his, but I didn't contradict him. I knew what he meant. The family he remembered most at Christmas, the family of his childhood, was gone. We stood together, each with our own memories, until the chill seeped under our coats, and the early dark began to fall.

"Papa!" I exclaimed, startling us both. "There's a perfume store at the mall. It's in the new wing, and I completely forgot about it this morning. They might have atomizers. It's worth a shot."

We passed from the December darkness into the overwhelming brightness of a tiny store crammed from floor to ceiling with loudly colored perfume boxes. Every surface not covered in merchandise was covered in mirrors, reflecting us, the perfumes and the impeccably dressed salesman behind the counter into infinity. We almost couldn't breathe for the clouds of scent in the air.

"Can I help you?" asked the salesman.

"Atomizers!" I gasped.

"So charmingly old-fashioned," he smiled, with a nod to Papa.

"Do you have them?" I persisted.

The salesman led us down the length of the sales counter and knelt to pull two boxes from a hidden far corner. He opened the boxes to reveal beautiful glass atomizers nestled in satin.

"Is this what you had in mind?"

"They're perfect," I said. I turned to Papa. "Buy both of them. Who knows if we'll ever be able to find them again."

Papa paid for the atomizers, his typical grin and chuckle restored, and we smuggled them into the house while Grandmama pretended not to know what we were up to. I wrapped them in the spare bedroom, with Papa keeping a lookout at the door, and hid them in the jumble of presents under the tree.

The atomizers met with Grandmama's approval and appeared soon after Christmas on a glass tray on her bathroom vanity. Several years later, after Papa's memorial service, I slipped into the quiet bathroom to find a few moment's peace in the packed house. I rested my fingers on the cool glass atomizers and closed my eyes, remembering all those years of Christmas journeys.

When my parents and I cleaned out the house after Grandmama, too, passed away, I knew which precious memento I wanted to keep. I got an old shoebox and some tissue paper and carried them into the bathroom. When I emptied the atomizers of perfume for transport, I was enveloped for a moment in my grandmother's scent.

I don't wear perfume, but I keep the empty bottles on their glass tray on my dresser, where they remind me of my grandparents every day. When I see them, I remember all those Christmas drives, visits, and shopping trips with Papa. And when I open them, I can still smell Grandmama. The long journey to find those atomizers is a cherished memory of Papa, one I wouldn't have if, years ago, I hadn't forgotten about the new perfume store at the mall. It was a gift that, like the atomizers, I almost didn't find.

— Courtney McKinney-Whitaker —

It Takes a Village

82

The Christmas Lights

Christmas is most truly Christmas when we
celebrate it by giving the light of love
to those who need it most.
~Ruth Carter Stapleton

I grew up in a small town in Kansas, with one main road and one set of traffic lights. During the holiday season, the main street was always decorated with lights and a huge Santa, reindeer and sleigh in the front yard of the courthouse. Santa had been the victim of kidnapping so many times that it had become almost a game by the time I was a teen. I can neither confirm nor deny allegations that I kidnapped said Santa, and may or may not have strapped him to the overhang by the high school with a sign on him that read, "Will work for eggnog."

I lived on a tree-filled, shady street where lawns were perfectly manicured in the summer, and snow was shoveled uniformly in the winter. I was taken in by my paternal grandparents when I was five. They were very stern people who frowned upon frivolity in most matters. They were not prone to charity as they had very little themselves, but they did believe in kindness and self-respect. They would never have accepted charity, but they taught me that giving quietly was better than shouting it from the rooftops. I really didn't know until many years later how much they lived what they taught.

Each holiday season, my grandfather could be found on a ladder outside the house hanging strings of lights on the many evergreen trees that encircled it. My grandmother watched him carefully to ensure proper spacing of the lights. It was accepted in our neighborhood that everyone should decorate, and she wanted it to look perfect. Every evening as the sun set, the neighborhood lights would all come on about the same time. Snow would have already fallen a few times by then, so the lights on the trees, in picture windows, and on decorated houses would cast multicolored shadows on the snow below. In the eyes of a child, the world was ablaze in color, and it was a fine time to be alive.

The year I turned twelve, about a week after the lights had gone up, we discovered the lights were gone, stolen from right under our noses. My grandfather was not inclined to buy more and redecorate, but my grandmother insisted. How would it look if our house was dark during the holidays when everyone else's was lit? Mumbling a commentary not fit to repeat, my grandfather trudged to the store to get more lights and rehang them as instructed.

Nothing else was said about the missing lights until about a week after Christmas. One of my chores was to bring in the mail from the front. On the stoop, I found a box containing every missing strand of Christmas lights, wrapped neatly in a ball. For the next five years, the pattern repeated itself. Lights would go up, go missing, and be returned to us in an unmarked box after the holidays were over. If I attempted to ask about it, my grandfather would shake his head, ending my questions immediately. After I left home and started my own path, I would wonder now and then what the story behind five years of missing and returned lights had been.

Some years later, I found myself back home having to clear out the old house after my grandparents had passed. The last place to empty out was the garage and its attic. Several of my childhood friends and neighbors were there to help me sort through seventy years of stuff, so the work went quickly.

At the end of the afternoon, only four of us remained — my closest pals growing up. Up in the rafters of the garage, tucked into a dusty corner, I found the box. The Christmas lights were old and many of them broken, but I knew instantly what they were. As I handed the box down, I asked if anyone knew what had happened all those years ago.

Over dinner that night, I learned the truth about those lights, and about what real friendship meant to a group of twelve-year-old boys.

The first year the lights went missing, my friend Dave lost his father in the Vietnam War. Their family had no income then, although his mom went to work later. For the first time in Dave's memory, there were no lights on the house for the holidays. Their house was the only one in darkness on a street full of lights, something his mother was ashamed of.

His friends, having no money to buy lights, decided to do the only thing they could think of. They "borrowed" the lights from our trees and decorated Dave's house with them as best they could, never telling him what they had done. When the holidays were over, the boys felt duty-bound to return the lights in good condition, but the next year it felt necessary to again "borrow" them for the happiness of their best friend.

The second year, my grandfather caught them returning the lights. The boys explained why they had taken them, after which my grandfather instructed them to tell no one, and it was understood they would return the lights in good working order. A gentleman's agreement had been made.

Years later, after my gran had passed and Grampa was in his late eighties, the four men got together with their kids and decorated his house for the holidays until his passing. They never spoke of what had transpired before; the gentleman's agreement was still in place.

Instead, they brought the lights of the holiday back around, to pay it forward, a gift from the past. Once again they were three young boys making Christmas merrier for someone who needed a little help.

— Cj Cole —

Grampy's Rock

*The greatness of a community is most accurately
measured by the compassionate actions of its members.*
~Coretta Scott King

In early December 2000, I was in a panic because I couldn't think of a thing to put under the tree for my grandfather. Grampy wasn't one of those people who already had everything, but rather one of those people who didn't *want* anything. I don't know if he was trying to make things easier for us, but his request (or, rather, lack thereof) threw the entire family into a tizzy. Every year. What to get for the man who wants nothing? I pestered and cajoled until he finally caved and said, "Fine, then. Get me a rock."

A rock.

Lucky for him, I knew of just the rock. I quickly did a Web search (in 2000, it was still cool to call it "the Web") and typed up an e-mail to a man who didn't know me from Adam, but whom I hoped would respond. Christmas was only two weeks away, and we still had nothing for Grampy.

Dear Colonel Ackman,

> *Please take a moment to review this e-mail. I know you take care of far more pressing matters each day, but I am working on limited time and would love to have just a moment of yours.*

My grandfather, Major Paul A. Weakland, loved the military. He is not only a decorated soldier but an exceptional human being. He was stationed in Fort Hunter Liggett in the 1960s, fell in love with it, and more than forty years later continues to bring his grandchildren (of which I am one) to visit every year. We have camped, stayed at the Hacienda, and roomed at the Officer's Quarters. He taught his children, grandchildren, and various neighbor children to shoot firearms, swim, and respect nature on the base — not to mention the hundreds of times that we visited the mission and the surrounding property. When we were very young, we often pretended that we were in the Army and came dressed head-to-toe in camouflage!

Here is where I begin to sound a bit strange. Sometime during his station, my grandfather ended up in the Indians with a private and a Jeep. He found a rock there that looks like God put a paint can down on it. It has a white circle on the top, with what looks like white paint running down the sides. He liked the rock so much that he and the private loaded it into the Jeep and brought it back to his quarters. The rock was too heavy to bring home, so he had to leave it behind. It still sits, nearly fifty years later, across the parking lot from the Fort Hunter Liggett PX and the movie theater by the road. (It sits in the cactus and rock display.) Whenever he brings us for a visit (we are nearly all adults, now), we still stop by to take a look at The Rock on our way home, and he laughs to see it standing there after so many years.

My grandfather is going to be eighty years old in the coming months and has begun to talk about how he won't be able to make the trip to Fort Hunter Liggett very much longer. My brother, sister, and I would very much like to show him how much he means to us and how much we appreciate all he has taught us — by bringing that rock home to him for Christmas. We didn't think it would be wise to steal from a military property, so I am writing to ask for clearance to pick it up in time for the holidays.

Please let me know how I can obtain permission to bring this piece of our family history home.

With utmost respect,
Shauna McGuiness

Four days later, I received his response:

Ms. McGuiness,

I have attempted to contact you by phone several times, but I have failed.

Your request to take possession of this rock is approved. We did discuss the wisdom of granting this request. We do not want to be in the business of providing the public large mementos of any kind of the post. However, your grandfather's service to this post and the Army, his continuing interest in both Fort Hunter Liggett and the Army, can move even the most hardcore.

I ask that you contact [name and phone number]. You will need to schedule a time to make contact with them and identify the rock. You will need to ensure you have the means to safely transport it. Once the rock is identified, it becomes your posses-sion. You become responsible for transfer to your vehicle, and you become responsible for anything that may occur. Ensure you have the means to secure the rock for transport. We are not averse to assisting you, but this is under your direction, since the rock becomes yours, and the means of transport is yours. We are not sure which rock you refer to, so please ensure you have an understanding of the weight of this object and what will be required to make safe transfer and transport.

I salute your love and respect for your grandfather. Under normal circumstances, such a request would not be granted, but the love of a granddaughter for a man of service cannot be ignored.

Respectfully,
LTC Stephen M. Ackman

Three days later, my husband, my sister, and I left our home in the dark of early morning to make the two-hour drive to the base. We arrived as the sun became a pinkish purple smear in the sky, still dotted with stars. Showing our I.D. cards to the uniformed man huddled in the guard shack at the entrance, we were cleared for admittance.

Passing olive-green tanks and Humvees, we finally reached our destination: The Rock. Surrounded by dirt and cacti, it was part of a flower box of sorts on the outskirts of the PX/movie theater parking lot. It was there, as it had been for decades: round white paint splotch on the top. A tractor rolled up next to us, and a giant, friendly man named George helped us load the heavy gift into the bed of our El Camino (where it lived until Christmas Eve — we probably didn't get the best gas mileage for the following week and a half). The rear of the car was considerably lower, as we thanked him and drove away.

December 24th arrived. My siblings met my husband and me at Grampy and Lulu's house at midnight. It was very much a cloak-and-dagger affair. (In hindsight, we were probably very lucky that my grandfather didn't hear us and come out with a BB gun to order us off his property.) That rock was so heavy that it almost didn't make it out of the truck bed and onto the dolly that we brought. It took all four of us to hoist it, and it still threw my poor hubby's back out. (He managed to limp through the rest of our top-secret assignment, thank goodness.) Rolling and dumping The Rock into the front yard, we admired our handiwork and promised to reconvene in the morning.

Hours later, we all giggled as we passed our surprise on the way to the front door, trying not to look in its direction. We also made sure to push our grandparents into the house as we kissed and hugged and wished a "Merry Christmas." Grampy was dressed for the day in red pants and an impossibly shiny green shirt — complete with Christmas tie. When everyone finally arrived, we led him out into the yard.

Of course, he was confused. "What're we doing out here?" Then he saw it. It was as if he was being reunited with a long-lost friend. No, a long-lost *love*.

"My ROCK!" he bellowed in unhidden glee. He knelt to touch the spot where God's paint can had once been. "My rock..." Tears came to his eyes, and he ran a shaky hand through white hair.

"You said to get you a rock for Christmas." I kissed him on the cheek.

"Well, you got me just what I wanted."

How often can someone say that and really, truly mean it?

Grampy visited Fort Hunter Liggett and Lieutenant Stephen Ackman in the spring, bringing a photo that he asked me to find for him online so he could ask for an autograph. He got one. It reads:

Major (ret) Weakland,

> *I am so glad that the rock is where it belongs — with those who know and love it. May it energize your memories and those of your family of Fort Hunter Liggett — visit us often!*

LTC Steve Ackman

— Shauna McGuiness —

A Home for Christmas

*I would maintain that thanks are the highest
form of thought, and that gratitude
is happiness doubled by wonder.*
~Gilbert K. Chesterton

"You have one month," the landlord said with no expression. "I told the new family they could be in by Christmas."

I gave my husband that wide-eyed look of horror. We were not aware of any "new family" wanting our home. We were building a new home and had planned to move in after New Year's. Now we had less than two months.

My husband was building our new house himself. How was he going to finish everything and still keep his full-time job? We didn't have to wait long for the answer.

The Monday after Thanksgiving weekend, he came home two hours early with a solemn look on his face. "Tell me what happened." I urged him to the couch with a steaming cup of coffee.

"They let me go," he responded in monotone. "No reason. Just said they didn't need my kind of help anymore." His voice had a ring of defeat.

"We'll be okay." I struggled to keep my voice from quivering and appear calm for his sake. I was anything but. Now we had no income.

Soon, we'd be homeless too if the new house didn't get finished in time.

My husband suddenly had all the time in the world to work on our unfinished house, but it looked like there wouldn't be any gift-giving this year. I didn't mind for myself, but I worried for our two young boys. A Christmas tree, dinner, and trimmings were out of the question, too.

On the other hand, I was determined not to let circumstances get the best of me. I may not have been happy about the situation, but I wasn't going to allow it to steal my joy. We would make the best of it.

"When you pack your toys," I told my boys, "pick out a few that you don't play with anymore. There are less fortunate kids at the shelter in town who will love them." I planned to do the same as I packed clothes and other household things for our move. We could keep the spirit of Christmas in our hearts by giving to others. That was a matter of choice.

Word got around that we'd be forced to move early. Suddenly, friends began to show up at the building site. "Had a couple of spare hours," one said. "Thought you might need some help." Wonderful friends, new and old, joined in preparation for our move. Ladies came to help me pack and clean. The task became less daunting every day.

When Christmas was five days away our landlord knocked on the door to remind us. "I promised the other family they could be in this week. Make it happen."

December 23rd arrived, and our new house was complete enough to move in. There was still painting to do, but that was minor. As we moved things out, the new family moved their things in. They apologized for our inconvenience, but they had no other place to go. Several families helped us move and get furniture into place. That night we set up our beds and collapsed into them with mountains of boxes surrounding us.

The next morning, Christmas Eve, we dug until we found some cereal and bowls. We laughed as we used boxes as table and chairs. We decided to wait until after Christmas to unpack everything else. We had done it. We were in our new house. It was time to give thanks and celebrate.

The day began by visiting nursing-home residents, singing Christmas carols and offering a prayer at each room. Then we were off to the dollar store to let the boys pick out a few treasures. After a quick fast-food dinner, we attended our church's Christmas Eve service. On the way home, we took our time driving through the neighborhood to enjoy the festive lights. It was restful and restorative, and time to take a breath. But when we arrived home, we were delightfully surprised.

"Why is the house all lit up?" I asked.

"Steve asked if he could move some of the boxes to storage while we were away," Tim said. "I gave him a key. Maybe he forgot to turn off the lights."

When we opened the door, a fully decorated Christmas tree complete with wrapped presents underneath greeted us. Everything was neatly put in place. There was even a plate of cookies on the counter. Tears flooded from my eyes as I read the note on the tree: "Merry Christmas, friends. We're glad to be a part of your life."

It was a warm welcome home we would never forget. Out of love and generosity, we didn't just get a new house; our friends gave us a home for Christmas.

— C.A. Simonson —

Around the Tree

Nothing ever seems too bad, too hard, or too sad when
you've got a Christmas tree in the living room.
~Nora Roberts

"Christmas without a tree!" I said to my husband, who was half-listening. I had just returned from a party and learned that one of my brother's friends couldn't afford a Christmas tree this year. I knew this woman from my brother's parties. She was a single, hard-working mother of three. After her recent divorce, she and her three small children moved in with her sister, who also happened to be a single mom. Times were hard for all of them that year, and I overheard this lovely woman tell my brother that it was going to be a slim Christmas. They were going to save money by not getting a tree.

I know, first-world problems. All I could think about, though, were the hours and hours our family spent around a beautifully decorated tree at holiday time. The laughs we had. The songs we sang over and over again. The decorations we made, some of which were great, others… not so much.

And my heart sank when I thought of this sweet family not having one.

"I'm going to buy a tree, lights and decorations, and Secret Santa the tree to them!" I explained excitedly to my husband.

I went shopping for the perfect tree. Not too big. Not too small. With a stand. Next came the lights. Beautiful, sparkly lights. And an extension cord just in case. Finally, the decorations. Red, silver, white, gold, and green. The perfect Christmas colors. Decorations that kids could enjoy for years to come.

I delivered the tree to the family that very night. My husband and I drove to their house. We dropped off the tree and all the decorations in their driveway, knowing they would be home from work soon. We didn't leave a note. Or a card. Just the tree. Then we drove off.

Much like the Grinch, my "heart grew three sizes that day" when my brother called later to tell me someone had dropped off a tree for his friend's family. He said they were so happy and appreciative, and it really felt like Christmas. They were so grateful to whomever their Secret Santa was.

Thinking back, it wasn't about the tree. What I loved about the tree and what I wanted so much for that family was the family time. The tree was just the backdrop. But during the holidays, it's partially what brought us together as a family and kept us anchored together there. Sometimes, for a few minutes. Sometimes, for a few hours. It's where we made so many memories. Laughed and lived. Around the tree.

— Crescent LoMonaco —

86

Mending Hearts

Christmas isn't just a day, it's a frame of mind.
~Valentine Davies

Every winter, as inflatable snowmen popped up beneath the palm trees, and bells clanged outside overflowing stores, I became a Grinch just counting down the days until the holiday madness would end. Despite being surrounded by jolly friends who tried to share their Christmas cheer, I could never feel the joy of the season.

Growing up, I'd learned to be thankful when I had food that I didn't have to beg for. I knew I was lucky just to have a bed to sleep in most of the time. I had kind and compassionate teachers at school who went out of their way to make sure I had what I needed because my mom wasn't always around or able to provide those things for me.

Santa Claus wasn't someone I thought to write to when I needed help.

Christmas hurt my heart. The focus on family and gift giving made me painfully aware of how different I was, and of all that I didn't have. Once I became an adult, I thought it would be easier to escape those feelings. I'd volunteer to work on the holiday so that others could be with their families, or I'd go read stories to children in the hospital. Some years, I'd get together with another single friend, and we'd eat out wherever we could find an open Denny's and then go see a movie. We were usually the only people in the theater.

One December evening, while scrolling through Facebook, I came across a post from my friend Sam: "It breaks my heart that I can't give my daughter a Christmas this year."

Sam, like me, never asked for anything. She was a former soldier, strong and fiercely loyal, the best kind of friend to have. She and her husband Erik had been having a rough year financially. He'd been injured and unable to work, and Sam worked part-time in order to be home to care for their daughter, Skylar, who had Down syndrome.

They lived simply, focusing on needs instead of wants, taking care of each other and the people they chose to consider family. I was among that lucky few, and I didn't take it lightly. They'd chosen me from the moment we met the year before at the Mended Little Hearts 5K, a run to benefit a local charity for kids like Skylar, who was also born with a heart defect that required surgery when she was just hours old.

Skylar, not one to be defined by any diagnosis, was an amazing kid. She was a finger-snapping diva, a cheerleader, dancer, and honor student with a rock-star following of friends at school. She was equally happy watching *Star Wars* movie marathons or getting her nails done and was never afraid to tell you exactly how she felt about anything. And there was no better cure for a bad day than a Skylar hug. She could literally squeeze the negativity out of you. She loved without limits.

Seeing Sam's post melted my Grinch heart and sent my mind spinning into action. How could I help? What could I do? I knew she wouldn't take money, even if I tried to be sneaky and drop some cash into her purse when she wasn't looking. She was too much like me, and she knew me well.

The next day, I tried to secretly pay their rent for a few months, but their apartment complex wouldn't allow it. I needed help, so I enlisted some of the merriest elves I knew — friends from church who immediately jumped at the chance to gather some donations and decorations. Then the plan started to take shape.

I worked on the fireworks crew at Universal Studios Orlando, and with that job came the perks of free admission to the park and some pretty incredible discounts on merchandise. Skylar was a huge fan of Harry Potter, so her Christmas surprise would have a magical theme. I wandered through Hogsmeade and Diagon Alley buying robes, wands and a stuffed owl — everything wizardly and wonderful that I could carry. My co-workers, knowing my Grinch-like ways, thought they'd stepped into an alternate universe when they saw me having fun doing Christmas shopping.

When the magical night arrived, a photographer friend offered to come along to help capture the memories. We met at Sam's and unloaded my car, lugged all the gifts up to the second floor and kept them just out of sight. All I'd told Sam was that I was coming over with a surprise for Skylar. That wasn't out of the ordinary, so she didn't suspect anything. Instead of a Santa suit, I donned a Gryffindor robe and headed inside while Chris got his camera ready.

Skylar threw herself at me in a full-body hug, and after we twirled around for a minute, she noticed I was dressed funny. I reminded her about my special job that let me visit Hogwarts all the time and handed her a long, thin box. She tore it open and shrieked when she saw her very own Hermione Granger wand. She danced around and showed it to her mom and dad, and then I taught her a special spell.

She focused all her energy on the front door, twirled her wand in a heart shape, and yelled with all her might, "Christmas, come now!"

Then she ran to the door and threw it open. A mountain of brightly wrapped presents stood there with her name all over them. I don't know whether Sam or I was crying harder as we watched Skylar jump around, squealing with pure delight at the magic she'd just made. Our hearts were whole again.

That night may not have taken away every memory of Christmases past, but it gave us all a new holiday to celebrate. We call it "Skylarmas," and it's all about the magical healing power of friendship. It doesn't always involve mountains of presents. Sometimes, we just make huge messes with flour, dough and sprinkles in an attempt to bake unicorn-shaped cookies. Other times, we settle for spirited phone calls or videos of Skylar on Facebook if we can't be together.

But no matter what, when I think of Skylarmas, I am always thankful for the people who chose to consider me their family, and for that amazing girl who taught me to love without limits. Skylar's heart may have needed mending when she was just a baby, but it's the strongest one I know — strong enough to help mend my own, when I didn't even realize how broken it was.

— Tammi Croteau Keen —

87

Bilingual Christmas

*Let us have music for Christmas... Sound the trumpet
of joy and rebirth; Let each of us try, with a song
in our hearts, to bring peace to men on earth.*
~Mildred L. Jarrell

I found myself in a second-grade classroom about a week before
Christmas. Substitute teaching in an elementary classroom
right before Christmas break is never dull. The room was
nearly buried under holiday decorations, and the teacher had
left the kids with a mountain of holiday-themed assignments. We'd
already worked our way through cotton-ball snowmen and tissue-
paper ornaments as well as endless Santa coloring pages.

Now, at the end of the day, the teacher had left one more assignment. The students had to think of ten Christmas words, write them
down, and then draw pictures of them. I worked my way around the
room, giving encouragement and much-needed spelling help, when
I came to one little girl who looked close to tears.

"What's wrong?" I asked. She looked bewildered, and one tear
threatened to break free down her cheek.

I checked her name on the teacher's seating chart. Acting on a
hunch, I recalled my minimal Spanish. It was closer to Spanglish than
Spanish, but I suspected that the girl wouldn't notice.

"Problemo?" I asked.

Her face lit up at hearing an approximation of what was clearly her native language.

"Si," she said and pointed at the worksheet. "No Ingles."

I nodded. Yes, she had no English. She had no way to read the worksheet, much less do it. But maybe, with my help, she could.

Taking a deep breath and squeezing into a small chair beside her desk, I prayed that I would recall enough Spanish to manage an explanation. The other students stayed miraculously quiet, which freed me to quietly guide the young girl through the assignment. I asked her to think of ten words to talk about Christmas in Spanish and to write them down. She'd learned how to write in Spanish, and I translated her Spanish words into English, which she then copied onto her paper. She had ten words in no time, and the drawing and coloring that followed required few words to explain.

However, there was one more problem. The teacher had left instructions that each student had to share their list and pictures with the class. I could see the girl getting worried again, so I coaxed her up to the front of the classroom first.

As we held her paper together, I pointed at the Spanish word and told her to say it, and then I did the same with the English translation. By the time we got to the third word, I realized that her classmates were trying to speak the Spanish with her, so I encouraged her to say them one more time as the students slowly repeated them. Finally, we had made it to the last word on the list, actually a phrase.

"Feliz Navidad!" she said enthusiastically. Her classmates repeated the phrase after her. Then, to my surprise, several of the students started to sing a Christmas song familiar even to the English-speaking students, "Feliz Navidad."

I glanced at the class assistant who smiled and nodded, adding her voice to the song. I joined in, too. We were all singing together as we finished with, "I want to wish you a merry Christmas from the bottom of my heart!"

"Merry Christmas!" the little girl called out after the song ended. I found out later that those were the first English words she had said completely on her own, without prompting.

And her grin was a mile wide when her classmates responded with, "Feliz Navidad!"

—Anna Cleveland—

88

Things Will Work Out

And that, of course, is the message of Christmas.
We are never alone. Not when the night
is darkest, the wind coldest, the world
seemingly most indifferent...
~Taylor Caldwell

The only light came from the occasional passing car that illuminated the road ahead. I pedaled harder. Even at the brave age of fifteen, I was nervous. As I crested the hill, I saw the lone light of the convenience store.

I propped my bike against the wall and hurried inside. With its burning incense, foreign music, and dry meats hanging behind the register, it was the kind of store I would normally avoid, but now I found comfort within. I needed milk and bread, nothing more, yet I wanted to walk every aisle. It was two days before Christmas, and I'd never felt more alone.

I'd recently moved in with my best friend's family. I'd been arrested again for fighting, and my parents had had enough. I worked two part-time jobs and went to high school, and my only possession was a bike, so my diet was simple — cereal for breakfast, and peanut butter and jelly sandwiches for lunch and dinner.

I circled the aisles several times, got my milk and bread, and made my way to the counter. The cashier looked down at my large ankle bracelet—proof that I was on house arrest and could be located anywhere with the sheriff's office GPS—and then smiled at me anyway.

"Honey, take that milk back to the cooler," she said, pointing to the rear of the store.

"What?" I said belligerently.

She turned the milk so that the label faced me and pointed out the date. "That milk is going to expire in two days. Grab one from the back. It's fresher, tastes better and will last longer." Her smile was genuine and not condescending.

My ankle bracelet felt heavier than ever before. I felt like I deserved to wear it after being rude to this nice lady.

"You okay?" she asked.

I had been staring at the milk label longer than I realized, immobilized by my shame.

"I'll get it," she said with an even bigger smile, returning with another gallon. I stood there watching her on the ceiling's corner mirror, the kind of mirror that makes everyone look suspicious, all except her. It emphasized her waddle and made her smile appear even wider. She double-bagged the milk and instructed me to put a loop at each end of the handlebar, and then single-bagged the bread.

"Things will work out, honey," she said as I left the store, that pleasant smile still across her face.

On the bike ride home, I pedaled with no certain purpose other than to feel the cool night breeze across my skin. The milk hung perfectly from my handlebars according to her instructions, and the bread was next to it, not getting squished.

***

Ten years later, after four years in the Air Force, several years of college, and a nursing degree, I was in the hospital cafeteria on my break. It was nearly empty. I got my usual: two peanut-butter-and-jelly sandwiches with a glass of milk for two dollars. I sat alone, and as I put my sandwich to my mouth, I noticed a lady sitting three tables away from me. Her head hung as she nudged her fork back and forth through her food. She wore a visitor bracelet on her wrist. At that late hour, she had to be related to a patient there.

After years as a nurse, I learned three certainties: The healthy can die instantly; the ill can live for decades; and when the pain of a patient ends in death, the pain for the loved ones — especially young children — has just begun.

When she looked up, I was suddenly that fifteen-year-old again.

I put down my sandwich, walked over to her table and sat across from her. Even in her apparent pain, she managed to greet me with a smile.

"Did you work in a convenience store about ten years ago?" I asked.

She nodded, and her smile disappeared as if she was ashamed. "I was between jobs."

"I'm glad you were," I said.

She raised her eyebrows as if she found a moment in her past that correlated to my face, and she softly nodded.

I reached out and took her hand in mine. "Thanks for the milk."

Her grin swelled as tears ran down her face.

"Things will work out," I whispered.

She sat there, cried for several minutes and said nothing. Then, with a smile, she got up from the table and left.

I never saw her again. I'm not sure why she was there, but I knew for certain why I was.

— Charles R. Stieren —

89

The Toymaker

*When you joined the military, you joined
the largest family in the country.*
~Author Unknown

C hristmas 1991 was almost upon us at Holloman Air
Force Base in southern New Mexico. People decorated
homes, stores, and offices for the season. Real and artificial Christmas trees sprouted everywhere. Outdoor lights
were festive. Luminaria adorned churches. People booked restau-
rants for holiday parties. Fireplaces burned piñon with its wonderful aroma. Radio stations played non-stop Christmas carols. Our Air
Force squadron looked forward to the afternoon when I would play
Santa and hand a present to each of the young children of squadron
members.

However, America was still at war in Iraq after Desert Storm ended
earlier in 1991. Now, we supported Operation Provide Comfort to
help the Kurdish population with aid and protection. We continued to
provide people to Central Command in the Middle East, usually one
person at a time. We were ready to go: current wills, current training for
chemical warfare and weapons, immunizations up-to-date. Everyone's
mobility bag was always packed.

Just days before Christmas, as squadron commander, I received a
deployment task for a captain. Only one person possessed the required
rank and specialty — Captain Scott. This meant he would not be with
his wife, Barbie, and three young boys and little girl for Christmas. Our

captain did not complain or ask, "Why me?" or "Why now?" He knew he had a job to do. He would answer his nation's call. His character wouldn't allow him to whine.

As Captain Scott prepared for immediate departure, he was glad he'd already purchased presents. But then, with a mix of panic and emotion, he said, "We bought many presents that need to be assembled for the kids. The presents are stashed in my neighbor's garage. Barbie can't take care of the kids and assemble Christmas presents. Can you help?" I assured him Barbie would have help. Captain Scott left his family and went to war.

He knew we would help. Over the months of Desert Shield and Desert Storm, as many squadron members deployed, the remaining folks supported their families. Guys cut other people's lawns. People helped with carpools for sports and Scouts. If a family pet went for a vet visit, somebody would watch the kids so Mom wouldn't have to juggle toddlers, puppies and kittens.

Lieutenant Robert was a single, self-proclaimed handyman. I didn't ask. I just said, "Lieutenant, you are about to be a toy maker." With enthusiasm and his usual can-do attitude, he simply said, "Yes, sir, when and where?" I knew he understood the Air Force concept of service before self. His character was top-notch.

According to our plan, Lieutenant Robert would assemble the children's gifts on Christmas Eve. Scott's four children joined my wife, Carolyn, our young son and daughter, and myself for Christmas Eve supper. As I drove Scott's kids to our house, Robert went to Scott's neighborhood and parked his truck. As arranged, he walked into the neighbor's garage, toolbox in hand, and began his toy-making career.

At our house, we enjoyed little kid chatter and my wife's wonderful meal. After supper, we all piled into our station wagon and went to the new movie *Hook* at the mall movie theater. Everybody enjoyed the adventure story about Peter Pan.

After the movie, we made a pay-phone call to Barbie from the theater lobby to check on Robert's progress. Lieutenant Robert was still doing elf work. We took the kids for ice cream. The shop was ready to close for Christmas Eve, but the staff allowed us to order cones and scoops. Who would turn away a couple with six kids on Christmas Eve? By this time, the kids were well toward cranky, and the evening was late. We stalled and drove around to admire Christmas lights.

Another pay-phone call from a convenience store found Lieutenant Robert packing up his toolbox. I took my wife and kids home and drove Captain Scott's kids back to their mom. When I came around the corner on their street, I saw our lieutenant's tail lights as he pulled away from the curb. He had worked on bikes before, but this was his first-ever log-cabin playhouse project.

Barbie's kids excitedly told her about supper, the movie, and ice cream. They were tired and glad to be home. The older kids thanked me, and they were off to bed. Barbie said our support helped her "keep it together" for Christmas. She praised Lieutenant Robert as a toolbox hero.

I was happy Barbie received the help she needed. I knew their Christmas would be very different without her husband at her side. Our own Santa chores for our two believers were next. Before my kids' bedtime, Carolyn set out milk and cookies for Santa, as well as carrots for the reindeer. Our children went to bed.

Before our bedtime, I took our dog outside. I smiled as I looked at the stars and smelled piñon smoke. Hopefully, whoever was burning wood in their fireplace late on Christmas Eve didn't have small children in their homes who would worry about Santa.

With a follow-up Christmas Day phone call, Barbie said Christmas morning was more wonderful than she ever expected, considering she was flying solo. She thanked Carolyn, Lieutenant Robert, and me for our Christmas gift of help.

I passed Barbie's words to Robert. He was just happy to share his time and talent. Our lieutenant never bragged about what he'd done or complained that he'd given up his evening. This was a tribute to Robert's character. He simply demonstrated that we all do our best to help those in need, especially families of our deployed squadron members at Christmas.

—John Bowen—

90

Chicken Soup for the Soul

A Warm Welcome

We cannot live only for ourselves. A thousand fibers
connect us with our fellow men.
~Herman Melville

The refinery my dad worked at was closing, but the company offered him a job if he was willing to relocate. With a wife and three young daughters, he took it. We moved to a town that was 800 miles away from the only home I'd ever known. I was fourteen years old, halfway through Grade 9, and forced to leave my friends, my first boyfriend, the neighbourhood kids I grew up with, and all my cousins, aunts and uncles. And it was just before Christmas.

Everyone in my family was feeling the loss. My mom was sad to leave her sisters and friends, knowing it wouldn't be easy to start over.

My parents knew a few of the other families who also transferred, but my sisters and I didn't know anyone our age. School was out until the new year, so we had almost two weeks to unpack and get settled. Mostly we just felt sorry for ourselves.

We would all be going to different schools. My little sister was enrolled in the local elementary school, my older sister was in high school, and I was in junior high, which meant we wouldn't even have each other to lean on. Truthfully, before the move, we didn't spend much time together away from home because we were all busy with our own friends and activities. Now, we were feeling disconnected and alone.

December 24th arrived, and my mother cooked a chicken. She said there was no point making turkey since it was "just us." It was so depressing, especially since we knew what we were missing.

Christmas Eve back home had always been a huge celebration filled with special family traditions. We'd gather together with aunts, uncles and cousins, and there would be plenty of delicious food, fun, and kids our own age. We always had a wonderful time with lots of love and laughter.

Sadly, not this year.

I was too old to let anyone see me cry, but I missed my old life. After choking down supper, I announced that I was going for a walk — by myself. I just wanted to get away from my sad, pathetic family. I didn't know how to make them feel better, and I certainly didn't know how to make myself feel better, so why even try?

I put on my coat and gloves and headed out the door. I walked for miles until I wasn't really sure where I was anymore. There was a dusting of snow on the ground, and fluffy flakes wafted down all around me. Occasionally, I'd see someone else walking, but I refused to make eye contact.

I turned a corner and heard party sounds coming from one of the houses. I looked up, and there was a girl a little older than me hanging out her front door. "Hey, there — Merry Christmas!" she yelled over the music. "Where are you going?"

"Just walking," I answered, looking away. *Who does that? Hollers out their front door at total strangers!*

"You look frozen. Do you want to come in and warm up?" she asked. "We've got a warm fire, hot chocolate and homemade cookies. Everyone is singing Christmas carols. Why don't you join us? The more, the merrier!"

I looked around and realized I was lost. My fingers were numb, and I really didn't want to go home yet. "I guess I can come in for a few minutes," I said.

Even then, I realized it wasn't smart to go into a stranger's house, but that night I didn't care. I went in and saw people of all ages standing around a piano, eating cookies and singing carols. They were all wearing goofy sweaters, and most of them wore Santa hats. Before I could object, someone jammed one on my head and said, "There, now you fit in."

I stood beside the fireplace, sipping hot chocolate and watching, until someone pulled me up to the piano. I was feeling self-conscious, but before long I joined in the singing and even sat down and played a duet on the piano. I knew most of the songs, and it was fun to be around people who were laughing, singing and teasing each other.

There was so much joy in that room—enough to welcome a sullen young stranger into their midst and make my first Christmas in a new town feel special.

I stayed about two hours and then realized my family was probably getting worried about me. I asked someone if they knew how to get to my street and found out it wasn't far. Somehow, I had walked in a big loop. As I bundled up to leave, I thanked them for letting me be part of their celebrations.

I walked home with a little bounce in my step. The snow had finally stopped falling, and everything was covered in a fluffy white blanket. Funny, I didn't notice them before, but now I saw twinkling lights and Christmas decorations, and I passed a few people who were out walking. Almost everyone smiled and said, "Merry Christmas!" I realized I was smiling, too.

When I got home, there was a crackling fire in the new fireplace—something we'd never had before. And I went into my very own room to change—my first bedroom I didn't have to share. I was starting to realize that maybe there were a few things about the move that weren't so bad.

When I came out, my sisters were watching an old Bing Crosby movie, so I squeezed in beside them. Mom gave us each a wrapped present and said it was from the relatives back home. Mine was a red leather jewelry box filled with costume jewelry, perfume, and little trinkets. It was like getting a warm hug from far away.

It's been decades since that Christmas Eve when strangers welcomed a lonely teenager into their home. They showed me that Christmas is about caring and opening your heart—and sometimes your home—to people who need a friendly smile or a warm place to feel welcome.

We try to carry on that tradition. This year, we're expecting twenty people spanning four generations ranging in age from five to ninety-two. Over time, some of the names and faces have changed, but love and laughter and, of course, homemade Christmas cookies are always there.

—Lori Kempf Bosko—

91

Chicken Soup for the Soul

Christmas Alchemy

At Christmas, all roads lead home.
~Majorie Holmes

Our young family moved from the tropical heat of Asia to what we believed would be a winter wonderland. Our very first winter in Chicago was turning out to be a far cry from it, though, with gray skies and endless bone-chilling cold. The thrill of our first snowfall quickly turned into worry about navigating on slippery roads. The sense of adventure we had for our new life gave way to self-doubt and homesickness. And just as the animals were hibernating, it seemed that so were our new neighbors, withdrawing into their cloistered groups for the winter. As outliers, we felt alone.

In the midst of this unsettling time, though, at the beginning of December, something happened. It all began with a simple request from our eight-year-old daughter.

"Mommy, let's put up a Christmas tree at home."

At first, we didn't pay too much attention to this request. We had never put up a Christmas tree. In fact, we weren't practicing Christians. But something about my daughter's repeated plea made us go ahead with this first step. The only problem was we didn't know anything about what to do next, including where we could buy a tree.

After determining that chopping off a backyard evergreen tree that looked "Christmasy enough" wasn't an option, we headed out to walk around the block. Loaded with layers of clothing to ward off the unfamiliar cold, we tasked ourselves with finding a tree for our daughter.

We didn't realize it then, but that was the first time we stepped out to give ourselves a break and not just to tick off another item on our to-do list. We took time to meander around our block and familiarize ourselves with our new town. We began to pay attention to the fresh air and the approaching Christmas season.

When we finally selected our tree, we realized we didn't have a car big enough get it home. Of course, we had not considered that. It was our first time.

Standing sheepishly at the exit, we considered our options. Should we return the tree? Should we go back and explain our predicament to the store owner? No, returning was out of the question now.

So, we decided to carry it home. Huffing and puffing, we each held on to an unwieldy end. We had walked only a few steps when a gentleman who had seen us in our neighborhood stopped his truck and offered us a ride home.

Our first friend.

The Christmas tree was propped up in our living area for only a few minutes when a simple fact struck us: It was too dark. We needed Christmas lights! So, the next evening, we went back to the store and asked for lights.

The storekeeper was a kind soul who, after getting over the initial surprise of our seemingly daft queries, explained to us that we needed multi-colored, winding lights. Thanking the gentleman, we left with our lights and a little bit of his warmth.

Late into that night, we carefully wound the lights around the tree and excitedly held our breaths for the beauty of the first glow.

Still, the tree looked like it was missing something: pint-sized, dangling ornaments. Where would we get them? One of our neighbors across the block had put up a breathtaking, luminous and lush tree, carefully placed in a window for all to see. I spent unnatural amounts of time studying the bells and whistles adorning the tree, trying not to look like a stalker.

One evening, when I saw the lady clearing snow off her sidewalk, I went over to introduce myself and ask her seemingly inane questions about the tree's dangling adornments. If she was flummoxed at our ignorance, she hid it well and gladly gave store references.

A friendly face in our neighborhood.

Suddenly, winter didn't seem so bleak. Dusk meant it was time to turn on our Christmas tree lights. We no longer felt so alone in our new town. We had witnessed the stirrings of friendship, a sense of community and, most importantly, a feeling that this might truly become home.

The years have rolled by, and we have put up a tree every year since. It symbolizes a lesson for us to look for the stars rather than whine about the darkness. The winters are still gray and dark, but our Christmas tree outshines it all — every year.

Our tree has gotten grander and the decorations have gotten fancier, but, to this day, we gratefully reminisce about our first Christmas. It was a harbinger of hope, warmth, magic and, most importantly, made this windy, wonderful city feel like home.

— Amita Jagannath —

Treasured Traditions

92

Every Living Thing

I never thought it was such a bad little tree.
It's not bad at all, really. Maybe it
just needs a little love.
~Linus van Pelt

I n the living room, the flames flickered across the makeshift bed where my stepfather lay, dozing in and out of a morphine-induced state. We were told it was "a matter of time" before the cancer in Dad's brain would take him from us. The only thing we could do was to keep him as comfortable and pain-free as possible.

Dad faced the picture window where he could look out over the fields. The snow cast a silvery shadow over the acreage. He lapsed back into a restless sleep. The gray outlines of deer scampered between rows of trees to feast on apples that had fallen to the ground.

It was two in the morning, but my brother Johnnie and I pulled on our winter gear to go outside. We left the warmth of the wood-burning stove and ventured out into three feet of heavy snow. The sky was dotted with stars and the moon shone brightly over Schweitzer Mountain.

Pulling a small sled that made whooshing sounds, I followed Johnnie, who had an ax slung easily over his shoulder. We breathed through our noses because the cold would make our teeth and throat ache, so there was no conversation, only the sounds of our movement crunching through the snow.

As we trudged up the hillside, I thought about Dad. He was an independent logger by trade. It was hard, demanding seasonal work that had taken Dad into the Selkirk Mountains, and the Bitterroot and Cabinet mountain ranges.

Dad didn't talk a lot, but he was animated when speaking about nature and the need to care for and respect it. He loved the forest and all it provided. He had a tender heart, and many times he brought home a wounded squirrel, owl, rabbit, or other small creature that needed nursing before release back into the forest.

One December day eleven years earlier, Dad drove up the hilly driveway, and he clambered out of the truck, holding onto, well, a pine stick with two crooked branches.

He smiled broadly. "This little guy wasn't getting the sunlight he needed to grow, so he's gonna be our Christmas tree!" We understood Dad believed this little tree needed to be rescued and nurtured through the holiday season.

Each year thereafter, in mid-December, Dad brought home a stick with branches to decorate. And each year, the little tree was not strong enough to hold a string of lights, so Mom tacked the lights around the picture window, framing the tree, which only would support two blue bulbs.

I was brought back to the present as we approached a little tree that stood ghost-like, a pine stick with two crooked branches silently observing the snowy mountain and the twinkling lights of Sandpoint. My brother and I exchanged a nod — this was the little tree that needed a generous dose of love. Johnnie aimed the ax, and with one swift hit, the little tree leaned into his free arm. We laid the little pine on the sled and began our trek back down the mountain.

As we opened the door into the house, we heard Mom say, "Dad, look what's here just for you!" He opened his eyes as the snap of the switch turned on the lights that surrounded the picture window. Dad smiled as he watched Mom place two blue bulbs on the crooked limbs of the little tree for the last time.

That night in the mountains was nineteen years ago — and Dad's last Christmas. But the family tradition of nature's Christmas lives on.

Each little stick with its sparse branches reminds us of Dad's generosity of spirit, and that even the smallest living thing in nature is a gift.

— Sharron Read-Lambert —

The Santa Collection

I will honor Christmas in my heart,
and try to keep it all the year.
~Charles Dickens

"Where are all the Santas?" Nicholas asked. I chose to ignore my twelve-year-old son's question and focused on hanging the beaded garland on the Christmas tree. "Seriously, Mom, where are all our Santas?" he repeated.

Nicholas and his brother Gabriel started rooting through the packing boxes and bubble wrap that had gotten our Christmas decorations safely through the move. "It won't even be Christmas without the Santas," Gabriel declared. His eight-year-old face scrunched, and he blinked hard, trying to hold back the tears.

It was our first Christmas on our own since the divorce. Things were hard for all of us.

"Let's deal with the Santas later," I reasoned.

I put on my best smile and redirected the boys to the boxes full of ornaments. I plugged in the lights and watched the tree come to life.

The distraction worked, and for the next several hours my three boys and I decorated the Christmas tree, sang Christmas carols, and drank hot chocolate. Our house was brimming with Christmas cheer.

It was not the Christmas I had wanted for us. After thirteen years of marriage, it was just me and the boys now.

I was dealing well with the divorce. Everyone said so, but a part of me was struggling as a single parent. Money, time, and energy were in short supply.

And then there were the Santas.

I remember exactly how the Santa collection started. We didn't have a lot of money that first year we were married, and none of it was earmarked for Christmas decorations. I remember standing in this shop full of Christmas stuff and being completely overwhelmed with the idea of it all when my now ex-husband had a brilliant idea.

"Let's pick out one Santa that we love," he said. "Then, every year, we'll buy one more. Eventually, we'll have a whole collection to reflect all our years together."

We carefully picked out the perfect Santa. He was a very traditional old elf with bright colors and a bag of toys. We took him home and set him on a shelf.

Every year, we picked a new Santa, and as the kids grew, they helped pick the Santas. Eventually, we bought a small hutch, worked together to refinish it, and set it in the corner of the living room. For most of the year, it held some dishes and knickknacks, but at Christmas everything came off the shelves, and we filled it with the Santa collection.

I had never considered what would happen if we got a divorce and our family was torn apart.

I decided that the Santa tradition would have to end. I did not even unpack them. Someday, I would divide them up and give them to each of the boys, and they could start their own collections. But this year, I could not bear to look at them and be reminded of happier times.

We had picked the next day to finish up our Christmas shopping. I reminded all three boys on the way to town that this year we were on a tight budget, and we would have to be careful how much money we spent. We walked around the mall looking for everything on our list.

"What about the Santa?" Gabe asked softly.

"We can't afford to buy a new Santa this year," I said.

"But I brought my own money," he said. "Can't I please get him for you?"

He opened his hand, which was clutching a Santa he had found.

It was only three inches tall and made to look as if Santa was walking through a terrible storm. His robes, coat and beard swirled around him.

He looked old and worn, with a grave face and muted colors. If any Santa were to symbolize our year, this one was it.

"Please, Mom," Nicholas begged.

I took the little Santa to the cash register. The boys were all smiles as she wrapped the figurine in paper.

When we got home, we carefully cleaned the hutch and packed everything away. Then we brought in the moving boxes and carefully unpacked the Santas.

Usually, I was very particular about how I arranged the Santas on the shelf, but this was the year of letting go, so I let the boys have free rein on how to set up the Santa collection. They were thrilled.

Every time I walked into the living room, I was reminded of old memories and better times. While that led to some self-pity, it also helped me remember some of the good times.

The next year, putting the Santas up was a lot easier. We had gone on vacation at the beach, and we bought a beachy Santa in Florida to add to our collection. It was still a little sad to see all those Santas full of memories, but the boys refused to let the Santa tradition die.

More than a decade later, the Santa collection keeps growing, and we still decorate the same hutch every Christmas. The boys, who are now nearly grown, still fight over who gets to put the Santas on the shelf. Every year, we blare Christmas music, drink hot chocolate, and unwrap the Santas and the memories of all the Christmases past they represent.

The newer Santas mix with the old Santas, just like all our memories. The Santas do not make me sad anymore. Instead, just as intended, they remind me of all the beautiful years with my boys and the beautiful Christmases we have shared together.

— Theresa Brandt —

94

Chicken Soup for the *Soul*

A Silver Lining

Blended families: woven together by choice,
strengthened together by love, and each uniquely ours.
~Author Unknown

When I married for a second time, my husband and I combined a family of five children, ages fifteen to twenty-six. The only child still living at home was my fifteen-year-old daughter, so she and my husband had a chance to bond. I did not have that opportunity with his children, but I wanted very much to be accepted and loved by them. I was always on the lookout for ways to connect with them when we were together.

Our first Christmas, I put into practice a tradition I had grown up with. It was a hit! Now, thirty-three years later, I can honestly say that it is the single most cherished and loving tradition of our blended family.

As a first-generation American, I grew up in a home that continued to practice many European customs and traditions, not only during the holidays but all year long, according to the Julian Orthodox calendar. My parents were born in Macedonia and Bulgaria, and both immigrated to America in the 1920s where their marriage was arranged by two aunts. Although they met for a brief ten minutes (talk about speed dating!), they agreed to marry, and they remained married until my father passed away forty-six years later.

According to the Orthodox calendar, Christmas Eve supper was the last day of a forty-day Lent. As part of the dinner, a special homemade bread or strudel was served. It was special because a silver dollar was placed in it before baking. The belief was that whoever found the coin in their designated piece would have extra good luck the coming year.

My mother used to nestle the foil-wrapped silver dollar between layers of crispy, delicious phyllo dough and cheese. This was typically baked in a round pan, so even she didn't know where the coin was. Because we were only a family of four, and the round baking pan was large, the extra pieces were designated for the church and extended family.

As much as I loved this tradition, for whatever reason I did not continue it during my first marriage. But when we became a blended family of five children, I thought it might be nice to start something that would unite everyone and become a new shared tradition.

The first year there were only ten of us for dinner. I sliced a piece for each of the five children, two spouses, one grandchild, my husband and myself.

I also wanted to express my good wishes for what the New Year might bring for them, so I composed a simple two-line poem recognizing something uniquely important about each person at the table.

Now, some thirty-five years later, with twenty-seven of us, the tradition continues. I serve the cake and read the poem whenever most of us are around the table at one time during the holidays, sometime between Thanksgiving and New Year's. If someone cannot be present, one of the children takes a video to send to the others, or we put them on speakerphone. Today, in the year 2020, I am sure we would make it a Zoom event.

This became known simply as "The Poem," and now reading those poems of past years is like a mini-history of our family. We acknowledged births, graduations, weddings and, sadly, even deaths. But we always try to recognize a special accomplishment for each family member, be it ever so small, such as starting kindergarten, riding a two-wheeler without training wheels, or having their best golf score ever.

After the reading of the poem, everyone eagerly bites into their designated piece of cake to see who will be the "lucky" one. Since baking is not my strong suit, I never attempt the traditional homemade strudel. I think the first year the coin was hidden in a Bundt cake. One time, it was brownies. Another year, I took the coin to a local specialty bakery and asked them to make twenty-plus cookies that resembled a house and place the coin in one of them, commemorating a year when everyone in the family had a change of residence.

After slicing the cake into the allotted number of pieces, a number is placed on each one like a little flag with a toothpick. Then an identical set of numbers are placed in a basket from which everyone draws their number. When all the pieces are distributed, everyone bites in. Trust me, your family will find creative ways to do this that are as much fun as the first bite itself. And to guarantee that it is not rigged in any way, in all the years I have put this into practice, I have never once found the coin in my piece.

And don't let the thought of a poem intimidate you. Here's the simple opening and closing of the first poem, which you are welcome to use. In between, add just a few words about what is important to each family member at this stage in their lives.

Opening:
Along with all the Christmas cheer,
May 1987 be your best year.
To see your plans and dreams come true,
Here's a special wish for each of you:

Closing:
We love you all. We're glad you came
Come back next year — we'll do the same.
We'll gather round for old times' sake
And dig for silver in a cake.
Another year has ended,
Tomorrow we must part,
But the memories tonight
Will live on in our heart.

Or in lieu of a poem, each member can simply say what they

are hoping for in the coming year or what was the highlight of their previous year.

The second tradition we began was spreading a white tablecloth on our large dining-room table with a variety of colored magic makers. Each child and grandchild traced their hand and then wrote a little message into their hand drawing. Some wrote in the palm of the hand; others wrote something in each finger. Some couples intertwined their hands with a double message. The creativity was quite amazing.

Now, whenever a large group of us gather, we spread out the tablecloth and marvel at how the children's hands have grown and what our message was. And, of course, new additions to the family are added to the tapestry.

As this pandemic year has proven, those special days and holidays with family will never be taken for granted again. Nothing is more important than being with loved ones. And if there is any way we can make those moments even more special than they are, we are leaving a legacy that no virus or pandemic can destroy.

—Violetta Armour—

95

Chicken Soup for the Soul

It Smells Like Christmas

If baking is any labor at all, it's a labor of love.
A love that gets passed from
generation to generation.
~Regina Brett

I was walking past my favorite bakery in town last December, a week after Thanksgiving, when I had to stop to savor the sweet scent coming from the open door. The aroma brought me back to Christmases past, many years ago. I stood there on the sidewalk while many wonderful memories came flooding back to me. I felt the joy of Christmas. That single moment lifted my spirits for the remainder of the day.

One of my fondest childhood memories is the delightful scent of Mom's Christmas butter cookies as they baked in the oven. The tradition of baking the butter cookies together started when I was about eight years old. The sweet aroma of the cookies filled our apartment and made me feel cozy, safe and loved. I sat at the kitchen table, giddy with anticipation as I waited for the decadent morsels to be done. Finally, after what seemed like hours, the cookies were ready.

When I bit into the warm, soft cookie, straight out of the oven, I was filled with joy, knowing the holiday season had officially begun. With my nod of approval that the cookie was perfect, my mom announced cheerfully, "Let the decorating begin!" Then, we started to decorate the cookies with red and green sugar crystals and silver ball nonpareils. For the next three weeks leading up to Christmas morning, we would spend every weekend making batches of the butter cookies for family, friends, neighbors and teachers. It was a special time we shared together.

Our tradition of baking Christmas butter cookies continued throughout the years until the last Christmas we spent together. By then, I was married and a mom of two little girls, ages four and one. Mom was very patient as she helped my young daughters add ingredients, mix dough, and decorate the cookies. She never used her written recipe; she knew it by heart. She instructed my daughters just as she had instructed me: "Add just a little more flour, about a pinch or two," or "You might need another egg. It seems dry." She would improvise the recipe measurements. However, it never failed; the cookies always tasted the same.

As the cookies baked and their sweet scent filled the apartment, I couldn't help but smile, remembering when I baked the same cookies with Mom. I was brought back to the present when my daughter Heather jumped up and down with excitement and shouted, "It smells like Christmas!" She was only four years old at the time, but she described the aroma perfectly.

After my mom passed and the years rolled by, I baked the butter cookies every Christmas as our family grew to five children. My husband, Harold, liked to join in when it was time to decorate. Although the cookies were good, they didn't taste like my mom's.

That December morning, as I stood outside the bakery, I decided it would be the year I baked my mom's butter cookies to taste exactly as hers did. I was determined! Now a grandmother, I planned to bake the cookies with my grandchildren when they came to visit for a few days during Christmas.

Christmas Eve finally arrived. My daughter Heather, the mom of my three grandchildren, would arrive shortly with her family. I set up a folding table in the kitchen for baking. Everything was laid out and ready for when my grandchildren arrived. I couldn't wait to get started. I took out my mom's recipe that was now yellowed with age. I looked over the recipe once more, wondering what I could do differently to make it taste like hers. I put the recipe aside when the doorbell rang.

My grandchildren ran into the house with excitement. They wanted to get started baking right away. They settled around the table eagerly waiting while I looked for my mom's recipe. I had hastily put it down when the doorbell rang, and now I couldn't find it. After five minutes of looking, the kids were beginning to get antsy. I had no choice but to improvise the recipe, just as my mom had done. I'd been making the cookies for so long that I knew the ingredients by heart.

So, the fun began. While we were measuring the ingredients, I suggested, "Maybe we can add more nuts," and "Add a little more butter to make it creamier." It was then I realized that I was doing exactly as my mom had done with me as a child and then with my children when she helped us bake the cookies.

We slid them into the oven and the anticipation began. My grand-children were so excited to take the first bite of the butter cookies they had made. As we sat in the kitchen, the distinct sweet aroma filled the air. My granddaughter Eleanor, age four, giggled and yelled, "It smells like Christmas!" just as her mother said at the same age. At that moment, I realized it wasn't about the cookies tasting just like my mom's. It was the time we shared as we made them.

I didn't need the recipe; I was baking just like Mom.

— Dorann Weber —

96

The Legacy of Mom's Christmas Stocking

Carve your name on hearts, not tombstones.
A legacy is etched into the minds of others
and the stories they share about you.
~Shannon L. Alder

As a small child, I remember hanging stockings over the fireplace on Christmas Eve. It did not bother me that they looked a lot like my dad's work socks. However, using my dad's socks bothered my mother.

She taught herself to knit for the sole purpose of providing each of us a beautiful Christmas stocking. For months, we saw our pretty, forty-something, redheaded mother bent over a sheet of instructions as she created that first sock. By early December, Mom had knit seven stockings. Each of us was thrilled to have our name embroidered across the top of a red, green, and cream-colored work of art.

I was the first to marry, and my husband was the first in-law to receive a stocking. Despite a marriage certificate and a wedding ring, we joked that he wasn't officially a member of the family until his name was embroidered on one of Mom's creations.

With each marriage and grandchild, Mom created a new Christmas sock. By that time, she only needed to refer to the instruction sheet every so often. Each stocking was a ticket to the happiest, most chaotic celebration in our growing family.

Mom even made a couple of extra stockings, tucking them away for the next in-law or grandchild to join the family. From time to time, we'd have guests for Christmas. They were usually from another country and had no place to go for the holiday, so they were invited to join in our celebration. Mom would print their name on a plain piece of paper and pin it on a spare stocking. Santa made sure our guest had a sock filled to the top with oranges, walnuts, gum, socks, paperback books, and other goodies.

Sadly, we learned that stockings could be taken out of circulation. They were not exempt from estrangement, divorce and/or death. Our beloved brother's stocking was sadly retired after he was killed in a tragic accident.

The family was delighted in 1996 when three new babies were born, and a splashy wedding brought in a new granddaughter-in-law. Mom's red hair was turning white but her arthritic fingers continued to slowly work the yarn. The soft, rhythmic clicking of metal knitting needles was music to our ears as she demonstrated her love with every knit and purl.

When Mom passed away after a short illness, none of her daughters had learned to knit the stocking. We put her bag of knitting supplies in a storage box along with a small spiralbound notebook in which she had written the names of everyone for whom she had created a stocking. Through the years, she had crafted forty unique works of art.

Two years ago, one of Mom's youngest granddaughters became pregnant with her first child. The text messages flew back and forth about who could knit a stocking for the new baby. My pretty, red-haired niece Angie called me to ask if I had directions to make "Grandma's Christmas Stocking." Shortly after that conversation, Angie began the task of creating the first sock, knitting as she pored over the directions, just as her grandmother had.

When the new baby arrived, one of his very first gifts was a personalized Christmas stocking. It had been created using his great-grandmother's pattern by another pretty, forty-something redhead carrying on the decades-old legacy.

—Nancy Emmick Panko—

97

The Christmas Box

*Anyone who believes that men are the equal of women
has never seen a man trying to wrap
a Christmas present.*
~Author Unknown

"I can't believe this!" exclaimed my soon-to-be daughter-in-law, Heather. "Why would they wrap a gift like this?" The "this" to which she was referring was a birthday present from one of my young adult sons: a brown paper grocery bag, stapled along the top, with my name written across the front in black magic marker. I was unfazed because that is how all three of my sons wrapped gifts to me. Personally, I didn't think anything of the bag wrap, simply grateful they cared enough to remember me in some way. I also thought this re-use of a paper bag was good for the environment.

That was in August. By Christmas, Heather was determined to show her now husband and two brothers-in-law how a gift should be wrapped. She outdid herself. On Christmas morning, the most beautiful box I had ever been graced to receive was under the tree. It was a tall rectangular box perfectly wrapped in shimmering paper with a stunning matching ribbon and elegant bow. A matching tag displayed my name.

I was speechless. The mother of three boys, I had been the only female presence in our home for twenty-nine years. Frills had been absent for a long time.

"I can't open this," I declared. "It's far too beautiful to dismantle." After much prodding and cajoling, I gingerly unwrapped only the top, creating a space just big enough to open it. I was careful not to rip the paper or dislodge the ribbon in any way as I gingerly reached in to pull out the gift.

I guess it was the care with which I opened my gift that tipped my kids off that this box might be re-used in the future. "Oh, Mom, don't tell me you are going to save it!" one of the kids spouted, referring to my reputation for saving things because I might have use for it in the future.

The next Christmas, the box appeared under the tree again, only this time it bore a different name tag. The recipient groaned as he was instructed to be careful and open the top just enough to remove the gift. And so, without any formality or fanfare, a new tradition was born in our household. This was now the official Christmas Box.

The box has appeared almost every year, and each time the recipient's name and year are inscribed on the inside flap. Seventeen years later, there are fourteen names with the years they opened the box. Each year as we prepare to surround the tree to begin our gift exchange, someone speculates on who the year's recipient might be. Each year, when it is passed to the giftee, the others comment, "So you get the box this year!" Surprisingly, the couple of years it has been absent, someone has remarked, "Hey, no one got the box. What's going on?"

Every time I have placed someone's gift inside the Christmas Box, I spend time looking at the individual names of our family written on the flap. I reflect on the events of their life that particular year. I say a prayer of thanks for how blessed my world is because of them. And, yes, I calculate how many times someone has gotten the Christmas Box so as to keep it fair.

The beautiful gift box is no longer just a box. It holds priceless memories and treasured family history. It would not be Christmas in our home without that box underneath our Christmas tree.

My grandchildren are now old enough to begin being recipients of the family talisman. This past Christmas, my oldest granddaughter, now a teenager, was the one to have her name on the tag. She seemed apprehensive, but I imagine it was because she had five adults watching her every move. Gently, she placed the box in her lap to begin her unwrapping and abruptly stopped as five people cried out in alarm: She had begun to un-tape the side rather than the top. Carefully, she resumed opening from the top, leaving the package intact for next year — but not before checking to see that her name was now indelibly written inside the Christmas Box.

— Rose Robertson —

98

Boxing Day Reinvented

Life is better in pajamas.
~Author Unknown

After seeing so many television commercials and hearing the stories of friends tracing their family roots, I decided to study my own. In my middle-class neighborhood, located in northern New Jersey, my heritage seemed rather bland: British Isles on both sides of my parentage — English, Welsh, and Irish — and not even a single ancestor on the European continent itself!

Nevertheless, it was a legacy, and I decided to study some of the traditions of my forefathers and incorporate them into my daily life. Hence, my recent observance of Boxing Day.

Celebrated on December 26th, the day after Christmas, Boxing Day has been observed principally in countries related to the United Kingdom. According to tradition, back in Victorian times, along with their time off, the servants were given Christmas gifts contained in "boxes." These boxes, filled with money, food, clothing and trinkets, were tagged, decorated, and filled on Christmas night, ready to be taken "home" the following day — known as "Boxing Day." This was also a way to make up for the servants working on the actual holiday.

Other historians dispute the claim that the tradition began with Queen Victoria and attribute its creation to a much earlier time period, sometime during the latter Middle Ages.

Regardless of how or when Boxing Day began, I started to integrate parts of this tradition into my own Christmas holiday several years ago. Truth be told, I was growing weary of the hustle and bustle of the holiday season. With endless, nonstop shopping, baking, and decorating, I was yearning to turn to a simpler celebration — if that even existed.

For several years, I tried to observe the Winter Solstice — the longest night of the year — which occurs sometime around December 22nd. While that observance does cause one to pause and admire the winter beauty — especially where I live in the Northeast — it still falls right before the Christmas rush. Rather than enjoying the stillness of a winter's evening and appreciating the stark beauty of nature, I still found myself rushing about, attempting to accomplish more chores on my never-ending holiday to-do list. So much for slowing down to enjoy the longest night of the year!

Enter Boxing Day, the day after Christmas, and the holiday my British ancestors observed at least 150 years ago. Full disclosure to any *Downton Abbey* fans — when I refer to my British ancestors, I'm certain my lineage consisted of those living in the attic rooms and dining in the basement areas! In essence, they were the ones receiving the Christmas boxes on Boxing Day, not preparing them.

My first attempt to honor this holiday, along with saluting the servant class of my ancestors, occurred five years ago. The day after Christmas, I assembled my immediate family, telling them that we were going to spend a low-key, relaxing day together. No running out to the mall to exchange holiday gifts, no elaborate cooking or cleaning-up, no extra chores at all. Just hanging out and enjoying each other.

Looking back, I don't even think that we ventured out of our pajamas! It was a restful, low-key day, and one that was well-deserved after the non-stop holiday madness. I was surprised how much our usually high-powered, high-energized family enjoyed the solitude, along with the holiday leftovers and afternoon naps for everyone.

A week later, during a New Year's Eve celebration, I happened to mention our modified Boxing Day to our next-door neighbors. I was taken aback when they asked if they could participate in our Boxing Day sabbatical, and the next year they joined us — in their pajamas! We built a fire in the living room hearth, feasted on a simple potluck buffet, and shared a relaxing, winter afternoon over holiday ham sandwiches and Christmas cookies.

The following year, our neighbors joined us once more — in their comfortable clothing, along with their delicious contributions to our holiday buffet. That year, however, we expanded on the Boxing Day theme. Rather than exchanging a Christmas present that was not "quite right," everyone brought a "gift box," in keeping with the Boxing Day tradition. That year, we donated several toys, two bathrobes, six pairs of pajamas, and a cuckoo clock to a local shelter.

While the donations were certainly an added bonus to our Boxing Day celebration, I didn't want that to detract from our central focus of our newly launched holiday — enjoying the simple things, like family, friends, food, and conversation — so I was adamant about keeping the day as effortless as possible. No new additions allowed!

It's been five years since we started celebrating Boxing Day. Year after year, the fire is lit in the living-room hearth, a simple buffet is served on the dining-room table, conversations flow through the house among family and friends, boxed gifts are donated to a local shelter, and I silently toast the wisdom of my British ancestors.

Life certainly does not get any better than this — especially when all this can be enjoyed while relaxing in our pajamas!

— Barbara Davey —

99

The Christmas Letter

The best of all gifts around any Christmas tree:
the presence of a happy family
all wrapped up in each other.
~Burton Hillis

When the kids became preteens, Christmas seemed to morph into a long list of gifts they wanted. After they opened their name brand clothing or electronic gifts, they'd run off to their rooms. I was disappointed by our commercialized Christmas routine, and I wanted to find the magic again. I wanted Christmas to be about love and happiness, but mostly about coming together as a family.

Then I remembered the red box.

I have a red velvet box with sequin designs all over it. I am positive no one else would find it pretty, but to me it is the most beautiful box in the world. The red box held the very first Christmas present given to me by the love of my life. Inside the box was a letter. The letter was written in scribbled handwriting and contained no poetry or elaborate words. Instead, the letter contained real emotions from the heart. It was authentic and personal and meant more to me than any store-bought gift. Twenty-five years later, I still have the red box. It is a bit tattered, but it still holds that Christmas letter along with many more that special someone has written to me over the years.

I had my answer—a way to bring my kids back to what Christmas is all about: love. I implemented the new Christmas letter tradition. Each of us writes a letter to each person in our family. The letter has to be at least one page and can contain a favorite memory as well as why we are thankful that person is in our life. The letters are placed in each stocking hanging on the fireplace. The stockings are then handed out at the end of Christmas Day so that we can each read our letters privately.

The first Christmas, there was a lot of grumbling about having to write the letters. The next Christmas, there was a little less protesting. By the third Christmas, I didn't even have to tell them to write their letters. They looked forward to getting their stocking full of letters and even asked if they could open them early. The magic was back!

The letters may not seem like much of a gift, but they benefit the giver *and* receiver. The giver must sit and think about what each person in our family means to them and why they love them. For the receiver, they get a stocking full of reasons they are loved and important. We don't need fancy gifts; we need to know we are loved and important to someone.

— Michelle Bruce —

Holiday Spirit for Two

*Appreciation is a wonderful thing. It makes
what is excellent in others belong to us as well.*
~Voltaire

My husband is a bit of a Grinch, but I could double as one of Santa's elves. Christmas decorations, caroling to neighbors, baking holiday treats for the office — you name the Christmas activity, and I'll be there with a themed sweater.

As the third of ten siblings, the Christmas season always brings up some of my favorite memories with my family, like learning to wrap presents with my mom and older sisters and working with my younger siblings to deck the entire house with festive decor. Christmas music was an essential component, and in our musical home, there was always someone willing to belt out "Jingle Bells" or any number of holiday songs.

But spending Christmas with a Grinch can be a tough balancing act. My husband didn't have the same cheerful holiday memories as me, and I'll admit that working retail for years probably didn't help my husband see the kinder side of people, no matter the season.

However, he never tried to stifle my joy in the Christmas season and was indulgent when I covered our tiny apartment in holiday wreaths, tinsel, and a stubby, fake tree that took up too much space. I did keep my Christmas playlists — yes, I have several, depending on what type of Christmas spirit I'm feeling — to myself.

That was our compromise for several years until there was a Christmas season when all my holiday gusto deserted me. We weren't going to be able to see either of our families that year, which is one of the highlights of the season. Also, I was going through a stressful time at work that left me drained and often in tears by the end of the day.

So, by the time that December 21st had rolled around, our apartment was bare of any holiday decor except for a handful of Christmas cards from family and friends. Not even a long drive to see Christmas lights was enough to revive my spirits.

As I trudged up the steps to reach my apartment door, I contemplated mustering the energy to at least dig out a Christmas wreath. But as I opened the door, I found out that there was no need.

The first thing that caught my eye was the stubby, fake tree that took up too much space. It was cheerfully lit up with multicolored string lights, random ornaments I had collected over the years, and a handful of stuffed animals. Christmas bunting was hung, holiday table decor was set, and there was a plate of green and red Christmas tree cookies on a plate. One of my Christmas playlists was even playing on the wireless portable speaker.

Naturally, I burst into tears.

My dear husband rushed to hug me and apologize for decorating without me, while I could barely sob about how sweet it was that he put in so much work for me. It was a little messy, but we managed to get the door closed, and both of us sat down to drink hot chocolate with a Christmas cookie.

When I hadn't started Christmas decorating the day after Thanksgiving, my husband said he knew something was seriously wrong. Yet, there was nothing he could do about our ability to see our families for Christmas or the issues at my workplace. So, attempting to lift my spirits, he set aside his usual dislike for the trappings of Christmas and decorated our home for me.

From then on, our holiday tradition has been to decorate together and even do some other Christmas activities, too. He'll taste test Christmas cookies with me and will even put on some Christmas music and dance with me. He draws the line at caroling, though.

I was happy enough with our compromise before, but I have to say that it is much more fun to do it together.

—Diana K. Peterson—

A Second Chance at Childhood

*A wise lover values not so much the gift of the lover
as the love of the giver.*
~Thomas á Kempis

My husband Paul tells me that when we first met, he was immediately drawn to my quirky sense of humor. To which I replied, "I didn't have toys as a kid. I had to entertain myself." While this quip was meant to be lighthearted, there was a darker story behind it.

Not long ago, I came across an old picture from the last Christmas I celebrated in Vietnam in 1974 as a happy four-year-old. In this picture, I was holding a doll I had received as a Christmas present. I was exuberant, having a wonderful holiday.

Months later, I was playing with that doll when my mother ran toward me in a state of panic, blurting out, "We have to go NOW." I had no idea what was going on. I asked my mother if I could bring my doll to wherever it was that we were going. The answer was an unequivocal "NO." What I was too young to understand was that a Communist government takeover had occurred and we had to leave the country immediately.

One hour later, the Vietnam War was officially over and we had left our precious homeland. Those close to me believe I lost my doll, and my childhood, on that day.

A year later, my family and I were living in California as refugees, trying to rebuild our lives after losing almost everything we had. My parents did the best they could, but money was always scarce.

At age six, I had become accustomed to our new normal — constantly worrying about our day-to-day existence. I was not a happy, playful child anymore.

While my parents dealt with the challenge of making ends meet, I was doing my best to fit in, to grow up as a "normal" American kid. As far as I understood, American kids played with toys. Lots of toys. But given our finances, "lots of" was no longer part of our vocabulary. I made do with some crayons and the quintessential 1970s toy — the water ring toss.

Fast forward to 2016. The date was December 25th. The condo that Paul and I shared was filled with whimsical Christmas decorations and holiday accessories. A multitude of beautifully wrapped presents sat underneath our enchanting Christmas tree. Colorful lights and sparkling knickknacks abounded. We had created the Christmas spirit we had both always wanted.

Soon, it was time to open our presents. With a twinkle in his eye, Paul handed me my first package. I enthusiastically ripped off the wrapping paper to reveal *Battleship*. I chuckled as I held the game in my hands.

"Open another one," Paul said with a smile. Eagerly complying, I opened another present to reveal a checkers set. I laughed as he handed me yet another present. I opened it to reveal *Connect 4*.

"Since you didn't get enough toys as a kid, I gave Santa some helpful hints on what to get you for Christmas," Paul said. What a husband! You see, months before, I had shared with Paul that I had always wanted these toys as a child.

"Santa is totally awesome," I exclaimed.

"He sure is," Paul agreed.

"Wouldn't it be fun if we played with your new toys right now?" he asked.

We opened my new games. I felt like an exuberant kid again. About two hours later, and after much gleeful laughter, I had bested

Paul not once, but twice. I am still the undefeated checkers champion of our household.

Paul and I agreed that playing with my toys would be our new Christmas tradition. It is very fitting because I have always felt that Christmas is about new beginnings and rebirth, among many other wonderful things. My rebirth included seeing my world through the eyes of a child again. Except now, this child is carefree and joyful.

Some people say that the magic of Christmas happens when kids come to believe in happiness and joy. Well, this forty-nine-year-old kid could not agree more.

Consequently, if you ask me if my childhood was lost at age five, I would reply with a resounding "No!" Innocence, much like toys, can sometimes be collateral damage of a war-torn past. While I may have lost some of my innocence as a child, I did not lose my childhood. It has been alive and well, living inside my heart all this time. It just took a very long detour.

— Kristen Mai Pham —

Meet Our Contributors

J. Ross Archer is a retired colonel from the U.S. Army where he served for twenty-three years. He holds a master's degree in psychology, and he is an active Rotarian and Gideon. He is the author of three books and numerous short stories and essays. His hobbies include skydiving, motorcycling, and SCUBA diving.

Violetta Armour fulfilled a dream of owning Pages, a bookstore in Phoenix, AZ in the early 1990s. She resides in Sun Lakes, AZ where she enjoys all the activities a retirement community offers, especially pickleball. She has published four novels, including the award-winning *I'll Always Be with You* and two mysteries.

Debbie Ashley received her Secondary Education degree from Clarks Summit University in 1985. She enjoys being with her husband of thirty-four years, her two sons and their wives and her daughter in college. Debbie's hobbies include gardening, cooking and visiting Lake Michigan beaches. She hopes to write a nonfiction book someday.

Dave Bachmann is a retired special education teacher who taught English and creative writing in Arizona to youth with emotional disabilities for forty years. He now writes children's stories, grown-up stories and poetry in California where he lives with his wife Jay, a retired kindergarten teacher, and their one-year-old Lab, Scout.

Kelly Bakshi is a freelance writer and author of several children's nonfiction books. She is a proud boy mama to her two sons and a Bouvier des Flandres named Sirius Black. She lives in the beautiful

Hudson Valley where she and her husband enjoy hosting Christmas each year. Find her on Instagram @kellybakshibooks.

Maxwell Bauman is Editor-In-Chief of *Door Is A Jar Literary Magazine* (doorisajarmagazine.net). He earned his MFA with a focus in publishing from Wilkes University in 2015. When not reading, writing, or editing, Maxwell loves to play guitar and make LEGO art. You can follow him on Twitter @maxwellbauman.

Nancy Beach received her Bachelor of Science in Bible, with honors, and is working on a Master of Arts in counseling. She has been married for twenty-seven years and has two grown children. Nancy enjoys reading, sunsets, and sand between her toes. She writes devotionals and inspirational fiction. Learn more at www.filledtoempty.com.

Cindy Bear is retired and lives in Iowa. She is married and has three children, twelve grandchildren and two great-grandchildren. She enjoys reading, traveling, and baking cookies.

Lisa Bell is a published author and works as an editor for *NOW* Magazines, LLC, covering two of their nine local markets. She enjoys working with other authors as a book editor and coach and leading two writing groups in the Dallas/Fort Worth area of Texas.

Lori Kempf Bosko is a Canadian writer living in Edmonton. This is her fourth contribution to the *Chicken Soup for the Soul* series. She loves reading, writing, travelling, and spending time with friends and family, especially her four amazing young grandchildren: Halley, Austin, Kain, and Mila.

Cyndi Bowen is an ordained minister who leads a prayer team at her local church as well as being a registered nurse in a hospice program. She lives with her two sons in Southeastern Ohio and enjoys writing inspirational devotions and poetry.

John Bowen served in the Air Force as a career financial officer in various states, Asia, and Europe. He is a proud husband, father, father-in-law, and grandfather. John belongs to a legacy writing group in Ohio.

Theresa Brandt is a writer and mother of three terrific young men. Theresa loves reading, writing, gardening, crafts and cooking. Besides her three handsome boys, she shares her life with the best boyfriend ever and lots of furry friends. E-mail her at tbbrandt1972@yahoo.com.

Michelle Bruce is a retired registered nurse, wife, and mother of four children. Michelle enjoys refinishing furniture, antique shopping, writing, and her many animals on her Nebraska ranch. E-mail her at brucefamily6@gmail.com.

Helen L. Burgess received her Associate degree in Applied Library Science, with honors, from Illinois Central College in 2008. Helen enjoys writing poetry, reading mysteries, researching genealogy and is currently working on a family memoir. She is retired, living in Illinois.

Eva Carter has worked in the telecommunications industry as a Financial and Budgets Analyst. Born in Czechoslovakia and raised in New York, she now lives with her husband in Dallas, TX.

Kandace Chapple is the editor and publisher of *Grand Traverse Woman* magazine. Her essays have been published in *Writer's Digest*, *Literary Mama*, *Motherwell* and more. She loves to mountain bike on Northern Michigan trails, hike with her dog Cookie, and spend time with her husband and two sons.

Anna Cleveland received her Bachelor of Science in English from Appalachian State University in 2004. She is married and works as a teacher in North Carolina. Her main interests are reading and writing, especially poetry, and she hopes to publish more in the future.

Cj Cole lives on the Eastern Shore of Virginia, home of the Chincoteague wild ponies. For over fifteen years Cj served the shore as a morning radio host, newspaper advice columnist, children's librarian and tribal storyteller.

Gwen Cooper received her B.A. in English and Secondary Education in 2007 and completed the Publishing Institute at Denver University in 2009. In her free time, she enjoys krav maga, traveling, and backpacking with her husband and Bloodhounds in the beautiful Rocky Mountains. Follow her on Twitter @Gwen_Cooper10.

Melissa Cutrera, MDiv., is a pastor's wife and homeschool mom. She is the author of *God's Great Plan*, a picture book that shares the gospel with children. She enjoys reading, hiking, visiting museums and parks, and teaching for her local homeschool co-op. Melissa writes weekly devotions for women at www.melissacutrera.com.

Barbara Davey is an adjunct professor where she teaches English and professional writing to undergraduates. She retired in 2020 after a lengthy career in marketing, public relations, and community outreach. She loves swapping out her "dress-for-success" wardrobe for yoga pants and sneakers. She and her husband live in Verona, NJ.

Octo-generation writer **NancyLee Davis** is still writing. She feels life is a series of stories. As a former farm wife, horse breeder, race car driver, teacher, mom, grandmom, great-grandmom, NancyLee has a million stories and is still adventuring for more. She feels memories make the best stories.

Lola Di Giulio De Maci is a retired teacher whose stories have appeared in numerous titles in the *Chicken Soup for the Soul* series, the *Los Angeles Times*, *Reminisce* magazine, children's publications, and in newspapers as a columnist. Lola earned a Master of Arts in education and English and writes overlooking the San Bernardino Mountains.

Anissa Deshpande is pursuing a Bachelor of Science degree at University of New Haven. She is inspired by her friends and family. She loves writing, painting, going to the beach, and adventures.

Kathy Dickie is the proud grandmother of two amazing granddaughters, who fill her life with never ending adventures. She enjoys globetrotting with her husband, family visits, quilting, research, and writing. Kathy and her husband live in South Surrey, British Columbia.

Pat Dickinson lived in northern New York for thirty-eight years. She and her husband retired in 2016 and moved to North Carolina. They have been married for forty-eight years and have two adult children. She has had three novels and a gift book published.

From Cleveland, OH, **Joan Donnelly-Emery** graduated with a BFA in Musical Theater from Syracuse University. She now lives in Franklin, TN with her husband Alan, Terrier Dottie, and birds: Baker, Carl, and Ellie. She loves Christmas with an obsession that scares her family, and counseling may or may not have been recommended.

Melissa Face is the author of *I Love You More Than Coffee*, a gift book for parents who love coffee a lot and their kids (a little) more. Her essays and articles have appeared in local and national publications, and she teaches world literature at the Appomattox Regional

Governor's School. Learn more at melissaface.com.

Bonnie Jean Feldkamp is an award-winning freelance writer and columnist. She is the Communications Director for the National Society of Newspaper Columnists, member of the Cincinnati Enquirer Editorial Board, and a board member for the Cincinnati Chapter of the Society of Professional Journalists.

Glenda Ferguson received her education degrees from College of the Ozarks in Missouri and Indiana University. She lives in Indiana, and her brother, Mike, lives in Missouri. They both miss the handmade Christmas tradition since their mom passed away. The wonderful Christmas memories have outlived most of their mom's handiwork.

Carole Brody Fleet is a multi-award-winning author, media contributor and five-time contributor to the *Chicken Soup for the Soul* series. An expert in grief and life-adversity recovery, Ms. Fleet has made over 1,200 radio appearances and additionally has appeared on numerous television programs as well as in worldwide print and web media.

Carole Fowkes is originally from Cleveland, OH but has lived in Tampa and Chicago. She currently resides in the Dallas area with her husband. She is the author of a humorous cozy mystery series titled *The Terrified Detective*. E-mail her at cmsldfowkes@gmail.com.

Linda Gabris is a writer whose work has appeared in publications across North America and England. She has instructed creative writing workshops and international cooking courses for sixteen years. Linda currently writes general interest articles and food columns for numerous publications in Canada and the USA.

Anna Elizabeth Gant is a writer and academic editor. She's a summa cum laude graduate of Regent University and is pursuing her M.A. in English at the University of Nottingham. She recently completed her first children's novel. Anna loves community theatre and was thrilled to play Mrs. Darling in *Peter Pan*. Find her on Twitter @Anna_E_Gant.

Lea Gillespie Gant is wife to Neil and mother to Anna. She is a writer and a lover of flowers. Lea is the author of the Thomas Nelson children's book *Never Say Goodbye* and a graduate of Blue Mountain College with a B.A. in history and psychology. She enjoys music, photography and baking for the annual county fair.

Robyn Gerland is the author of *All These Long Years Later, Hand-Me-Downs,* and *Change-The Face of Time,* all of which are available in libraries across Canada. She has been a columnist for several magazines and newspapers and taught creative writing classes for both Conestoga College and Vancouver Island University.

Jenna Glatzer is the author or ghostwriter of more than thirty books, including Celine Dion's authorized biography. She lives in New York. Learn more at www.jennaglatzer.com.

Rob Goldberg is a graduate of the University of Delaware. His avocations are acting as an advisor/representative to a local community organization, advocating for alternative energy and serving as a director of a plastic recycling company. He belongs to the Brandywine Writers Circle, where he writes essays and memoirs.

Josh Granovsky is a Toronto-based screenwriter. His writing has earned him the Telefilm Canada New Voices Award, a Canadian Community Newspaper Award, and a Twitter follow from rapper Missy Elliott. He is currently working towards an MFA in screenwriting at the University of Southern California.

Award-winner **Melody S. Groves** is a full-time freelance writer living in Albuquerque, NM. She writes fiction and nonfiction Westerns and magazine articles. When not writing, she plays rhythm guitar, tambourine and backup vocals with the Jammy Time Band.

Sharon Harmon is a poet and freelance writer. She writes for the *Uniquely Quabbin* magazine and has been published in *Flash in the Can: Number One* and *Flash in the Can: Number Two.* She is currently working on two children's picture books.

Victoria Hathfield is a high school student in Canada. In her spare time, she enjoys reading, dancing, fishing, and writing personal anecdotes as well as short fiction stories. In the future, she aspires to become a university professor and to use what power she has to make a difference in the world.

Crystal Hodge is mother to two adult daughters, grandmother to four rescue fur babies and, by virtue of marriage to an Australian from Tasmania, is considered an expert on the mysterious habits of the Tasmanian devil. Connect with Crystal at crystalhodge1202@gmail.com.

Shonda Holt lives in rural Oklahoma with her husband of twenty-one years, and her sixteen- year-old son and fourteen-year-old boy/girl twins. She has a bachelor's degree in sociology and is currently working toward a certification in Bible and theology from Global University. She enjoys travel, flower gardening, and baking cookies.

Kristin Baldwin Homsi lives in Houston, TX with her husband and three children. She is a strategy manager in the oil and gas industry and an avid runner. Kristin began writing after the premature birth of her twins drastically altered the trajectory of her life. You can find her on Facebook and Instagram as Raising Trinity.

Rose Howe was born in Newcastle-upon-Tyne, England. She settled in the United States in 1985, where she met her husband Darrell. For the past twenty-five years they have lived on their Triple H Ranch in the small community of Monument in Eastern Oregon.

Alisha Isaacson is a yoga enthusiast, loves to read, and is a mother of two. Her family is her whole world and she is forever a student of life.

Amita Jagannath is an obsessive-compulsive reader who is a software engineer by profession, paranoid parent by choice, and a seasoned spouse critic according to her husband. She currently lives in Chicago with her husband and daughter.

Sheryl K. James retired from a thirty-five-year career with the Federal Government. She has one daughter and two granddaughters. Sheryl enjoys playing her electric piano and writing music, painting with acrylics, and gardening with her husband of fifty-five years. Throughout her life, she has written poems for family and friends.

Linda Baten Johnson grew up in White Deer, TX, where she won awards for storytelling. She still loves telling tales. A tornado destroyed her hometown, and the faith-based action she witnessed as people rebuilt homes and lives influences her writing. Check out her historical fiction and romance at lindabatenjohnson.com.

Tammi Croteau Keen is an author of children's books promoting acceptance, inclusion, and kindness. She is an avid runner, a devoted "fur-mom" to three cats and a dog, and a doctoral student in leadership at City University of Seattle.

Judy Allen Kemp is a retired registered nurse with almost thirty years of experience in various fields. She received her MSN five days after her sixtieth birthday. She has two adult children, two adult grandchildren, a toddler grandson, and a great-granddaughter. Her hobbies include family, fishing, writing, and beginner quilting.

Lori Ann King is the author of *Come Back Strong: Balanced Wellness after Surgical Menopause*. This is her second story published in the *Chicken Soup for the Soul* series. She is currently writing a memoir about the evolution of an athlete as well as a collection of cycling short stories. Learn more at www.LoriAnnKing.com.

Angie Klink is the author of eight books, including *The Deans' Bible: Five Purdue Women and Their Quest for Equality*, *Kirby's Way*, and *Divided Paths, Common Ground*. She was the scriptwriter for *Rise Above the Mark*, narrated by actor Peter Coyote. Klink holds a B.A. in communication from Purdue University. Learn more at angieklink.com.

Bobbie Jensen Lippman is a professional writer who lives in Seal Rock, OR with her cat Purrfect and a robot named Waldo. Bobbie's work has been published nationally and internationally. She writes a weekly human-interest column for *The News-Times* in Newport, OR. E-mail her at bobbisbeat@gmail.com.

After spending thirty-three years working as an illustrator and graphic artist for *The Tonight Show*, first with Johnny Carson and then Jay Leno, **Don Locke** now enjoys retirement with his wife Susan and their two dogs. He is the author of two novels: *The Reluctant Journey of David Connors* and *The Summer the Wind Whispered My Name*.

Crescent LoMonaco used her knowledge from years working behind the chair and owning a hair salon to write the "Ask a Stylist" column for the *Santa Barbara Independent*. She is a frequent contributor to the *Chicken Soup for the Soul* series. She lives on the California coast with her husband and son.

Irene Maran is a freelance writer, retired, and living at the Jersey shore with her cats and turtles. She currently writes two bi-weekly newspaper columns, runs a prompt writing group and is a professional storyteller. A grandmother of five she enjoys sharing her humorous stories with adults and children.

Linda Maxwell teaches English at Georgetown High School and freelances for the *Georgetown Times* in coastal South Carolina. She has published work in Eastern Kentucky University's *Chaffin Journal*, UNLV's *Wordriver*, *Catholic Digest*, *Poetry as Prayer*, *Southern Women's Review*, *The Litchfield Review*, and *Tidelands*.

Nicole Ann Rook McAlister is a homemaker and homesteading mama who resides in her log cabin in the Pine Barrens. She grows a garden full of wild herbs, fills walls with her art, and plays endless board and card games with her family. She spends her free time camping with her daughter Midnight and niece Bailey.

Jane McBride considers writing her dream job. The mother of five children and grandmother of ten, she spends her time being with family, going to garage sales, and, of course, writing.

Shauna McGuiness is a professional theater person, who has penned hundreds of theatrical pieces for all ages and, since 1994, has served as resident playwright for various Bay Area schools. She published a YA novel titled *Frankie in Paris*, which spent a week as a #1 top selling Kindle YA book.

Courtney McKinney-Whitaker is an award-winning author of fiction, essays, and poetry. She lives, writes, and celebrates the holidays in Pennsylvania with her family. Learn more at courtneymck.com or on Twitter @courtneymckwhit.

Angela McRae is an award-winning writer and editor in Newnan, GA. She writes cozy mysteries and books about teatime, and she is currently at work on a cookbook of vintage Christmas recipes.

Baylie Jett Mills is the author and illustrator of *The Adventures of Max* children's book series available for sale online. Baylie is an accomplished pianist and plays the guitar, ukulele, and harmonica as well. She loves reading, writing, and spending time with her family and four adorable little dogs.

Sue Mitchell swapped her teacher's desk for a writer's desk. Her short stories have appeared in several publications, but her tribe of cats remains in luxurious isolation, declining publicity. Sue has a growing Twitter following @pagancatmommy.

Laura Moehrle has a Bachelor's in English and writing. She is happily married to a wonderful, supportive husband and has three grown children. Laura is a freelance writer and hopes to one day become a novelist. She is very excited to have her work appear in the *Chicken Soup for the Soul* series.

Sandy Lynn Moffett is a poet and inspirational writer. She spent more than forty years in the funeral industry as a singer. She received her Associate of Arts with a major in English at the age of sixty. She and her husband Greg have four children and twelve grandchildren. Sandy loves to travel and is working on a children's book.

Jesse Neve is a lifelong Minnesotan. She is a wife and mom to four "kids" who are all inches taller than her now. She has been writing forever and tries to bring joy and smiles to everyone who reads her words. E-mail her at jessedavidneve@frontiernet.net.

Caitlin Q. Bailey O'Neill is a long-time contributor to the *Chicken Soup for the Soul* series, published in eight titles so far. A writer and editor at heart and nonprofit communications coordinator by day, Caitlin's proudest role is mom to Reilly and Ainsley and aunt to Quinn, Alexa, James, Bradley, Wesley, and Christmas surprise Avery.

Joanne Padley is an observer of life from both ends of the spectrum, as a staff member at the University of Buffalo as well as at Asbury Pointe Retirement Community. A mother of five, she enjoys writing in her spare time. E-mail her at joannepadley@yahoo.com.

Nancy Emmick Panko is a retired pediatric nurse with fifteen *Chicken Soup for the Soul* stories to her credit. She is the author of award-winning *Guiding Missal* and newly released *Sheltering Angels*. A member of the Cary Senior Writing Circle, Nancy enjoys being in, on, or near Lake Gaston with her family.

Diane C. Perrone is a Christian, mother of five, grandmother of sixteen and great-grandmother of one. Her Master of Arts degree is from Marquette University in Milwaukee, WI. Retired from teaching, marketing consulting and sales, she currently writes from Phoenix, AZ.

Diana K. Peterson earned an undergraduate degree in English and is currently pursuing a master's degree in education and curriculum. As a teacher in Las Vegas, NV, Diana works to inspire her students with a love of reading, creativity, and hopes to touch more lives with her writing.

Like her father, **Kristen Mai Pham** loves to write. When she isn't penning inspirational screenplays for film/television and short stories, she enjoys dreaming of her imaginary pet Corgi and anything with chocolate on it. Follow her on Instagram @kristenmaipham or e-mail her at Kristenmaipham3@gmail.com.

Stephanie Pifer-Stone is an Interfaith minister with a degree in holistic theology. She studied Religious Literacy at Harvard Divinity School. *Becoming Egg-straordinary* is her first book about releasing your inner butterfly. In addition to her husband and their furry kid, her passions include yoga, writing, and cooking.

Connie K. Pombo is an inspirational speaker, freelance writer and frequent contributor to the *Chicken Soup for the Soul* series. When not speaking or writing, she enjoys combing the beaches of Florida for shells and visiting her four grandchildren in Pennsylvania. Learn more at www.conniepombo.com.

Shannon Scott Poteet is wife to an incredible husband and mother to three amazing children. She is passionate about women and children's causes and spends her free time working with both. She loves seeing others realize their potential and delights in spreading light and laughter everywhere she goes.

Sharron Read-Lambert is co-author of her husband's memoir, *Badge of Color,* and two free-verse poetry books. Retired from training law enforcement K9s, she lives in Southern California with her husband and four loving dogs. Sharron enjoys traveling and is working on a second memoir. E-mail her at lambz1309@gmail.com.

Sasha Rives is a writer living in Southwest Missouri with her husband and three cats. She loves taking an idea from concept to completion and all the details it takes to make the big picture. She enjoys travel, knitting, reading and possibilities.

Rose Robertson and her husband enjoy a wonderful family of three sons, two daughters by marriage, and four grandchildren. Rose enjoys gardening, reading, writing, and needlework. She volunteers with teens who have experienced the death of someone significant and also works with parents who have suffered the loss of a child.

Lucy Rodriguez is a proud mother of three who walks through life with strong faith, a love for life and a passion for writing—all which have helped her through some of her most trying moments. She enjoys nature, gardening, walking, laughing, eating ice cream and spending quality time with her family and friends.

Nancy Roenfeldt received her Bachelor of Arts from Vanderbilt University and has worked as an English teacher for more than thirty years. She has twin girls and five grandchildren. She enjoys cooking and golf. She attends church regularly where she serves as a Eucharistic Visitor.

John M. Scanlan is a 1983 graduate of the United States Naval Academy and retired from the United States Marine Corps as a Lieutenant Colonel aviator with time in the back seat of both the F-4S Phantom II and the F/A-18D Hornet. He is currently pursuing a second career as a writer.

C.A. Simonson writes Christian fiction and inspirational nonfiction. Her human-interest stories appear in seven anthologies with over 400 articles in magazines. Author of four novels, she lives in the beautiful Ozarks of Missouri. When not writing, she loves to fish in her backyard pond.

Stacey Sisk has four children who are growing way too fast. She and her husband of nineteen years co-own an online marketing company and enjoy life in rural Missouri combining recreation with the best of modern technology. She received her B.A. in Communication, with honors, from Missouri Baptist University in 2002.

Diane Stark is a wife, mother of five, and freelance writer. She is a frequent contributor to the *Chicken Soup for the Soul* series. She loves to write about the important things in life: her family and her faith.

The desire of three-time award-winning author **LD Stauth's** heart is to encourage her readers. An avid camper, she continually marvels at God's creation revealed in nature. All three books in her *Campground Mystery* series have won awards for romance, mystery or suspense, and are a light-hearted, fun adventure.

Charles R. Stieren lives in Orlando, FL where he works as a nurse case manager and is a single parent of two children. He enjoys the outdoors. His fictional short stories have appeared in *Adelaide* magazine, BoomerLit.Mag, *Thorny Locust, The Avalon Literary Review, Fairy Tales, the Sequel*, and many others.

Lynn Sunday is a writer and animal advocate who lives near San Francisco with her husband and senior rescue dog. Fourteen of Lynn's stories have appeared in the *Chicken Soup for the Soul* series.

Regina Velázquez is a writer and editor living in western Massachusetts. She received an M.A. in English from the University of Tennessee. In addition to raising her two children and working full-time, she enjoys baking, making popsicles, singing, and reading. She is currently working on a play and a young adult novel.

Molly Mulrooney Wade earned her M.A. in 1998 and her J.D. in 2001. She is the Director of Communications and Marketing at a Catholic high school in New Hampshire. Molly most enjoys writing about topics that fuel the soul with joy and that remind readers of God's surrounding love.

Beth A. Wagner is an elementary librarian and small business owner of GO STEAM! in Pennsylvania. She has been married to her husband Chris for sixteen years. They have two sons and one daughter. Beth enjoys reading, being outdoors, game nights, and spending time with her family and two dogs, Clementine and Winston.

Pat Wahler is a Missouri native and proud contributor to eighteen previous titles in the *Chicken Soup for the Soul* series. Pat is the author of three novels and is currently at work on her next book under the supervision of two rescues: a bossy cat and a spoiled Pekingese/Poodle mix. Learn more at PatWahler.com.

Dorann Weber is a freelance photographer who lives in the Pine Barrens of South Jersey with her family. She's a contributor for Getty Images. Her photos and verses have appeared on Hallmark cards and in magazines. Contributing stories to the *Chicken Soup for the Soul* series has ignited a passion for writing.

Louisa Wilkinson is a story lover, curious traveler, mom, soon-to-be grandma, writer and human resources professional living in the rural Midwest. Her works include *Alice & Frosty: An American Adventure* published by The Iowan Books, as well as magazine articles and stories in the *Chicken Soup for the Soul* series.

Cass Wingood is a single mom of six. Her stories are spin-offs from life with loads of children where there is never a dull moment. Cass enjoys great coffee, rainy days, watching sunsets and of course her six kids and seventeen chickens.

Nemma Wollenfang is an MSc post-graduate and prize-winning writer who lives in Northern England. Her usual realm is speculative fiction and her work has appeared in several venues, including: *Beyond the Stars*, *Abyss & Apex*, and *Flame Tree's Gothic Fantasy* series. She also enjoys rambling about ancient ruins like Stonehenge.

Donna Womack is an elementary library media specialist in central Missouri. Prior to that, she taught third, fourth and fifth grades. She is a graduate of Central Methodist University, Southwest Baptist University and the University of Missouri-St. Louis. Donna loves to read, travel, bake and spend time with her family.

Meet Amy Newmark

Amy Newmark is the bestselling author, editor-in-chief, and publisher of the *Chicken Soup for the Soul* book series. Since 2008, she has published 168 new books, most of them national bestsellers in the U.S. and Canada, more than doubling the number of Chicken Soup for the Soul titles in print today. She is also the author of *Simply Happy*, a crash course in Chicken Soup for the Soul advice and wisdom that is filled with easy-to-implement, practical tips for enjoying a better life.

Amy is credited with revitalizing the Chicken Soup for the Soul brand, which has been a publishing industry phenomenon since the first book came out in 1993. By compiling inspirational and aspirational true stories curated from ordinary people who have had extraordinary experiences, Amy has kept the twenty-seven-year-old Chicken Soup for the Soul brand fresh and relevant.

Amy graduated *magna cum laude* from Harvard University where she majored in Portuguese and minored in French. She then embarked on a three-decade career as a Wall Street analyst, a hedge fund manager, and a corporate executive in the technology field. She is a Chartered Financial Analyst.

Her return to literary pursuits was inevitable, as her honors thesis in college involved traveling throughout Brazil's impoverished northeast region, collecting stories from regular people. She is delighted to have come full circle in her writing career — from collecting stories "from the people" in Brazil as a twenty-year-old to, three decades later, collecting stories "from the people" for Chicken Soup for the Soul.

When Amy and her husband Bill, the CEO of Chicken Soup for the Soul, are not working, they are visiting their four grown children and their grandchildren.

Follow Amy on Twitter @amynewmark. Listen to her free podcast — "Chicken Soup for the Soul with Amy Newmark" — on Apple Podcasts, Google Play, the Podcasts app on iPhone, or by using your favorite podcast app on other devices.

Thank You

W e owe huge thanks to all of our contributors and fans. We received thousands of submissions for this popular topic, and we spent months reading all of them. Our editors Laura Dean, Crescent LoMonaco, and Jamie Cahill read all of them and narrowed down the selection for Associate Publisher D'ette Corona and Publisher and Editor-in-Chief Amy Newmark.

Susan Heim did the first round of editing, D'ette chose the perfect quotations to put at the beginning of each story, and Amy edited the stories and shaped the final manuscript.

As we finished our work, D'ette Corona continued to be Amy's right-hand woman in working with all our wonderful writers. Barbara LoMonaco, Mary Fisher and Kristiana Pastir, along with Elaine Kimbler, jumped in at the end to proof, proof, proof. And yes, there will always be typos anyway, so please feel free to let us know about them at webmaster@chickensoupforthesoul.com, and we will correct them in future printings.

The whole publishing team deserves a hand, including our Senior Director of Marketing Maureen Peltier, our Vice President of Production Victor Cataldo, and our graphic designer Daniel Zaccari, who turned our manuscript into this beautiful, entertaining book.

About Toys for Tots

Your purchase of this *Chicken Soup for the Soul* book supports Toys for Tots and helps create Christmas miracles for children who might not receive gifts otherwise! The mission of the U.S. Marine Corps Reserve Toys for Tots Program is to collect new, unwrapped toys during October, November and December each year, and distribute those toys as Christmas gifts to less fortunate children in the community in which the campaign is conducted.

You can contribute to your local Toys for Tots campaign in several ways. You can donate a toy at one of the area toy drop locations, host a Toys for Tots event at your office or other venue and collect toys for Toys for Tots, or volunteer at the local warehouse. You can also donate by visiting toysfortots.org.

Local campaigns are conducted annually in over 800 communities covering all 50 U.S. states, the District of Columbia and Puerto Rico. Local toy collection campaigns begin in October and last until mid to late December. Toy distribution also takes place mid to late December.

Members of the community drop new, unwrapped toys in collection boxes positioned in local businesses. Coordinators pick up these toys and store them in central warehouses where the toys are sorted by age and gender. At Christmas, Coordinators, with the assistance of local social welfare agencies, church groups, and other local community agencies, distribute the toys to the less fortunate children of the community.

Over the years, Marines have established close working relationships with social welfare agencies, churches and other local community agencies which are well qualified to identify the needy children in the community and play important roles in the distribution of the toys. While Toys for Tots Coordinators organize, coordinate and manage the campaign, the ultimate success depends on the support of the local community and the generosity of the people who donate toys.

You can learn more about Toys for Tots by visiting their website at https://www.toysfortots.org.

Sharing Happiness, Inspiration, and Hope

R eal people sharing real stories, every day, all over the world. In 2007, *USA Today* named *Chicken Soup for the Soul* one of the five most memorable books in the last quarter-century. With over 100 million books sold to date in the U.S. and Canada alone, more than 250 titles in print, and translations into nearly fifty languages, "chicken soup for the soul®" is one of the world's best-known phrases.

Today, twenty-seven years after we first began sharing happiness, inspiration and hope through our books, we continue to delight our readers with new titles, but have also evolved beyond the bookshelves with super premium pet food, television shows, a podcast, video journalism from aplus.com, licensed products, and free movies and TV shows on our Popcornflix and Crackle apps. We are busy "changing the world one story at a time®." Thanks for reading!

Share with Us

We all have had Chicken Soup for the Soul moments in our lives. If you would like to share your story or poem with millions of people around the world, go to chickensoup.com and click on Submit Your Story. You may be able to help another reader and become a published author at the same time. Some of our past contributors have launched writing and speaking careers from the publication of their stories in our books!

We only accept story submissions via our website. They are no longer accepted via mail or fax. Visit our website, www.chickensoup.com, and click on Submit Your Story for our writing guidelines and a list of topics we are working on.

To contact us regarding other matters, please send us an e-mail through webmaster@chickensoupforthesoul.com, or fax or write us at:

Chicken Soup for the Soul
P.O. Box 700
Cos Cob, CT 06807-0700
Fax: 203-861-7194

One more note from your friends at Chicken Soup for the Soul: Occasionally, we receive an unsolicited book manuscript from one of our readers, and we would like to respectfully inform you that we do not accept unsolicited manuscripts, and we must discard the ones that appear.

Chicken Soup for the Soul

AGE IS JUST A NUMBER

101 Tales of Humor & Wisdom
for Life After 60

Amy Newmark

Paperback: 978-1-61159-071-5
eBook: 978-1-61159-305-1

More inspiration and entertainment

Chicken Soup for the Soul.

Miracles & Divine Intervention

101 Stories of Faith and Hope

Amy Newmark

Paperback: 978-1-61159-073-9
eBook: 978-1-61159-313-6

for your family and friends

Changing your world one story at a time®
www.chickensoup.com